"*Rethinking Worldview* throws off sparks able to light the dry tinder that many Sunday school classes and seminary seminars have become. J. Mark Bertrand's four worldview pillars, his explanation of how to move from consumer to critic to contributor, his discussion of personal unity and diversity within the Trinity, and much besides, make this book worth having and giving."
   —MARVIN OLASKY, editor-in-chief, *World* magazine

"The strength of Bertrand's book is its comprehensiveness, as the author turns the prism of worldview until every angle has been illuminated. Bertrand maintains our interest throughout his long discussion with an incipient narrative thread in which his understanding of worldview is told as the sum of his own discoveries and experiences in relation to worldview. The book actually has the quality of a suspense story in which the reader is led to wonder what Bertrand discovered next in regard to worldview."
   —LELAND RYKEN, professor of English, Wheaton College

"*Rethinking Worldview* is an engagingly written work to strengthen believers in their efforts to engage the world in a winsome and effective manner. Built around the themes of worldview, wisdom, and witness, this excellent book provides an illuminating and thoughtful way forward for the twenty-first-century church to think, live, speak, and worship. Mark Bertrand has made a splendid contribution to the ongoing conversation regarding Christian worldview thinking. After reading this book I wanted to shout "Yes, and Amen!" I heartily commend this book and trust that it will receive a wide readership."
   —DAVID S. DOCKERY, president, Union University

For those of you suffering from "worldview fatigue," or who think it's a theologically unhelpful concept, or who are new to the notion altogether, read this book. It's like a satisfying draught of ice-cold, refreshing water on a hot summer day! It offers reinvigorating approaches to the priceless Christian worldview concept, properly focuses our attention on its wisdom-giving properties, and propels us to full-bodied Christian witness and cultural engagement on its basis. Bertrand's book is a rich gift to serious citizens of the kingdom of God.
   —DAVID NAUGLE, professor of philosophy, Dallas Baptist University; author, *Worldview: The History of a Concept*

D0122031

Learning to Think, Live, and
Speak . . . Online!

If you have enjoyed *Rethinking Worldview,* be sure to visit the online community at:

www.RethinkingWorldview.com

You can contact author J. Mark Bertrand and access interviews, essays, and a number of web-only extras. The site also features a free annotated discussion guide to facilitate group study of *Rethinking Worldview.* Visit today!

(RE)THINKING

Learning to Think, Live, and Speak in This World

WORLDVIEW

J. Mark Bertrand

CROSSWAY BOOKS
WHEATON, ILLINOIS

Rethinking Worldview: Learning to Think, Live, and Speak in This World

Copyright © 2007 by J. Mark Bertrand

Published by Crossway Books
   a publishing ministry of Good News Publishers
   1300 Crescent Street
   Wheaton, Illinois 60187

Cover design: Josh Dennis

Cover illustration: iStock

First printing 2007

Printed in the United States of America

Scripture quotations are from *The Holy Bible, English Standard Version*,® copyright © 2001 by Crossway Bibles, a publishing ministry of Good News Publishers. Used by permission. All rights reserved.

All emphases in Scripture quotations have been added by the author.

Library of Congress Cataloging-in-Publication Data
Bertrand, J. Mark, 1970–
 Rethinking Worldview: Learning to Think, Live, and Speak in This
World / J. Mark Bertrand.
  p. cm.
 Includes index.
 ISBN 978-1-58134-934-4 (tpb)
 1. Ideology—Religious aspects—Christianity. 2. Theology, Doctrinal—
Popular works. 3. Apologetics. I. Title.
BR115.I35B47 2007
230—dc22   2007006233

VP		17	16	15	14	13	12	11	10	09	08	07
15	14	13	12	11	10	9	8	7	6	5	4	3	2	1

For Laurie

CONTENTS

MEDICINAE TEMPUS EST

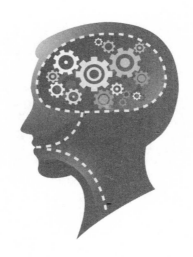

Preface
What This Book Won't Do

In the old days, authors introduced their books with an apology, taking advantage of the dual meanings of the word. They begged indulgence for the shortcomings of the work, and at the same time offered a defense of why it was written in the first place. If you ask me, that was a fine tradition, and I'd like to revive it here.

This is a book about worldview, which means it will touch on matters of theology, philosophy, and culture. These are deep waters, and I admit at the outset that I'm not the most authoritative guide. I make no claims to expertise. Instead, I am a fascinated amateur. In a field packed with professional ministers, theologians, historians, and philosophers, I am a layman. If anything, my sensibility is more artistic than academic—a fact that will no doubt drive some readers crazy, though I hope it will open up unexpected vistas, too.

As the title *Rethinking Worldview* suggests, these pages represent a two-pronged invitation. First, this is a call to rethink and reevaluate your own perspective on the nature of reality. You are right about some things, wrong about others; and perhaps this is an opportunity to ensure that the balance tips the right way.

Second, I invite you to think again about the idea of worldview itself. So much has been written on the subject—much good, some not—that it has become familiar, even commonplace. In some ways, the popular understanding of the concept is deficient, and as a result, those quick to dismiss it as old-fashioned might be operating without a good, nuanced grasp of what worldview thinking really is. Hopefully, reading this book will stimulate a desire to take a second, deeper look.

What to Think, How to Think

For all its ambition, there are some things this book will not do, and we might as well establish them up front.

This book will not tell you what to think.

It does not include a catalog of official Christian viewpoints on theological, philosophical, or political matters. For the most part, it is not polemical. We will not be considering the shortcomings of various public policies and formulating idealistic alternatives. That really is the realm of experts, and while I am as opinionated as the next man, and as convinced that my ideas, if implemented, would usher in a golden age, I know that everybody else thinks the same thing, and for reasons just as sound (or unsound, as the case may be).

No, this book will not tell you what to think—but that is a common enough caveat. Most authors say something along these lines: "I won't teach you what to think; I'll teach you *how* to think."

Noble as that sentiment might sound, this book will not teach you *how* to think, either.

As a young man, I read many, many books that made this claim and never found one that actually delivered. Later, when I became a writer and teacher myself, I always tried to be careful never to set such ambitious goals. My aim is to inspire reflection and action; so think of this book as a conversation, where you are free to elaborate and dissent.

The greatest compliment I have ever received came from a student who sat quietly in the back of a weekly Bible study I once taught for college students. He approached me after a particularly long group discussion and said, "What I like about your class is that you don't talk down to us. You treat us as equals." Those words stuck with me, and whenever I find myself straying from that ideal, I try to shut up.

As a result, in the chapters that follow you will discover my thoughts on a variety of topics, and you will encounter them in the way I think them—which might not always be the best method of explaining. I make no apology for this; consider it a sign of respect for the reader.

But I do apologize for the inevitable fact that, like many authors, I have bitten off more than I can chew. This book covers subjects too wonderful for me to express, and there will be rough patches along the way, places where my limitations are shown to least advantage. I have attempted to smooth them out, to provide the most reliable account possible, but there is a virtue in allowing some of these shortcomings to make it onto the page. It is my way of saying, "I think this is so, but I could be wrong." It goes without saying that for final authority, look to God and not this book.

Parallel Reading

With that in mind, I have one request to make. If you are going to invest the time required to digest this book, I ask that you read it in tandem with Scripture. Many Christians read from the Bible daily as a matter of course, but if you haven't cultivated this habit, I ask that you adopt it at least temporarily. This book, after all, is ultimately a derivative work, a book about a book. It leans against Scripture as an injured man leans on his crutch. To make the most of it, you as a reader will need to do some leaning of your own.

There are many reading plans available to guide you through the Bible, and there is always the option of starting at Genesis 1 and moving forward. If you have a method of your own, by all means employ it. If not, let me suggest an expedient. Begin in the New Testament with the Gospel of John and then keep going through Acts, Romans, and beyond. This will keep the good news of Christ, the history of the early church, and the essentials of sound doctrine in the forefront of your mind as you read *Rethinking Worldview*. I have tried to create a book consistent in every way with that parallel reading, but being finite and fallen I have no doubt failed. Where you find friction between your Bible reading and what you see here, set aside my errors in favor of truth.

An Introduction and a (Re)Introduction

This book is an introduction to worldview thinking and its implications for people new to the concept, and a reintroduction to those who, like me, have not always found particularly helpful the ways the idea is expressed and applied in the mainstream. It is divided into three parts—worldview, wisdom, and witness—with the conviction that any treatment of the intellectual dimensions of worldview that doesn't lead into a discussion of how to profitably live and speak in this world is incomplete. If there is one thing I will reiterate time and again, it is the organic relationship between these things.

If worldview thinking is to prove valuable in our lives, it must help make us better believers and doers of the truth. Otherwise it becomes a mental exercise that breeds arrogance and shores up the false security of intellectual elites.

Before We Begin

I've noticed an interesting trend among some twenty-something evangelicals, a tendency to snigger behind the hand whenever worldview is mentioned. It reminds me of how my generation reacted when older Christians talked about end times portents or rock music. We were jaded. We knew better. The Bible, as far as we could tell, backed our skepticism more than the certainties of our elders.

When I was first exposed to worldview thinking—a kind of Christian cultural critique that involves tracing back the philosophical assumptions that underlie cultural expressions—it was as exciting to me as, say, deconstruction. But then, I hadn't grown up with the idea of worldview. I had not persevered through a thousand youth group lectures on the topic, or been encouraged to diagnose and dismiss everybody else's *ism*. These younger evangelicals have, and to them it is old hat.

I do not agree, but I sympathize. In many ways, the worldview approach that has gone mainstream throughout evangelicalism deserves the sniggering. A lot of people without even rudimentary philosophical training are using pseudo-philosophical language in an effort to reassure equally untrained laymen that their belief systems will stand up to scrutiny. And they do—until they're actually tested. A lot of simplistic scorecards are handed out so that unsophisticated young people can discern the "hidden agenda" of the various scary elites. Worldview thinking has been co-opted by the culture wars, so it is no wonder that people disenchanted with those wars have grown indifferent to worldviews, too.

But it shouldn't be that way.

The Disconnect

When worldview analysis is properly applied, it operates as a kind of buttress to the moral argument for God's existence. The reader discovers "Christian" themes, assumptions, and structures in work done by people whose mind-set is anything but Christian, and this raises the question: *why?* Asking worldview questions is a way to open up the culture to deeper scrutiny. It ought to provide a fuller, richer experience of the world around us.

Instead, worldview critiques often function on the pass/fail level, like a bacteria filter which, applied to our entertainment, cleanses it of harmful influences. The worldview critic reduces what he reads to the level of theme then gives an up or down vote on whether the distilled meaning of the work fits into the biblical worldview. Unfortunately, this turns out to be a way not to engage with the work directly at all. Instead, the art is processed into a set of categories already familiar to the critic, who then applies the standard responses to them. The whole process is depressing to anyone who actually enjoys and benefits from the complexities of art.

If you are one of those people whose eyes glaze over when the "w-word" is mentioned—or worse, one of those people who uses it as a club to bludgeon ideas you haven't fully grasped—then *Rethinking Worldview* may be just the thing: an attempt to rediscover the benefits of worldview thinking without resort to the baggage that has accumulated over time.

PART ONE

WORLDVIEW

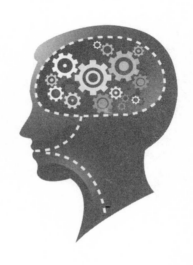

1

Things Unseen:
Rethinking Worldview

Reality can be only partially attacked by logic.
FRIEDRICH DÜRRENMATT

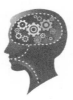

"So you're writing a book about worldview?"

I must have heard it a thousand times from a thousand different people, each one with a wide-eyed, uncomprehending stare. Not because they had no idea what a *worldview* is—it's a view of the world, obviously—but because it was hard to imagine why another book on the subject needed to crowd its way onto the shelves. After teaching Christian worldview for several years to high school and college students, I knew what they meant. There were already dozens of exceptional titles on this topic and hundreds of competent hangers-on. Everything that needed to be said about worldviews had already been uttered, emphasized, repeated, underscored, and capped with a series of exclamation marks.

What could I possibly add to all that?

Nothing, I found myself thinking. There was nothing more to say. The ancient author of Ecclesiastes bookends the problem succinctly: on the one hand, there is "nothing new under the sun" (1:9), and on the other, "of making many books there is no end" (12:12). Whenever people asked about my book, whatever explanations I managed to stutter through, the raised eyebrows never lowered and the tone of mild amazement never evaporated.

"So you're writing a book about worldview? Oh, dear."

Looking back, I am sure that many of the people who heard about this book were not so skeptical. It was my own doubts, my own cynicism, torturing me.

The problem is, I don't see the concept of worldview the way other people do. As far as I'm concerned, it's mine. Of course, I realize I did not invent it and up until now have done relatively little to promote it, but still I'm plagued with the blind, intimate regard of a lover for the object of affection. Yes, I am in love with worldviews. From the moment I first discovered the notion, I have adored it. No matter how often I think about them—no matter how many of their problems and shortcomings become apparent to me—I can never seem to exhaust my fascination with worldviews.

My discovery of worldview, however, was like G. K. Chesterton's discovery of orthodoxy. In his famous book by the same name, Chesterton compares himself to a man who has set sail on a quest and made landfall on an isle of mystery, only to find that it is already inhabited and well known to everyone else. By the time I planted my little flag on the beaches of worldview, there were already skyscrapers towering over the tree line.

So when the urge to write, to contribute a slender volume to the growing literature on the subject, finally came to me, I harbored doubts. Whatever there was to say had already been said. Writing another book would be like composing a sonnet in honor of a beauty queen: you are not telling people anything they don't already know.

But I was wrong. The more I studied and taught, the more I realized that there *was* something more to be said, something urgent. As much as I love the worldview concept, and as much good as I believe it has done, I am convinced that the time has come to rethink our assumptions about worldviews. We need to take a second look and make sure that, in adopting the concept so widely and making it such a staple of evangelical discourse, we have not gutted it. I suspect that we have. In streamlining the idea of worldviews for mass consumption, we have been simplistic. We have been pedantic. And worst of all, we have been overconfident.

I know because I have been guilty of all this and more, and writing *Rethinking Worldview* has helped me see it.

What is left to contribute to the conversation about worldview? Plenty. First, we need to recapture a more complex, nuanced appreciation of what worldview really is. Without that, we can't proceed. Second, we need to situate worldview in the larger context of a lived faith, finding out how all this intellectual labor should affect not only the way we think but also how we act. To do this will require a renewed focus on the biblical concept of wisdom, which is one of those things we tend to talk about rather than practice. Finally, this book will explore the organic connections between worldview and wisdom, and how they express themselves in witness.

As Christians, we want to talk to the world about the gospel of Jesus Christ, and we want them to listen. I believe that a new understanding of worldview coupled with a life of wisdom leads inevitably to profound, powerful witness—and where witness is lacking, perhaps worldview and wisdom are, too. So in these pages we will rethink worldview, restore wisdom to its central role at the heart of Christian living, and seek to regain a credible and creative witness in the culture where God has placed us.

"So you're writing a book about worldview?"

You better believe it.

Worldview and Its Discontents

What makes the worldview concept, pioneered by philosophers, appropriated by theologians and apologists, and now embraced by evangelicals around the globe, so compelling? Of all the insights that have percolated within the ivory towers over the last century, why has this one captured the imagination of so many thinkers—and why has it found such traction in the popular mind?

In part, the reason lies in how obvious the concept is once explained: the notion that everyone has a unique perspective, that we interpret facts through the lens of some theory about life, seems self-evident. "It's common sense," people say. This is something the average man already knows without needing some academic to tell him so.

Another reason for the popularity of worldview thinking is that, in a fragmented society where each of us feels embattled on some point or another, it is comforting to realize that our opponents in the culture war—whoever we conceive of them to be—are, by definition, blinded by their own perspective. No one is purely objective. Our view of the world is colored by upbringing, class, ideology, and experience. So what if our enemies muster powerful arguments against us? So what if "facts" and "reason" seem to be on their side? They are starting from their own prior commitments, and we are starting from ours. Ultimately, none of our basic assumptions are subject to challenge. We may not be able to prove "them" wrong, but they cannot prove us wrong, either. Or so the thinking goes.

When an idea hits the mainstream, it is invariably simplified and streamlined. This has happened to the worldview concept in spades. At one extreme, it becomes a form of relativism: everyone has a worldview; worldviews are inherently subjective, so everyone's perspective is equally valid. At the other end of the spectrum, the worldview concept becomes the key to establishing the priority of one perspective over all the others: everyone has a worldview, but only one is ultimately coherent, so all the others are equally invalid. The irony is that partisans on each end of the divide employ similar terminology, but to different purpose.

Evangelical Christians have tended toward the latter extreme, and no wonder: the worldview concept offers a way to assert the superiority of our faith and deconstruct every opposing ideology, religious and secular, in one fell swoop. In addition, because it is such a bookish, educated notion, worldview thinking offers a much-needed counterweight to the tradition of anti-intellectualism that so many evangelicals now want to leave behind.

That is certainly what attracted me. My first exposure to worldview came through Christian apologists like Francis Schaeffer, a voice in the late twentieth-century wilderness who gave evangelicals permission to use their minds again in church. Here was a believer who did not shrink from an intellectual challenge. He did not cloister himself in some faraway spot where his faith need never be defended. At the high tide of modern confidence in science and rationalism, Schaeffer was arguing that after all, none of it—the world, life, the mind, the imagination, the body—made any sense unless God, as revealed in Scripture, really existed. Like many others, I was swept up in the confidence of that proposition, buoyed by the hope that, even if I myself could not understand the reason why, ultimately, intellectually, one simply *must* accept the truth of the Christian faith.

I knew that there was more to faith than intellectual assent. I knew that when Jesus commissioned the church to "make disciples," he had more in mind than changing people's worldview. But as an apologetic tool—and frankly, as a psychological crutch, as a justification for why a well-read, middle-class, academically minded man of the late twentieth century, with an advanced degree and more than a passing knowledge of philosophy (including Nietzsche, who had searched for God's pulse and found none, and Bertrand Russell, who had written emphatically, if not always persuasively, about why he was not a Christian), should not be scorned and dismissed out of hand for his faith—worldview thinking was a panacea.

The first thing worldview thinking established in my mind was that Christian faith is coherent. What the Bible teaches about God, man, and the world holds together. It has the strength of internal consistency. If anything, it is too consistent, too neat, since every challenge, every paradox, can be explained by the fact that God is omnipotent and we are finite. There are some matters, as God emphasized to Job at the tail end of the Bible's account of that righteous man's suffering, that are simply too dark for us to probe.

This sense of consistency was important to me, and still is, because the modern assumption that religion is simply myth and superstition runs strong in our culture. In the early twentieth century, liberal and fundamentalist alike agreed on the radical divide between faith and reason, each seeking to neutralize one by means of the other, and today we still live in the shadow of that settlement. Americans accept, for example, that a person elected to public office will make decisions based on his ideological framework. But if that framework is religious, we grow suspicious. Faith is a private affair, a matter of the heart. In the public square, reason is the arbiter—in name, if not in practice. Is it any wonder that, growing up in these circumstances, thoughtful Christians are drawn toward anything that might explain that we are not unsophisticated dupes—or at least, that our position is defensible from the point of view not only of faith but of reason too?

Evangelicals see themselves as an embattled people. Later, I will take up the topic of siege mentality and how our fear of impending collapse has sometimes led us to justify what in Christ's name is unjustifiable. For now, suffice it to say that we often find ourselves on the defensive, and defensive people tend to be shrill, uncertain, and unconvincing. So the worldview concept instilled me with confidence: there was no need to feel threatened by the world outside—the world that, as a Christian, I was called to be in, but not of. My Christian worldview was intellectually respectable. In fact, it had given birth to a rich and varied (though by no means spotless) tradition. Men and women with a faith like mine and a hope like mine were responsible for much of the good in the culture I had inherited. Instead of apologizing for my faith, worldview thinking convinced me to speak up for it.

When I did, I uncovered another obvious truth: other people have a worldview, too. They are not as impressed as I am that Christianity is a coherent way of seeing the world. The same could be said of Nazism or Stalinism. It is all very well to argue that Christians have a defensible theory of life, but what makes my worldview better than anyone else's? In fact, how can I argue with credibility for the Christian worldview when my own co-religionists cannot agree on what it is? We evangelicals are noted for our divisions—and our divisiveness—so to an outsider, all talk of a monolithic Christian worldview seems absurd.

So I said, "The Christian worldview is coherent."

"Which one are you talking about?" they wanted to know.

For lack of a better answer, I could argue for plain vanilla orthodoxy, the faith embodied in the ancient creeds, or generic evangelicalism, the thin consensus between the denominations that lets us all (mostly, kind of) get along. "That's the Christian worldview I'm talking about."

"Well," they would say, "that's just your opinion. You have your worldview, and I have mine."

Being an astute culture warrior, I pointed out: "That's relativism. You can't say I have my truth and you have yours. There's only one truth, and this is it."

"Says you."

Those two little words—*says you*—are the most powerful argument in any discipline: theology, philosophy, even domestic harmony. They are powerful because they are true. Whenever you say something, it is *you* who says it. You. And what do *you* know? Who are *you* to speak? Please, get real. You? Why should I listen to you? It is the perfect come-back—just ask your spouse. One of the beauties of the "says you" defense is that if your opponent responds that it is a logical fallacy or some other such rationalist nonsense, you can fold your arms, smile knowingly, and declare, "You've just proved my point." Argument won, game over.

You say your worldview is better than mine? Well, who are you?

Point taken. Somewhere along life's journey, I realized that I could denounce people as relativists for only so long before even I grew bored. After all, it is hard to dismiss as an imbecile the very person you are trying to win over. It is one thing to defend Christianity as a viable option, but quite another to cast it convincingly as the one, the only, option.

We do not fully understand an idea until we grasp its limits.

In coming to terms with this difficulty, I was starting to grasp the limits of the worldview concept. As a defensive measure, it was brilliant. As a contemplative measure, it was also superb. By thinking of the implications of my faith systematically—to the extent that anything can happen systematically in something as disorganized and inefficient as my mind—I was reminded that to be a Christian is, first and foremost, to be one who follows or imitates Christ. My faith involved a transformation: I was called to be like Christ, to be "conformed to his image." That is what we call sanctification. It implies a lifetime pursuit of godliness, and I found that worldview thinking overlaps helpfully with this idea. It reminded me that God's perspective on reality is the correct one—as creator, he has the first and last word—and that my own viewpoint (like my own actions) would be measured against that standard. Worldview consciousness encouraged me to pursue the mind of Christ.

In a sense, worldview thinking helped to justify my position as a believer. I did not come to faith as a result of it, but once I was there, it gave me a way to understand what had happened in my life. It also provided a way to understand why what happened to me did not happen to everyone. But I could not find a way to communicate this insight to anyone who did not already share it.

If you are already a Christian, then worldview is a revelation, but if you aren't, the concept alone will not move you. In fact, it might do just the opposite, driving you to the other extreme where everyone has a worldview and all worldviews are equally valid.

Some worldviews are better than others. This much was obvious. But if I said as much, or if I went further and said that the Christian worldview (however you defined it) was the best of the lot and, as Schaeffer said, the only one that makes sense of the world as it really is, then the unbeliever had a ready answer, one that I could not easily dismiss.

He said: "Oh yeah? Prove it."

I am not such a cynic that I believe this cannot be done. There are arguments—a host of them—that reinforce Christianity's claim. During the course of this book, we will look at more than a few. But this is the moment to shift gears and look at what worldviews really are. Already, we have established that everyone has a worldview. How did we get it? How is it formed? Is it possible by persuasion and logic to change it? Important questions, and before we can begin to talk about "proving" the Christian worldview, we need to explore worldviews at greater length.

How Worldviews Are Formed

Here's how they work: first, things happen. Events occur.

You observe them happening to other people; you experience them happening to you. These events produce emotional responses: joy, sadness, fear, worry, scorn, mirth. They also serve as catalysts for thought. When you think about what happens, you arrange events. You search for meaning, or at least for patterns, in what has taken place. You begin to draw conclusions about the way the world works.

Based on these conclusions, you face the future with certain expectations and prejudices, hopes and anxieties. New experiences, new ideas, new people are all interpreted in light of the conclusions you've already reached. A kind of belief system emerges, and you are only partially aware of how it works.

When certain things occur, you expect particular results to follow. If they don't, you might adjust your system—or, as sometimes happens, you might refuse to see. You trust certain people and distrust others, scorn certain messages and revere others, and all this happens in the shadow of what has gone before.

Our image of ourselves as neutral, unbiased observers is naïve. We are engaged and engulfed in the world around us, not detached from it. Whether we realize it or not, we have taken sides. Just like a political party, we have created a platform, a platform that draws from many sources, a platform about which we have an incomplete awareness. And this process creates what we call a worldview.

Interpreting Reality

A worldview is an interpretation of influences, experiences, circumstances, and insight. In fact, it is an interrelated series of interpretations—and it becomes a method of interpreting, too. A worldview is something you are aware of only in moments of crisis or contemplation. In ordinary time, it is like a pair of glasses or contact lenses. You are so accustomed to looking *through* it that you barely notice it's there.

Eyeglasses are an often-used metaphor for worldview. The famous French chanteuse Edith Piaf is best known for her standard "La Vie en Rose," life through rose-colored glasses. When we describe someone as wearing rose-colored glasses, we mean that he doesn't see the world as it really is; instead, everything takes on the rosy hue of the lens through which he views it.

This metaphor applied to worldview suggests that every perspective is like a pair of tinted shades. It only serves to color your perception of the world. But there is a better way of approaching the question. Don't think of your worldview as sunglasses. Instead, think of it as a pair of prescription lenses. The task of every worldview is to see the world as it is, to correct your vision. The test of a good worldview will be whether it brings reality into sharp focus or leaves things blurry.

And I happen to be speaking from experience.

Growing up, I was the kid who preferred reading to recess and chose the library over the playground whenever possible. My parents always warned me about reading in poor light, but let's face it: low lighting sets the mood. I'm not sure when my vision began to deteriorate, but at some point, perhaps as early as junior high, I became nearsighted.

This isn't a problem when you read—to this day, I can read without the aid of glasses—but it can definitely cause trouble when you're trying to catch a football. Fortunately, bookworms don't do much of that, so it wasn't until I learned to drive that my vision became a problem.

One afternoon I was riding home from high school with my cousin Jeff. He had recently gotten glasses and as he drove, he read off the signs that we passed. I was amazed at how far he could see. Up until that moment, I had never suspected that my own vision was faulty, and to be honest, I didn't wonder even then. Instead, I remember thinking that Jeff's glasses must have given him better than 20/20 vision, since he could see even farther than I could. I just assumed that whatever I could see was the objective standard.

When I was behind the wheel, my poor vision wasn't as much of a handicap as you might think. Because we lived in a small town, I had the streets memorized long before I had to drive them. I never had to consult street signs, and so it never bothered me that I couldn't read them. To make matters easier, I attended a church school where students worked in individual workbooks instead of in traditional classes, so I never had to strain my eyes to read what was written on the blackboard.

It is amazing to think that a young man with what I later discovered was 20/80 vision was capable of performing normally in every area of life (aside from catching footballs), never suspecting the deficiency of vision.

But when I left the closed system of a small town and headed for college, my assumption that I was seeing things clearly was challenged. I had to sit near the front of the classroom to have any hope of reading what professors wrote on the board. My slit-eyed concentration made up for the years when I should have had to squint but didn't. Still, I didn't realize my eyes were the problem—I just figured *everybody* at the back of the room had a hard time reading the blackboard.

The crisis only came to a head when my father visited in the middle of my first semester. Before leaving for college, I had sold my car, so I traveled as a passenger through my new surroundings, never really grasping the lay of the land. When my dad let me borrow his rental car to give my friends a ride, a disaster was in the making. It was eight o'clock at night in a town where I had never driven before. Snug behind the wheel, I worried about getting lost on the way from his hotel to the campus—but I stopped worrying the moment I backed into the truck behind me!

Busting the tail light in a rental car is not a good feeling, but I didn't blame myself. After all, I never saw the truck behind me. Fortunately, all the damage was to my car, and the truck was unscathed. So I scooped up the pieces of the tail light, put them in the glove compartment, and headed out into the night, still oblivious.

And that's where the real problems started.

When you have 20/80 vision, you don't see very well at night. The headlights up ahead dazzled and disoriented me. The unfamiliar roads took on a sinister aspect. Soon I was gripping the wheel convulsively to keep from shaking, and I was driving slow—very slow. Grandmas were blowing past me on the highway. My forehead beaded with sweat and I plunged into the depths of panic. I prayed out loud, promising never to drive again if I could just make it to the campus alive. Approaching headlights grew so big I thought they would engulf me. By the time I made it to the college to pick up my friends, I was a nervous wreck. I still didn't know what had happened, but I was ready to give up driving forever.

Fortunately, my dad suggested glasses as an alternative.

The Standard for Seeing

During my visit to the optometrist, I was never asked how I would like to see the world. Eye doctors do not have much of an appreciation for subjectivity; they are sold on 20/20 as an objective standard. Unfortunately, they *did* ask me what kind of frames I would like, and this resulted in a pair of large glasses with gray plastic frames that made me look like a wannabe science teacher.

Nevertheless I could see. In fact, with my glasses I was able to discover some things for the first time. Street signs were a revelation, for example, and I was now free to sit in the back row of the lecture hall, where I could not only read what the professor wrote on the blackboard but also see the smudges of chalk on his pants. Thanks to my corrected vision, I was also able to see and recognize people as they approached me in the hallway, so the reputation I'd had for snubbing them (when, in fact, I simply didn't recognize their blurry faces) disappeared.

Ideally, a worldview should serve the same purpose as my glasses. It isn't there to turn reality pink; instead, it brings things into focus. Of course, not every worldview accomplishes this, and the metaphor of eyeglasses suggests a reason why: worldviews disagree on what the standard or starting point of interpretation should be. Unless you adopt 20/20 as the standard, you won't achieve clear vision. By the same token, to account for the world as it really is, a worldview must share certain standards that are built into reality.

Building a worldview is a tricky business, and we are not entirely in control of it. Imagine this: your optometrist diagnoses your nearsightedness and then leaves you with some glass and a grinder and tells you to make your own lenses. That's what constructing a worldview is like, and that's why it is a lot easier to *talk* about worldview than to understand it. We are all fashioning a pair of glasses, but we do it badly, with unfamiliar tools and conflicting ideas about what clear vision really is.

Do I Choose My Worldview or Does It Choose Me?

When we talk about worldview, too often we make the assumption that human beings are in complete control of the way they view the world. We envision some ideological buffet stocked with different worldviews—Buddhist, Christian, Atheist, Marxist, Agnostic, Muslim, and so on—and each of us gets to pick one. As Christians, of course, we should pick the Christian worldview, and we should also be telling people what's wrong with the other views on offer, so that they will pick our worldview, too.

But do I choose my worldview or does my worldview choose me? Now this sounds like a trick question, doesn't it? I sure hope so, because it is. On the one hand, we have already seen that worldviews are shaped by our circumstances as much as by our choices, so it seems too simplistic to declare, "I choose my worldview." Then again, my worldview isn't some force of nature outside of me—without me, it can't really exist—so how can I say, "My worldview chooses me"?

And if I can't say yes to either proposition, there is another sense in which I *must* say yes to both. Yes, I choose my worldview. My choices (or, at the very least, my reactions) shape my subsequent approach to interpretation. Yes, my worldview chooses me. The circumstances to which I react form the range within which I operate, the conclusions to which I am likely to come, and (through the process of refinement) the stronger parts of my worldview assert themselves over the weaker ones, straining toward consistency.

The Aggressive Environment

Man is an interpreter. Place him on a desert island and before long, he will develop systems and stories to explain how he got there, why he is there, what he should do, and what is happening around him. So we might say that forming worldview is our natural response to our environment. But a lot depends on what you think that environment is doing.

Is it sitting back at a safe distance from us, waiting to be observed? If that's how you view it (and many people do), then you might think of forming worldview as tinkering with a car engine. It's something you do deliberately, perhaps on weekends, and the raw material waits for you to rebuild it. This is actually a very comforting image. You can make this adjustment or that one, change this or that filter, rev the engine, listen to the sound, and fine-tune your worldview until it really purrs. In the meantime, you can store it in the garage. According to this model, forming worldviews is a classroom exercise, not unlike a problem in engineering.

But is this a convincing account of how life shapes us?

Of course not.

Instead of waiting until we are at leisure to consider it, our environment constantly moves in on us, forcing itself on us, exerting pressure. Forming worldview is an active response to this aggression. It is not an academic exercise; instead, it is a form of mental self-defense. Forget about the car mechanics and imagine one of those martial arts movies where the hero holds the center while adversaries circle and rush in for the assault. Every kick and punch, every block, parry, and evasion is a worldview response.

This model does justice to the rough and ready nature of worldview thinking, to the core principles we cling to like a set of reliable moves that, executed consistently, will exploit gaps in the opponent's attack and use his own momentum against him.

If we keep this sense of struggle in the foreground of our concept of worldview, the question of whether we choose our worldview or it chooses us can be answered with a resounding (and seemingly inconsistent) yes. To the extent that we exert ourselves against the pressures, we are forming a worldview, and to the extent that the pressures are shaping our responses, they are changing and polishing and demolishing that worldview. And this is happening constantly, whether we are alive to the struggle and engaged in it or not.

Ambiguities remain: How much of your worldview is conscious, how much is unconscious? Is your worldview a set of fundamental beliefs or doctrines, or is it some kind of substructure beneath these doctrines, enabling them? Is your worldview just a myth, a story you tell yourself to allay your fears? To answer these questions, we have to pose another: What is worldview for? As simple as it is, this question is often overlooked. Why do we form a worldview? What good is it? What purpose does it serve?

The Navigational Chart

Your worldview serves the same purpose for you as a navigational chart does for a sea voyager. It tells you where you're going, what to expect, and how things are related to one another. Comparing your worldview to a modern map can be misleading, though. There are so few gaps in our geographical knowledge and so many in our view of the world.

So instead of a modern atlas, think of the old nautical charts mariners once relied on, the ones with sketchy outlines of unknown coasts, uncharted islands, and sea serpents coiled in the margin. We sneer at such things now, but think of the remarkable men who traveled the world with no better idea of its true dimensions than this. They were ready to plunge into the unknown and chart the course as they went. The way they navigated through unknown seas is quite similar to the way we navigate life.

Back then, the world was just so much uncharted territory, the maps based as much on speculation, guesswork, and tall tales as on observation. Sometimes the maps were right, but often they were wrong. A sailor who trusted in them uncritically might be lost. But as his map proved useful, he learned to trust it more. Over time, the maps were corrected until they became increasingly accurate, and today we think of maps as utterly reliable—so much so that we tend not to prefer one brand (for example, Rand McNally) over another, since we assume that they are all equally accurate.

The sailor's relationship to maps can teach us something about our own understanding of worldviews:

1) *Worldviews should be trusted, but not uncritically.* Maps change as new discoveries are made. No nautical navigator would insist, for

dogmatic purposes, that his map could never change, that it had to be right no matter what. You don't refuse to believe in the coral reef that just tore open your hull just because it wasn't on the charts! By the same token, our fixed ideas should not be so inflexible that we cannot make new discoveries.

2) *Much remains to be discovered.* Navigators of old understood that a map didn't lose its value just because it left some details sketchy. In a good map, there is always something left to be discovered. Our belief systems function in a similar way: they are incomplete but constantly growing. Admitting this does not devalue the Christian worldview; rather, it acknowledges that individual Christians realize how far they have to go before claiming to have the mind of Christ.

3) *The scale of objects and their relationship to each other is sometimes distorted.* The perfect belief system would not only get everything correct, but it would also organize things in right relation to one another. Our imperfect understanding, however, is distorted in the same way that Antarctica and Greenland are on a globe—the perspective of the map makes them appear larger than they really are. Sometimes you can hold to true beliefs and still lose perspective.

We navigate life with imperfect worldviews that sometimes help and sometimes hinder our understanding of what's happening around us. When we are young, our maps are filled with uncharted territory—and sometimes we fill them in carelessly, because we aren't always good and attentive observers. In spite of their faults, we often cling to our maps even when they take us to the wrong place again and again, even when they throw unexpected obstacles in our path. So the question becomes, how do we deal with these unreliable maps?

Making Better Maps

I've mentioned already how reliable maps are today. Perhaps I spoke too soon. There is a type of map we all encounter that is notoriously unreliable and yet essential to our daily existence, that is, the maps our friends draw for us.

How many times have you set out for a friend's house with nothing but a hand-drawn map to lead the way? When your friend drew it, she was rushed. Her mind was on other things. She couldn't remember all of the street names (and at least one that she thought she remembered is actually wrong), so instead she gave you landmarks: *Turn right at the*

gas station and then go straight until the second red light; then you'll see
a movie rental place—but keep going until you reach the fire station and
turn right again; then take your first left and our house will be the one
with all the cars parked in front. The diagram looks like a mix between
a pirate's treasure map and ancient hieroglyphics. And to make matters
worse, all of your other friends say that instead of getting their own directions, they'll follow you. I have been there too many times to count.

But why should this be? After all, we have such reliable charts available. Shouldn't all of our maps be accurate?

The reason our hand-drawn maps are so unreliable is that they are
not drawn with reference to the standard. Sure, if we copied them out of
an atlas, they would be perfect. But often we rely on memory. We sketch
things the way we *think* they are without really knowing. We approxi-
mate, even though we know that our maps will get our friends to the right
destination only if they happen to correspond to the established standard,
in this case the lay of the land.

The word *standard* has already come up in reference to optometry,
and now it is making another appearance. The more we acknowledge our
subjective limits, the greater we feel the need for some standard outside of
that subjectivity upon which to base our knowledge. We look for measuring sticks, for ways of checking a map to tell if it's good or not.

Testing Worldviews

You can test a worldview the same way you would test a map, by asking
yourself if it matches reality, if the proportions are right, and if it gets you
to the right destination. In more formal terms, we would call these tests
correspondence, coherence, and productivity.

If worldviews interpret reality, then the observations from which they
are drawn should correspond to reality. Given what we observe in the
world around us, what explanation can give an adequate account? Would
you trust a belief system that starts from the premise that man is intrinsi-
cally good, even altruistic? This is a widely held belief, but even its fervent
adherents do not usually behave as if it were true—they've had too much
experience with actual people! If we look at people as they really are,
we see that they're imperfect, that even the best of us have a propensity
toward evil. To correspond to reality, a belief system needs to account for
this intrinsic flaw in its description of humanity.

If correspondence appeals to an outside standard, the test of coherence checks for internal consistency. The various pieces of a worldview should *fit*. To the extent that it is cobbled together, flawed by the kind of inconsistencies and contradictions we have already noted, it is naturally unreliable. The logical law of noncontradiction, which states that something cannot be both true and false in the same way at the same time, is an expression of the principle that coherence is a hallmark of truth. Christian apologists attempt to deconstruct other worldviews by showing that their axioms contradict one another. For example, many people want to assert that murder is always wrong, but they reject the underlying assumption that would justify such a belief. After all, how can a worldview that rejects transcendent moral standards say that anything is *always* wrong?

In addition to asking whether a worldview gives adequate explanations for the world around us and is internally consistent, we can also test worldviews by measuring what kind of results they produce. A good belief system should produce good results. It should solve philosophical problems, resolve dilemmas, and put adherents in a better position to understand the world and act within it. This is not a test of pragmatism *per se*—the truth is the truth whether it gets you anywhere or not; but the ability to shine light in dark places is another hallmark of truth. In a sense, the earlier example applies here, too. By condemning murder in every circumstance while denying there are any transcendent moral standards, a person opens up an inconsistency in his viewpoint. By embracing these contradictions, the adherent is confronted with a dilemma, a problem. Worldviews that continually create such problems come to be seen as unreliable, while those that *solve* them are deemed more trustworthy.

These three tools are good as far as they go, but they are not necessarily conclusive. Sometimes a lie seems more coherent and consistent than the truth, so when we ask whether worldviews correspond to reality, whether they cohere and produce results, we have to admit that we're the ones asking—i.e., subjective people and, according to Christian doctrine, fallen too. This is all part of the struggle that is worldview. We are constantly wrestling with ideas while we question our own ability to judge, always acting decisively only to look back with doubts after the fact.

Uncertainties

There is an uncomfortable degree of uncertainty in all of this, which is perhaps one of the reasons why so many Christians who talk about worldview gloss over the problems inherent in such realizations.

I am no different. This chapter is really not the kind of introduction to worldview that I had in mind, but as I prepared for the task I found there was no other kind I could write. The only way to properly prepare the reader for the sense of gratitude that comes from having a God-given, transcendent standard upon which to rely is to dwell first on the doubts inherent in a situation where such a standard is lacking.

Even when we turn to Scripture for guidance, we are called upon to be interpreters, but it is an interpretation informed by the stories and structure of revelation, focused on one whose knowledge is perfect. Where we have doubts, we can rely, not on some point of logic, but on the person of Christ.

Worldview and the Supernatural

My first reservation about popular worldview thinking was the confidence with which it ignores the environmental factors that go into forming our viewpoints. Now, I want to take on another challenge: the way we often suppress the role of the supernatural in worldview formation.

Christians profess faith in a God who is sovereign. We say that God is in control of the circumstances in our lives. If those circumstances contribute to forming our worldview, then we might as well say that God, in what he commands and allows, is active in shaping it, too.

This goes to the heart of the idea of revelation. Theologians distinguish between two types of revelation: natural revelation and special revelation. Not surprisingly, natural revelation consists of the knowledge we receive from living in, observing, and testing nature. Note that it is not nature itself that is revealed, but God who reveals himself in nature—which is why, in Romans 1, the apostle Paul could speak of men plainly knowing God through creation:

> For what can be known about God is plain to them, because God has shown it to them. For his invisible attributes, namely, his eternal power and divine nature, have been clearly perceived, ever since the creation of the world, in the things that have been made. So they are without excuse. (vv. 19–20)

That is a remarkable statement when you stop and consider it. Paul is saying that from the moment God created the world, his eternal power and divine nature have been "clearly perceived" in the things he made. The reason mankind is "without excuse" is that we have denied what is perfectly obvious all around us. Few Christians today, I think, would argue for such an extreme. After all, it isn't true, is it? You don't go out in your backyard, smell the fresh-cut grass, feel the cool breeze, see the divine nature of God and his eternal power, and then fire up the grill. But Paul, in a sense, says that you do. It is a testimony to the mind-clouding effects of sin that we don't see what we are, in fact, seeing.

If natural revelation holds so much power, then imagine how formidable special revelation must be. Special revelation is the category of knowledge that God has revealed outside of nature, specifically in the Bible. There are things in Scripture, points of doctrine, that cannot be known apart from our reading them in its pages. The knowledge of God that comes from nature is, as the theologians say, sufficient to condemn, but not to save. Saving knowledge comes from Christ and the Word of God. We will have more to say about creation and salvation in the pages ahead.

God is at work in the world around us, which means there is a spiritual dimension to every discussion of the gospel. We are not converted to faith by clever arguments. We are not converted even by "evidence that demands a verdict," as important as such evidence may be. Two men can hear the same arguments and see the same evidence, but one believes and the other doesn't. Ultimately there is a mystery in all of this. When Jesus describes the work of the Spirit in John 3:8, he speaks in terms of the wind:

> The wind blows where it wishes, and you hear its sound, but you do not know where it comes from or where it goes. So it is with everyone who is born of the Spirit.

There will be many moments in life where, in the middle of some conversation—perhaps in some argument you are not handling very well—you will hear that sound, without knowing where it came from or where it is going, and the whole complexion of the encounter changes. When it happens, just hold your tongue and respond in awe. The Spirit's work is the unpredictable X-factor in our worldview discussions. It quickens what would otherwise be a dead exchange.

Changing Our Worldview

On top of the outside pressure and our response to it, our worldview is shaped by the Spirit's work, and there is simply no way to quantify these efforts. But the outcome of the whole process is that *worldviews never stand still.*

So the question isn't whether they can be changed, it is whether *you* can change them—and if so, how?

In a sense, we have already answered the first part. If your choices and responses contribute to the shaping of your worldview, then you have the power to change that view at least to the extent that you can make different choices and react in new ways. Now, your choices and responses are not all that goes into your worldview, so this is a qualified affirmative. Yes, you can change your worldview, but only insofar as you can change your actions (and only insofar as your actions actually shape your worldview). Is that complicated enough for you? I am not being intentionally obscure, but I think these qualifications are worth making, so that things don't look simpler than they really are.

To be blunt, some people give the impression that you can change your worldview through study and reason. As valuable as they are, study and the application of reason are not enough. Your worldview is not simply the product of study and reason, so it's wrong to suggest that changing it is a simple intellectual exercise. As you know, it is possible to argue any position convincingly, to twist logic in whatever direction you like, and even to back up every falsehood in the book with brief, thundering proof texts from the Bible. All of these forces lie in that shadowy, subjective realm we have already touched on.

Real transformation, though, comes from outside that realm, originating in the transcendent God. In fact, it might be more precise to say that transformation takes place when the personal, transcendent God goes to work inside a subjective, immanent man. Let's turn again to the apostle Paul. In Philippians 2:12–13, Paul gives this insight into the process of sanctification:

> Therefore, my beloved, as you have always obeyed, so now, not only as in my presence but much more in my absence, work out your own salvation with fear and trembling, *for it is God who works in you, both to will and to work for his good pleasure.*

The sentence in italics speaks volumes. Paul urges the Philippians to apply themselves, to work—literally, to work out their salvation, to bring all of their life into submission to that salvation. This is no exhortation to passivity. Paul does not say, "Sit back, relax, and let God work within you." Instead, the Philippians work, and God works in them. They want to please him, they want to work for his pleasure—they really do *want* it—and it is also God working in them so that they want it. The lines between what we do and what God does are blurred to the point that the two things become indistinguishable, inseparable.

So the key to changing your worldview turns out to be, not some profound philosophical quest, but the fundamental journey to Christlike sanctity that every Christian is called to undertake. If you want to change your worldview, to make it a more consistently biblical worldview, then the first and most important thing you must do is work out your salvation in fear and trembling, knowing that it is God working in you, both to will and to work for his good pleasure. The concept of worldview is one that Christianity inherited from philosophy. We couch it in high-sounding words. But it would be a mistake to think that this intellectual language describes an essentially *intellectual* process.

In life, you encounter unlettered Christians who possess a much greater grasp on the Christian worldview than the scholars who talk so much about it, myself included. Worldview is a spiritual process, and the path to consistent worldview thinking is not intellectual but spiritual.

The Second Look

The French novelist Marcel Proust once set out to change a young man's worldview, and there is something we can learn from his approach. Alain de Botton tells the story in his book *How Proust Can Change Your Life,* a whimsical application of the famous author's insight to the self-help genre. The young man in question had a taste for the finer things in life, for beauty and art, but he was trapped in a lower-middle-class home where there was no money for such "frivolities." He was driven to despair by the thought that he was condemned always to be on the outside looking in, that he would never live a life surrounded by beauty.

This is a common and entirely understandable form of despair. As the invulnerability of youth adjusts to life's realities, there is a sense of loss even for the things we never had—we mourn that they will never be ours. But suppose that the things we long for really are a part of our lives; we simply do not see them.

According to Proust, the young man who longed for beauty was actually surrounded by it, if only he could learn to see the beauty of everyday things. To remedy the problem, Proust advised the young man to gaze at the still-life painting of Jean-Baptiste Chardin. Chardin was an artist who shunned exotic settings in favor of simple arrangements of fruit; but through his eyes, there was nothing simple about them.

> In spite of the ordinary nature of their subjects, Chardin's paintings succeeded in being extraordinarily beguiling and evocative. . . . There was a harmony, too, between objects: in one canvas, almost a friendship between the reddish colors of a hearthrug, a needle box, and a skein of wool. These paintings were windows onto a world at once recognizably our own, yet uncommonly, wonderfully tempting.[1]

If the young man could take a second look at his everyday surroundings, if he could see them through Chardin's eyes, then his despair would give way to delight. As Alain de Botton concludes, it all came down to taking that second look:

> The happiness that may emerge from taking a second look is central to Proust's therapeutic conception. It reveals the extent to which our dissatisfactions may be the result of *failing to look properly* at our lives rather than the result of anything inherently deficient about them.[2]

Failing to look properly—these four words sum up the human condition nicely. Certainly, the whole worldview struggle boils down to a battle for perspective, a fight to see things properly. The passage quoted above lends itself to misunderstanding: you might read it and think that, for therapeutic reasons, we should learn to see the silver lining even in discouraging circumstances, and failing that we should simply choose to see bad as if it were good. *Surrounded by the mundane world and cut off from beauty? That's all right: just pretend that everyday things are delightful to behold!* That is not the point. Failing to look properly is the fault, which implies that there is a right way to see things.

The right perception of reality, however, may not always lend itself to cheerful ends. Sometimes reality is very bleak indeed, and there is enormous social and spiritual pressure not to see it properly. Take, for instance, man's fallen condition. Christian theologians have always strived to convince others to see man as God sees him; from that vision all the rest of Christian doctrine follows. But reaching even this small concession is hard. The eighteenth-century theologian Jonathan Edwards,

---

[1] Alain de Botton, *How Proust Can Change Your Life* (New York: Pantheon, 1997), 135.
[2] Ibid., 140 (emphasis added).

perhaps the greatest American thinker of his age, fully appreciated this difficulty. According to biographer George Marsden,

> Ever since the first glimmerings of his own awakening, [Edwards] was acutely aware that the human problem was to see one's condition in its true perspective. Human self-centeredness was so overwhelming and this world was so alluring, that each person was by nature incredibly short-sighted, self-absorbed, and blinded by pride. People had to awaken to their true interests.[3]

To awaken to our true interests, to see our condition in its proper perspective, demands the ability to take a second look. There is a spiritual dimension to this: throughout Scripture, blindness and sight are used as signs of unbelief and belief. But at its simplest level, taking a second look requires only a willingness to see things differently, to entertain (at least tentatively) a different interpretation of reality. I say that it requires "only" this, not because it is easy to do, but because the effort is small; what is difficult is recognizing the need to take a second look in the first place.

Changing Other People's Worldview

If we acknowledge that power over our own worldview is only partly in our hands, though fully in God's, then we must also concede that our ability to change other people's worldview is limited. Fortunately, we understand that the Holy Spirit often uses precisely the limited means at our disposal to bring about such changes. This is one instance where an honest assessment of our limitations serves more to encourage than to discourage engagement.

Limiting ourselves to the part of the task that remains in our power, what can we do to change other people's worldview? We can ask gracious and persistent questions and respectfully encourage others to see through new eyes. To do this, we must realize that, while worldview is a proposition, it is also a perspective. It is also a story.

---

[3]George Marsden, *Jonathan Edwards: A Life* (New Haven: Yale University Press, 2003), 120.

2

The Four Pillars:
Worldview as Starting Point

*I preach there are all kinds of truth, your truth and somebody else's.
But behind all of them, there's only one truth and that is that there's
no truth.*
HAZEL MOTES IN FLANNERY O'CONNOR'S *WISE BLOOD*

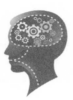

[1]

With only a scrap of bone for a weapon, Samson killed a thousand men.
I can hardly imagine killing one, let alone a legion. In fact, armed only
with a donkey's jawbone, I wouldn't fancy my chances against a sedentary sheep. It just goes to show what a remarkable feat Samson's victory
was. And a long one, too. Today we are accustomed to mass slaughter.
To wipe out a thousand men might be the work of an hour for a machine
gun, or the work of a moment for a bomb. But for an improvised club, a
weapon that must be raised in the sweep of a muscled arm and brought
down with brute force again and again, a weapon that must crush iron
helmets, smash skulls, and send men down to their knees in death throes
over and over, to dispatch a dozen men is a labor, a hundred a miracle,
and a thousand a triumph of Herculean proportions.

This is one battle scene it is difficult to imagine translating onto film.
I would not envy the director who took it on. My childhood book of
Bible stories could not help but illustrate it—what artist could pass up
such a scene?—but the carnage is limited to a single Philistine sprawled
at Samson's feet and another rushing up behind for a piece of the action.
Surely, this is a failure of imagination! But I do not blame the illustrator

for reducing the action to a manageable scale, because quite frankly I cannot imagine how Samson could have accomplished such a thing. Even if you assume one of those improbable moments from a martial arts movie where the bad guys circle menacingly around the hero, assuming a series of intimidating acrobatic poses, all the while politely waiting their turn to move in and be slaughtered, a circle of a thousand men would stretch to quite a circumference. And the bodies would really stack up after awhile! How did Samson do it?

Swords have always fascinated me, and over the years I've had the privilege to visit some notable museums and private collections of medieval and Renaissance edged weapons. Once, I accompanied some friends to the home of Ewart Oakeshott, one of the twentieth century's preeminent authorities on the sword. Oakeshott was in his eighties at the time. He was a small, sprightly man who reminded us a little bit of Yoda—particularly since we had devoured his books and considered him something of a guru. He lived with his wife in Ely, a town in the heart of the fens not far from Cambridge, the site of a magnificent Norman cathedral. On his wall, displayed with the same lack of ceremony with which a hunter might display a deer's head as trophy, Oakeshott hung one of the fifteenth-century swords found in a French river near the site of the Battle of Castillon in 1453.

When a sword spends centuries at the bottom of a river, the blade emerges looking a lot like an anchor: barnacled, eroded, withered. But I handled a couple of these weapons, including one at London's Wallace Collection that dated as far back as the ninth century, and while they may look bad, they feel wonderful. The superb balance of the weapon remains, and once you clasp your fingers around it, it is easy to imagine yourself cutting down one horseman after another. Your arm wants to move; it takes quite a struggle to remain calm and dignified. Oakeshott's sword from Castillon was like that. It was the kind of tool a warrior like Samson would have appreciated.

Of course, Samson had nothing of the kind. His weapon was humble and wholly inadequate, and his victory was a testament to his God-given strength and nothing else. We could speculate about *how* it was done, but that would be beside the point. It was impossible. It couldn't be done. The fact that Samson did it is intended to astonish us. And the more we know about war, the more astonishing it is.

But even more remarkable is the fact that the slaying of a thousand with a donkey's jawbone was not the greatest of Samson's achievements. The zenith of his fame came at his life's lowest ebb.

For the Philistines, Samson was a scourge; the sooner he was eliminated the better. But every attempt met with disaster. Until they could find a way around his remarkable brawn, Samson would stand between the Philistines and their dreams of domination, and he would cast a shadow over the power of their god Dagon, too. Representations of Dagon depicted him with the body of a man from the waist up and the body of a fish from the waist down—a bit like a bearded mermaid. It was to Dagon that praise went for the victories of the Philistines, though recently the fish-god had not given his followers much reason for thanksgiving.

Samson's fall was fated to come, not on the battlefield, but entangled in the arms of Delilah, the prototypical temptress, a Philistine beauty he should have avoided at all costs. After her insistent prying, Samson finally revealed to her the secret of his strength: his uncut hair. She waited until he was asleep, cut off his hair, and then passed the news on to the enemies who waited outside. They pounced on the powerless Samson. Now, deprived of his strength he was at their mercy—though, of course, there was no mercy to speak of. They promptly gouged out his eyes, mocked him, and kept him in chains as the local laughingstock. The man they once feared was now their jester.

Knowing Where to Push

To celebrate their deliverance, the Philistines offered up a sacrifice of thanksgiving to Dagon. They cried, "Our god has given Samson our enemy into our hand."[1] It occurred to someone that it would be the height of irony to parade the humbled Samson around in Dagon's temple for the crowd's entertainment, and so he was brought. This was a celebration of epic proportions, with some three thousand men and women packed into the temple.

When Samson arrived, however, it was not for the scene of his greatest humiliation, but for his final triumph. Though blind, his hair had begun to grow in captivity. Reading between the lines, it seems that his pride, too, had been checked, and it was a change for the better. Samson now remembered that his strength depended upon the Lord.

The account in Judges 16 is concise but heartbreaking. When Samson arrived, he asked his keeper to let him lean against the pillars that support

---

[1]Judg. 16:23.

the weight of the temple. Through the genius of Phoenician engineering, these columns held up the entire structure. Samson asked God for the power to topple them: "O Lord GOD, please remember me and please strengthen me only this once, O God, that I may be avenged on the Philistines for my two eyes" (v. 28). The image of Samson toiling between the pillars is one that has intrigued artists ever since. Imagine a dark, heavy ceiling that traps the aromas of blood from the sacrifice and sweat from the people, a structure large enough to house thousands of revelers. A network of columns supports the weight of the building, with the bulk of it resting on the two middle pillars. Hearing Samson's prayer, his keeper must have panicked, the alarm spreading throughout the crowd choking off their laughter. But it all happened too quickly for the Philistines to do anything. With a final cry—"Let me die with the Philistines!"—Samson pushed against the pillars with such force that they crumbled. All the weight of that mighty temple came down on the worshipers, drowning out the echo of Samson's words in a crash of masonry.

The writer of the book of Judges ends the account with this simple observation: "So the dead whom he killed at his death were more than those whom he had killed during his life" (v. 30). It strikes the ear like a thunderclap. Samson, the man who once slew a thousand men with a donkey's jawbone, has, at his final moment, outdone the carnage of a lifetime. And unlike the earlier victory, which required at least a thousand blows, this was accomplished with a single push. Before, he had reduced their army to a pulp blow by blow, but this time he does not strike a single man. Instead, he releases the weight of their own temple, and the Philistines are crushed as it falls down on them.

Samson killed more Philistines than he had in his whole life—and himself along with them—all by knowing where to push.

The Weight of Worldview

The moral of the story? Our belief systems are load-bearing structures. In a sense, they carry the weight of the world. And every day they are subject to assault: our beliefs are questioned, our conclusions mocked, our convictions dismissed. If they are not defended, our worldview will, over time, show the effects of this attack. But there is a quicker way to undermine a belief system, and all it requires is the toppling of the pillars that support its weight.

These pillars are not made of stone. They are ideas. They are axioms.

They are the underlying assumptions that make our worldview work. To believe the things we do, we must assume that certain principles are true. Often, we are not conscious of these necessary assumptions; they are simply "given." We accept them without question because it seems impossible, even unimaginable, for them not to be true.

Have you ever wondered if you are the only real person in existence and the rest of us are just figments of your imagination? It is a liberating thought. Not only would this mean that you are the most creative and attractive person who exists—a genius of monumental proportions—but it would also signify that you had never failed at anything in life, that no one despises you, and that all of the setbacks you have encountered up until now have really been clever plots invented by your subconscious mind to make your life more interesting. After all, if you're alone in the universe, you've got to do something to keep busy.

Let us hope you have *never* given this possibility much thought. As a rule, we all assume that other people are not figments of our imagination. If you come to the conclusion that they *are*, and that beyond the frontiers of your own consciousness there is nothing, then the rest of us are likely to put you in an institution. The reality of other people and the outside world seems to be a necessary assumption. You can't get along without it. If you act as if it is true, things work out well, and if you deny it, things go badly.

And yet, if you really believed that the rest of us were illusions, imagine how hard it would be to talk you out of it! What argument could possibly convince you? The evidence of your senses could not be trusted, since it is the principal means by which the illusion is maintained. You couldn't rely on reason or logic, because your logic teacher in school was *another person* who clearly did not exist. That means you basically invented logic, and if you made it up, how do you know it is reliable? The fact is we assume that other people exist, and any hint to the contrary is dismissed as ridiculous. But not because we can prove it.

We accept it as true because to embrace the contrary would be absurd.

Not every assumption is so straightforward. Although most people will acknowledge the existence of these necessary assumptions in theory, in practice we disagree on what they are. There are people who believe that the laws of logic are fundamental to our ability to think and know, but there are others who believe that logic is some kind of construct, and is not a necessary precondition for coherent thought. Some people think that to make sense of reality, we have to assume a creative intelligence guiding it, while others see this not as a case of logical necessity but existential weakness. Explore the world of ideas and you will find that there are huge disagreements about even the most basic principles.

As If

The funny thing is, even though there are many assumptions people would challenge in theory, they live their daily lives as if these assumptions are true. They are willing to make use of them, but not to acknowledge them. For example, there are people who believe that because there is no God, there can be no binding, transcendent moral code. Morality comes not from a creator but from the collective: society constructs our ideas of good and evil. What is right for me may not be right for you, and vice versa. To those of us who take morality seriously, this kind of thinking is downright chilling. If more people thought like this, we tell ourselves, the world would descend into anarchy.

But many people *do* think this way, and the world isn't nearly as bad as it could be. Why? It is because people who reject the idea of a transcendent moral code still behave as if there is one. Christians would argue that this is because man, whatever he might think of himself and his origins, is made in God's image and is, in some sense, instilled with a moral sense. Though he is corrupted by sin and suppresses the truth, on some level man continues to operate "as if."

Perhaps it is just force of habit, but Christians have suggested another explanation. It is necessary for a man, no matter what his ideology, to act as if certain things are so, because *they are,* and he cannot operate in the real world without making some concession to that fact. Worldviews are a way of interpreting reality, but not every worldview is equally valid because not every worldview interprets correctly. This is something we have already observed in the last chapter, and now we need to take it a level deeper. Our goal here is to see which pillars support the weight of the Christian view of reality, what forces seek to topple those pillars, and how even those who want to undermine the Christian worldview are often forced to act as if it is true.

[II]

I sometimes daydream about starting my own publishing imprint. For as long as I can remember, books have fascinated me—not only their contents, but their form: type, paper, binding, the smell and feel of a well-made book in the hand. If I break down one day and set up as a gentleman publisher, I will have to name my imprint Desert Island Books, because my goal would be to publish the kind of work that readers would gladly choose when stranded on the proverbial desert island.

Have you ever given serious thought to the question of what book, or what five books, or what ten books, you would take with you during an island exile? My walls are lined with creaking bookshelves, so it is a fearful question for me. How do you choose? Should you select books you have never read but always wanted to, or should you take trusted favorites that will stand up to many rereadings? If you are practical, you will no doubt include some kind of survival guide on your list. Personally, I look for the longest books, and I try to argue with the hypothetical genie who makes the choice possible that multi-volume works should only count as one! So my desert island list might look something like this:

The Holy Bible
War and Peace, by Leo Tolstoy
Remembrance of Things Past, by Marcel Proust
The Chronicles of Narnia, by C.S. Lewis
The Idiot's Guide to Desert Island Living

The Bible is a given; I wouldn't like to be stuck anywhere without it. *War and Peace* is one of those massive books that instill the people who have read it with a colossal sense of superiority, simply because no one else has managed to finish it. If I could find an edition that binds *War and Peace* along with *Anna Karenina*, so much the better. After all, you don't want to run out of reading material ten years into your twenty-year stay.

Remembrance of Things Past is a tricky one, too, because it consists of several thick volumes. Only a handful of readers have gotten beyond the first one, *Swann's Way,* but we all accept on faith that Proust, whom we encountered in the last chapter, is a genius, and his life work amounts to one of the greatest literary achievements of the twentieth century. An alternative to Proust might be James Joyce's *Ulysses,* but I read it in graduate school and don't think I could understand it again without the help of a guidebook, and it seems a shame to fill one of my five slots with a book about a book already on the list!

The Chronicles of Narnia, of course, is another multi-volume epic and a Christian classic to boot. For sheer escape value (and I imagine there

are times on a desert island when one wants nothing more than to escape),
Narnia can't be beaten. A good alternative, now that the Peter Jackson
films have induced a revival of interest, would be J. R. R. Tolkien's three-
volume *Lord of the Rings*. I have friends who would not consider two
decades on a desert island sufficient time to plumb the depths of those
books.

If you have not realized it by now, I create fantasy book lists the way
some people make up fantasy baseball teams. There are infinite combi-
nations, and every time you put together a list, you approach it from a
different perspective and come up with an entirely different selection of
titles. My lists are constantly being revised. In fact, now that I've mentioned Tolstoy and Proust and Lewis, all I can think of are other authors
I should take instead! And I have omitted the one book you simply must
take to the desert island: Daniel Defoe's *Robinson Crusoe*.

Unfortunately, *Robinson Crusoe*'s classic status has led many readers
to think of it as an adventure book for young readers, a somewhat less
accessible version of *The Swiss Family Robinson*. In fact, it's much more
than that. If the only thing you remember about Robinson Crusoe is that
he was stranded on a desert island, then you're missing something significant. And you're not alone. For years, I missed it entirely, and I never
would have discovered it if it hadn't been for a friend's chance remark.

I picked up a copy of the Oxford Pocket Classics edition of *Robinson
Crusoe* in a bookstore a couple of years ago and decided to reread it.
When I mentioned to my friend Luke what I was doing, he decided to read
it, too. Unfortunately, I didn't persevere. After about fifty pages (which
were surprisingly good), I mislaid the book and went on to other reading. I had forgotten about it entirely until one day Luke happened to ask,
"What did you think of Robinson Crusoe's conversion?"

"His *what*?" I asked.

"You know, where he comes to faith in Christ."

I remembered the shipwreck. I remembered Crusoe salvaging some
Bibles and prayer books from the wreckage. But I didn't recall a conversion scene. I had stopped too soon. So naturally, I dug through my piles
of books until I found *Crusoe* and started reading again. Sure enough, he
did repent of his sins and believe in Jesus Christ, and it is one of the most
remarkable conversions in all of literature. In fact, studying Crusoe's conversion will give us insight into the assumptions that make the Christian
worldview work.

He Has Appointed All This to Befall Me

After the first shock of his ordeal is over and Crusoe establishes himself on the island, he has time to think about the events in his life that have led to this catastrophe. As he ponders, Crusoe comes to see his circumstances more and more in theological terms.

This is not surprising. All of us, when faced with personal tragedy and hardship, sift our suffering for slivers of meaning. Why has this happened? What did I do to deserve it?

Crusoe is no different. At first, he labors industriously, imposing order on his wild surroundings, but when illness lays him low, and the strength he has relied on up to now is gone, he's left with all the time in the world to think. His thoughts turn to God, and he utters his first prayer in a long while: "Lord be my Help, for I am in great Distress." He begins to study his Bible, but as he reads, his sense of sin deepens. He realizes that he is guilty before God. At the same time, his life was spared when all his fellow voyagers perished, so his island imprisonment is also a deliverance—a salvation he owes to the Lord.

The way that Crusoe works through his situation and applies what he learns from Scripture to his own life is truly impressive, perhaps because it is so rigorously theological. Here is an excerpt of Crusoe's thinking, a passage that will serve as a key to unlock the foundation of the Christian worldview:

> What is this Earth and Sea of which I have seen so much, whence is it produc'd, and what am I, and all the other Creatures, wild and tame, humane and brutal, whence are we? Sure we are all made by some secret Power, who form'd the Earth and Sea, the Air and Sky; and who is that? Then it follow'd most naturally, It is God that has made it all: Well, but then it came on strangely, if God has made all these Things, he guides and governs them all, and all Things that concern them; for the Power that could make all Things, must certainly have Power to guide and direct them. If so, nothing can happen in the great Circuit of his Works, either without his Knowledge or Appointment. And if nothing happens without his Knowledge, he knows that I am here, and am in this dreadful Condition; and if nothing happens without his Appointment, he has appointed all this to befal me.[2]

Notice the progression of themes. Crusoe begins on the cosmic scale with

---

[2]Daniel Defoe, *Robinson Crusoe*, Oxford World's Classics (Oxford: Oxford University Press, 1999), 93–94.

earth and sea and creatures of every kind. Where do they come from? God has made them. If he made them, then he must govern them. If God is that powerful, then nothing can be outside his power, which means that not only does God know that Crusoe is stranded on the island, but he is stranded by God's decree. Beginning with the wide world, he ends by locating himself in the "great Circuit of [God's] Works." In other words, from the doctrine of creation, he arrives at God's sovereignty and providence. And from there he discerns that his proper relationship to God is that of reverence. He cries aloud: "Jesus, thou exalted Prince and Saviour, give me Repentance!"

I trembled the first time I read the words, experiencing anew the joy of my own salvation. And eventually it dawned on me that, in writing this passage, Defoe had described an *ideal* conversion, a movement through a series of realizations that are philosophically necessary for the believer, although most of us come to them unconsciously all at once, rather than by reasoning aloud as Crusoe does. These necessary assumptions are what I will dub the four pillars of the Christian worldview. They are the doctrines that hold up the weight of our entire system of belief: creation, order, rationality, and fear.

Crusoe begins by contemplating creation and from there he turns to the Creator. From the fact of God's having made the world, he reasons that God must also have the power to govern it. And it follows that if we are God's creation and he is all-powerful, we ought to fear him, as the Old Testament authors insisted. Throughout this line of argument, it is assumed that man can legitimately reason from the evidence of his senses to the transcendent, which is why I add rationality to the list: Crusoe's entire line of thought would be impossible apart from the possibility of real knowledge and the ability to work from known premises to discover new truths.

Hear, My Son

When Daniel J. Estes, an associate professor at Cedarville College, wrote his book *Hear, My Son: Teaching and Learning in Proverbs 1–9,* he included a chapter on the worldview that underlies the first nine chapters of that collection of wisdom. Estes identifies the same four assumptions found in the passage from *Robinson Crusoe:*

- *Creation*: The universe is Yahweh's creation.
- *Order*: Yahweh is sovereignly controlling the world.

- *Rationality*: Yahweh's world is knowable, but also mysterious.
- *Fear of Yahweh*: Humans must reverence Yahweh in their lives.

These four points are not necessarily the explicit teaching of Proverbs 1–9 (although each of them, as Estes shows, is explicitly taught), but they are the necessary assumptions of the author. In other words, if you consider the entire scope of what is said in these nine chapters, you will find that it only stands up if these four assumptions—these four pillars—are in place.

Together, these pillars tell us about who God is and what he does. They tell us about the world he has created and how we operate within it. They also tell us about our right relationship to God. While it is impossible to boil down the whole teaching of Scripture to a handful of concepts, the more you think about these four things, the more you will see how many different areas of thought they touch upon.

My thesis is simple: creation, order, rationality, and fear are the pillars that hold up the entire edifice of the Christian worldview. They are the necessary "starting points" of Christian thought. For that reason, they are all under attack. And because the Christian worldview, ideally speaking, corresponds to the way things really are, to the extent any unbelieving system corresponds to reality, it must borrow strength from these pillars—behaving as if they are true while officially denying them.

[III]

The first thing the Bible tells us about God is that he is the creator: "In the beginning, God created the heavens and the earth." In the New Testament, the Gospel of John echoes the creation account. Of Christ, the apostle John says, "All things were made through him, and without him was not any thing made that was made." God has revealed so much about himself to us, but the foremost fact is that he made us. In the book of Romans, the apostle Paul uses the metaphor of a potter and his clay to describe our relationship to God. He has formed us in a creative act, an expression of himself. When the Genesis account describes man's creation, we are told that God makes us in his image. Theologians debate the precise nature of this image in man, but whatever the details, the language of Scripture communicates a profound idea: that what we are is a reflection of who he is.

When Dorothy Sayers, a contemporary of C. S. Lewis noted for her successful series of detective novels, tried her hand at apologetics, she wrote a book titled *The Mind of the Maker*. One of the things Sayers does is attempt to understand God's creative act by seeing it through the lens of human creativity, which must surely be a legacy left in us from having been made in his image. In our urge to make things, we reveal our origin in the mind of the Creator himself. Students at Lakeland, Florida's, Cambridge Study Center can study the fine arts in a course called *Creative in His Image*, a play on words that echoes the same point Sayers makes. We are creative because we are made in the image of the Creator.

Why Creation?

But have you ever wondered *why* Scripture tells us about the creation of the world? After all, what is the practical value of this knowledge? Does it change the way you live your life? If you take two people, one who believes the world was created by God and the other who believes it came into being through chance, and study their daily activities, you will not notice any differences that can be directly traced to the book of Genesis. You cannot tell by looking who believes in creation and who believes in evolution, unless they are helpful enough to affix the appropriate fish—the standard version, the fish with the word *Darwin* inside, or the big fish eating the fish with *Darwin* inside, etc.—on the back of their cars. What you believe about the details of the creation story seem irrelevant to everyday life, too. People who believe in twenty-four-hour solar days do not get more (or less) sleep than those who believe that the "days" were metaphorical. So why is the creation story, which seems to cause so much trouble for Christianity in this scientific age, even included in the Bible?

We find the answer when the psalmist sings, "The earth is the LORD's and the fullness thereof, the world and those who dwell therein, for he has founded it upon the seas and established it upon the rivers."[3] Creation tells us something important about ourselves: who we belong to. God is omnipotent, but his right to dictate what we should and should not do comes, not from his strength, but from the fact that he made us. It is not that he has taken us by force, but that, through giving birth to us, he owns us.[4]

Paul's epistle to the Romans is the key theological text of the New Testament. Here, we find the most detailed expression of some of

---

[3]Ps. 24:1–2.
[4]And in redemption, where Christ's blood ransoms us, we say that God purchases again what was his by right of creation.

Christianity's most important doctrines. To grasp the importance of the doctrine of creation, we must turn once more to the first chapter of Romans, where Paul describes the fundamental fault of the unbeliever:

> So [sinful men] are without excuse. For although they knew God, they did not honor him as God or give thanks to him, but they became futile in their thinking, and their foolish hearts were darkened. Claiming to be wise, they became fools, and exchanged the glory of the immortal God for images resembling mortal man and birds and animals and creeping things. Therefore God gave them up in the lusts of their hearts to impurity, to the dishonoring of their bodies among themselves, because they exchanged the truth about God for a lie and worshiped and served the creature rather than the Creator, who is blessed forever! Amen.[5]

The whole of man's problem, it seems, can be summed up under the heading of *false worship*. Man, who is made in God's image, sins when he worships what is made by man. This passage conjures up images of ancient idols—not unlike the fish-god Dagon—but it is easy to see how the more sophisticated inventions of our own age qualify. When we worship such things, we exchange something breathtaking and glorious, God Almighty, for a mundane and disappointing evil. The true object of our worship and our service is not man but God. Why? Because we are creatures and he is the Creator.

So the logic is simple. If you know who made you, then you know whom you must worship and serve. Genesis tells us: *Go to the beginning, and you will find God.* The Old Testament adds: *Fear God, and you will find the beginning of wisdom.* In the New Testament: *Christ, by whom all things were made, is the wisdom of God.* In revealing creation, God points both to his Trinitarian nature and to the proper trajectory of a creature's life. The doctrine of creation serves not only as an answer to the philosophical question, *where did I come from?* but also (more significantly) as the basis for our obedience in this life. There is nothing abstract, remote, or impractical about it. It is a fundamental of the faith—perhaps *the* fundamental, since so many other doctrines flow from it.

Is God Necessary?

Ockham's razor is the sharpest tool in the philosophical toolbox. Actually, it is not a razor at all; it is an idea, a principle espoused by the fourteenth-

---

[5]Rom. 1:20b–25.

century philosopher/theologian William of Ockham, who insisted that entities should not be multiplied beyond necessity. In other words, the simpler the explanation, the better. If the reclining chair in front of your television can be adequately explained without an appeal to Plato's ideal chair, then leave all the Hellenistic philosophizing out and keep things simple. Ockham used this razor-sharp notion to slice away at the metaphysical speculations of his Scholastic predecessors, the ones who today are remembered (inaccurately) as the fellows who argued over the number of angels who could dance on the head of a pin. Ever since then, Ockham's razor has been the best friend of commonsense thinkers who have had it up to their eyeballs with all things obscure and convoluted.

I can certainly sympathize with them. To me, it seems axiomatic that the simplest explanation is always the best. But I once sat in on a high school classroom discussion that made me wonder if I was right.

The discussion was about Thomas Aquinas and his proofs for the existence of God. As a visitor, I received the handout students had read before class, an excerpt from Aquinas explaining the cosmological argument: *There is no effect without a cause, so there must be a first cause, and that cause is God.* Naturally, the argument was complicated, and on top of that the prose was a bit stilted and formal. As a rule, American high school students do not warm up to thirteenth-century theology without a fair amount of coaxing. I have to admit, I was having problems myself. With a lot more education and reading experience under my belt than the students had, I still found it necessary to read the Aquinas handout very attentively just to keep up.

From the outset, it was clear that as far as the students were concerned, the existence of God could not be "proven." Aquinas needn't have wasted his time. As one student pointed out, if you could prove that God existed, then what would be the point of faith? The teacher was prepared for this reaction.

"You don't have to agree with the argument," he said, "but if you think it fails, you need to explain *why*."

If you have taught long enough, you know that certain group dynamics always assert themselves. Every class has a few bright, talkative students who tend to dominate the conversation. These are the kids whose hands are up before the teacher finishes the question. And there are always a couple of students who never say a word. Maybe they suffer from clinical shyness, or maybe they are just profoundly bored—it's impossible to tell. In the middle, you have the students who are trying to follow along, who are always on the lookout for something to point out that won't sound too obvious or too dumb. Once they've had their say, they sit back with relief, knowing they can't be counted off for not participating. But of all the different types that emerge in any group, my favorite is the student who bides his time, lets the others think out loud, and finally jumps in with an observation that floors everyone, including the teacher. Often, these students manage to take something the teacher has said in an earlier class and use it to confound him now.

That's what almost happened here.

In the middle of the discussion, I noticed a young man who was slouched in his chair with utter nonchalance but who followed every movement of the conversation with his eyes. Several times his mouth began to form words, only to hold back at the last moment. He was waiting for the right opening. I remembered Luke Skywalker racing through the trench along the Death Star, voices crackling over the intercom: *almost there, almost there, stay on target.* Finally he struck.

The hand went up, and before the teacher had a chance to acknowledge it, the young man said, "What about Ockham's razor?"

"What about it?"

"Well, doesn't it blow Aquinas out of the water?"

The teacher shrugged. "Explain."

As the student outlined his argument, I could see that the others were nodding. Aquinas was making a stretch. He already believed in God, and he wanted to come up with reasons to make other people feel logically compelled to agree. But how do we know there is some cosmic law of cause and effect? How do we know that there cannot be an effect without a cause? It is semantically true, because effects assume the existence of causes, but we can explain the fact that things happen without some abstraction about cause and effect, and therefore without God. Aquinas was multiplying entities without necessity. The truth is always simple.

I admit it: I was impressed. As I already said, Ockham's razor has always seemed an imminently sensible dictum, so I imagined that a young man schooled in its use would go far in life. Genuine surprise overtook me when the teacher proved to be unimpressed.

"That is sophistry," he said. "What you're really saying is that because this is so complicated, it must be false."

"I'm not saying it," the student said. With a grin, he added, "Ockham is saying it!"

"Now you're shifting the blame! You better be careful using Ockham's razor or it will cut you, too." The classroom erupted in laughter, but to be honest, I didn't see why. It seemed to me that the objection had been dismissed too lightly, and that the student might have had a point. Maybe Aquinas was making things harder than they needed to be, because he wanted reality to prove more than it did.

About six months passed. One day, I mentioned this episode to a friend, along with my observation about the teacher not giving enough credence to the objection. It is dangerous to leave inquiring students with the impression that there are no answers, or that the teacher isn't interested in grappling with their questions seriously.

"Maybe you're not seeing the whole picture," my friend suggested.

"What do you mean?"

"The teacher knew the student well, and you were just a visitor. You're assuming the student grasped the argument and really believed Aquinas was guilty. But what if he was just using Ockham's razor because he didn't grasp it and wanted a clever way to dismiss what he did not understand? After all, sometimes things *are* complicated, and we have to face up to the complexity instead of banishing it with a clever trick."

On reflection, I think my friend is right. If we must avoid multiplying entities without necessity, who is to say what is necessary? Are we impartial judges of logical necessity, or are we more likely to dismiss what doesn't fit into our scheme and then justify the dismissal with logic? Aquinas and the cosmological argument had nothing to do with it. We were not sitting in the academy, where every student's head is in the clouds. No, we were in an American high school, with a group of students who were being asked to understand the minutiae of an argument they had already decided was wrong. And Ockham's razor was nothing more than a way to justify not having comprehended (or even completed) the reading assignment.

The reason all this is important is that, today, the concept of God is treated as an inconvenient anachronism, an aberration of the past on a par with (for example) the practice of slavery. Our ancestors condoned slavery, and we would rather not remember that awkward fact. Our ancestors believed in God—so much so that they inscribed him in our laws and bandied his name around in public discourse—but we prefer not to remember that, either. For centuries, for millennia, most people have looked at the world around them and believed that its very existence could only be explained by assuming a creator of some sort. This was not just the conviction of the uneducated; it was common sense among the *cogno-*

scenti. Today many people look at the world around them and believe that it can be explained apart from the existence of God. In other words, the concept of God is an entity multiplied without necessity.

You don't need a God to account for the universe.

Science and Spirit

The cold logic of mid-twentieth-century atheism has now given way to an era of renewed "spirituality," but it is an awakening more therapeutic than pious, more attuned to self-expression than self-denial. It is now fashionable to talk about God, though it is still deeply unfashionable to believe in him. Yes, Americans are a religious people, but we embrace religious beliefs in the same way that we adopt preferences for certain brands of product. The commitments are deeply personal without necessarily being deeply held. Our convictions are about identity, not reality. They suggest who we want to be rather than what we believe is true.

In some ways, the new, accessible spirituality may be the result of disaffection. In the same way that Europe's wars of religion paved the way for the emergence of pietism, the century and a half of struggle over the doctrine of creation has cleared a path for subjective, paradoxical expressions of faith. People want to explore spiritual things without getting bogged down in the culture war, so they look for modes of spirituality that do not step on the toes of science. As a result, they are receptive to the idea of religion as a metaphor, a way of adapting to and understanding life, rather than a coherent system of truth claims.

What this means is that the doctrine of creation, long under siege by scientists who believed that the theory of evolution adequately accounts for the universe apart from God, is also in danger of being classified as irrelevant by believers who adopt an approach to faith that emphasizes personal experience over the traditional doctrines of Christianity. In some ways, the second threat is greater than the first. When unbelievers deny the fact of creation, they are behaving as Christians expect them to act. But when believers begin to conceive of a Christianity without creation— arguing, in essence, that we can have our cake and eat it, too—then the risk of others being led astray multiplies significantly.

But what exactly is the risk? Let me spell it out. If the doctrine of creation is the basis upon which God can rightly demand our worship and service, then the collapse of the doctrine takes that claim to obedience with it. It robs God's actions in the world of any justification but power.

What right does he have to condemn sin? What right to judge? What right not to be judged by us according to our own standards? The Christian system of truth requires the doctrine of creation for coherence. Remove that pillar, and you lose much of the rationale for God's actions in history. If we are to be Christians who zealously embrace the whole of our inheritance, then we must guard the doctrine of creation against enemies both within and without.

[IV]

Thomas Hardy was one of those authors who are not afraid to let their worldview show. Reading *Jude the Obscure*, it soon becomes apparent that Hardy's universe is neither benevolently disposed toward man nor indifferent to him, but cruelly focused on crushing him. There is a phrase that ends the fourth chapter of part one of *Jude the Obscure* that has stuck in my mind since the first time I read it years ago. The young Jude, who spends his days gazing at the far-off glow of Christminster on the horizon, has just obtained the precious Greek and Latin grammars he has longed for. For Jude, Christminster is a "wonderful city for scholarship and religion," and when the books arrive from his former teacher Phillotson with the Christminster postmark, Jude opens them expecting some beautiful revelation of knowledge.

Ignorant of the nature of language, Jude has supposed that Greek and Latin were encoded forms of English, and that the grammars would provide him with the cipher that would turn the words of one language into the other. Instead, he finds that the ancient tongues are learned through rote; he must memorize tens of thousands of words, but Jude believes that his brain is not up to the challenge. He is plunged into depression, and Thomas Hardy chooses this moment to step back and, in an authorial tone, make the following observation:

> Somebody might have come along that way who would have asked him his trouble, and might have cheered him by saying that his notions were further advanced than those of his grammarian. *But nobody did come, because nobody does*; and under the crushing recognition of his gigantic error Jude continued to wish himself out of the world.[6]

But nobody did come, because nobody does. It is a heavy-handed piece of writing that leaves us in no doubt of the kind of world Jude finds himself

---

[6]Thomas Hardy, *Jude the Obscure*, 1.4 (emphasis added).

in. This is the beginning of a series of disillusionments. There is no help to come, either from the heavens or from one's fellow man. The novel climaxes with perhaps the most shocking scene in nineteenth-century literature, a tragedy that reduces the prior misfortunes of Jude to mere foreshadowing. But there is no help for it. In Hardy's world, there never is.

It is interesting to compare a book like *Robinson Crusoe*, where misfortune becomes a tool to educate the protagonist, with *Jude the Obscure*, where sorrows exist only to grind the hero under their wheel. The world comes in on Crusoe and he sees beyond the world to a benevolent, righteous Sovereign. The world comes in on Jude and he sees that there is nothing beyond it but malevolent chance. The theological reasoning that emerges from Crusoe's meditations would be out of place in Jude's mind, because his hardships are designed to cure him (and the reader) of such illusions. It is hard to imagine a starker contrast in perspective.

Fundamental to the Christian view of the world is the belief that God not only created all things, but through his power he upholds and governs them. The very idea of prayer is predicated on the assumption that God possesses the power to ordain what comes to pass. If he did not, then what use would it be to appeal to him? This power of God is called his sovereignty, and while there is debate within the various Christian traditions about its extent and manifestations, all agree that confidence in this power is essential to the faith.

As we have already noted, the Bible bases God's claim to man's obedience on the fact of creation rather than on brute force alone. We do not celebrate God's power for the sake of power itself, but because it is one of the many perfections of the one who made us. Even so, Scripture revels in God's power over creation, in the strong arm whose reach has no limit. Nothing is beyond his ability. With God, all things are possible. In his epistle to the Ephesians, Paul describes God as "him who works all things according to the counsel of his will."[7] To the Romans he declares that, "for those who love God all things work together for good, for those who are called according to his purpose."[8] The power of God is not a mere abstraction. It is not a force concerned with cosmic parlor tricks: God is not using his power to see if he can create a rock so heavy he cannot lift it. Rather, God's power is focused on the fulfillment of his will, and his will unfolds in time, in human history.

This concept of God's power requires his presence at the heart

---

[7]Eph. 1:11.
[8]Rom. 8:28.

of events. It is foreign to the divine as conceived by the deists, whose creator took a hands-off approach, letting things run themselves. It is also alien to the idea of the universe as a malevolent, impersonal force as witnessed in Thomas Hardy. Instead, it requires the Christian to believe that behind the circumstances of everyday life and the morally ambiguous developments we observe, there is a perfectly good and perfectly powerful force at work. There is a divine plan, and it is complex, unfathomable, and beautiful.

Direction vs. Intervention

There is a difference, of course, between what our faith requires us to believe and what we really practice. By and large, Christians view the world around them in the same impersonal way that atheists do. Things like the stock market, our love lives, and the weather are matters of indifference—the circumstances surrounding them are assumed to have little if anything to do with God. We don't blame God when a thunderstorm interrupts our satellite television signal during the NBA finals, just as we do not credit him when our favorite team wins. We may offer up a prayer that the satellite dish will regain its lock on the heavens, but this is a tongue-in-cheek petition, one we expect our buddies to smile at. If one of us suddenly threw himself down on his knees, lifted his hands, and implored Jehovah to intercede in the name of Jesus on behalf of the Knicks or the Rockets, the rest of us would figure he had gone crazy. And yet, in theory, we acknowledge that God is somehow sovereign over storms and satellites and basketball scores.

The reason for this reticence is not a lack of conviction about the power of God. It is a misconception about the nature of that power in relation to the world around us. We see God as a powerful force for intervention in a world that is ordinarily running its course. In other words, things just happen, and when they go wrong, God sometimes jumps in to set them right. But this is not the way God's power was conceived by Crusoe: "The Power that could make all Things, must certainly have Power to guide and direct them." God guides and directs the world around us—in the words of Scripture, he "works all things according to the counsel of his will."

It is simpler to limit God's role to intervention and not attribute to him the weightier task of direction. If God's primary role is to intervene, then he is there for us when things get bad but not a bother when they're moving along nicely. He also has less to answer for. If God is actually directing the awful mess we see around us, then it seems we must either come to suspect his motives or adopt the attitude of Voltaire's Dr. Pangloss, the master of "metaphysico-theologo-cosmolonigology" who could prove with absurd rigor that everything that happens is not only for the best, but is, in fact, the ideal. Since this leads down a twisted path where good becomes evil and evil good, better to let the world run on its own and reserve God for the occasional extraordinary intervention.

The only problem is that Scripture insists on a God who governs all things. It was from this conviction that Christians throughout the ages derived their concept of God's providence. Today, if you were to ask a contemporary churchgoer to explain the idea of providence, he might reply that it is, well, just what it sounds like: the way God provides for our needs. When we experience an unexpected stroke of luck, the pious among us attribute it to God's providence. There is nothing wrong with this, but it does not capture the full scope of the doctrine. In fact, providence is "God's maintenance, guidance and continuing involvement with creation and humans as means of carrying out divine purposes in history."[9] The difference might seem subtle, but it is significant. As creatures, we are not the sole focus of providence. God's providence, rather, aims at the accomplishment of his divine purposes, which are achieved through circumstances and through people, too. The purpose of the doctrine is to emphasize the fact that God is at work in the world, bringing about an appointed end, and the ways in which he provides for us are a part of that work—though not its sole function. We are meant to be God's servants and not the other way around.

Certainly, it is easier to see God's hand at work in extraordinary circumstances than it is to identify his workings on the mundane level. World peace or, depending on your inclination, world destruction, both seem exalted enough to inhabit the sphere of divine activity. Helping me reach the next gas station on the highway before the fumes in my tank give out does not. Even so, I imagine that more prayers are offered up each day for the latter. To interpret every positive (and, for that matter, negative) outcome in life as an act of God seems abominably nitpicky. And yet, if we do not cultivate the habit of seeing all of life under the dominion of God, we will never come to appreciate even a fraction of his mercy and power. As the theologian G. C. Berkouwer writes,

---

[9]Donald McKim, ed., *Westminster Dictionary of Theological Terms* (Louisville, KY: Westminster: 1996).

> There is a danger . . . that men subjectively and arbitrarily interpret
> history in the light of the extraordinary, that they seek only the special
> intervention of the finger of God instead of living with confidence in
> the hand of God which governs all things.[10]

Confidence in God's all-governing hand is at the center of a living faith. It
is a given within the Christian view of the world. As fallen creatures, we
have a tendency to see God only in the exceptional, but we should seek
him in the ordinary, too.

The Patience of Job

We must also learn to interpret, as Crusoe did, both the good and the bad
in life according to God's providence. When Crusoe came to acknowledge
God's sovereignty, he realized that if God is so powerful, then he must
have appointed the catastrophe that had befallen him. This is difficult
territory. We would like to see everything good that happens as part of
God's plan, and everything bad as the thwarting, albeit temporarily, of
his good intentions. But the Bible paints a different picture. God's sovereignty is total, even over evil. He chooses to permit evil and refuses
to justify this choice to man's satisfaction. When he is questioned, God
responds with greater questions, as he did to the long-suffering Job in the
Old Testament.

The story of Job is interesting because it depicts the limits God imposes
even on the actions of Satan. God puts Job forward as an example of a
righteous man and permits Satan to test that righteousness through torment. There is a prohibition against taking Job's life, but the lives of his
animals, his servants, and even his children are fair game. On top of his
grief, Job's body is afflicted, and then his wife (whom Satan has spared,
for obvious reasons) encourages him to curse God and die. Just when it
seems that Job's worries cannot increase, three talkative, philosophically
minded buddies show up and engage him in the conversation that takes
up most of the remainder of the book.

These dialogues are some of the most beautiful and troubling passages
in all of Scripture. They strip the human condition bare. They undermine
false piety and show that even the righteous question their Creator. In
my experience, teachers tend to focus on the beginning of the book and
its end, only vaguely sketching the outline of the heart of the dialogue.

---

[10]G. C. Berkouwer, *The Providence of God* (Grand Rapids, MI: Eerdmans, 1952), 162. For readers
interested in learning more about the doctrine of providence, Berkouwer's book is extremely helpful.

Perhaps this is because the final moments of the book, when God appears in answer to Job's questions and demands answers himself, when Job repents "in dust and ashes" and acknowledges the absolute sovereignty of his Maker, perhaps these moments are so overwhelming that it is impossible not to rush through the intervening matter to arrive at them. But if we rush, we miss the appearance of one of the most remarkable men in Scripture: a latecomer to the discussion, Job's young friend Elihu.

For a long time, Elihu has held his peace. He has listened while the older—and presumably wiser—men have had their say. By doing this, Elihu has recognized what the others have missed. Even Job, the paragon of patience and righteousness, has conducted himself badly. When Elihu speaks, it is as a judge, and God's appearance follows closely on his heels. But what fault does Elihu find with the others? The Bible tells us in the moment before Elihu finally speaks:

> So these three men ceased to answer Job, because he was righteous in his own eyes. Then Elihu the son of Barachel the Buzite, of the family of Ram, burned with anger. He burned with anger at Job because he justified himself rather than God. He burned with anger also at Job's three friends because they had found no answer, although they had declared Job to be in the wrong.[11]

Young Elihu is in the grip of righteous indignation. Over the course of the next six chapters he will rebuke Job and his three friends and defend God's justice and power. The cause of his bright-eyed rage is quite remarkable: he is angry with Job because he "justified himself rather than God." Grasp the importance of these few words, and you will appreciate how great the power of God must be. Job is a righteous man. His wealth and his loved ones are taken from him. His body is wracked with pain. The reader knows, because he has peered into the cosmic scene that laid the groundwork for this tragedy, that Job is not to blame for his suffering. And this is all Job has been saying. He insists that if only he could have his day in the celestial court, he could prove his innocence. It is a claim the reader knows to be true.

And yet, Elihu finds fault in him for making it. Why? Not because it isn't true, but because there is other work for Job to do. Rather than longing for the opportunity to prove his innocence to God, Job ought to be defending the actions of God to men. Even though he suffers unjustly,

---

[11]Job 32:1–3.

he should proclaim the rightness of God in allowing him to suffer. This is not to say that suffering is good; it isn't. But all things, good or ill, should be acknowledged as part of God's sovereign plan. There is no injustice in God—a point we must take on faith, since we do not have the faculty to judge his actions.

Job knows this. He has acknowledged it in his rebuke of his wife: "Shall we receive good from God, and shall we not receive evil?" In a sense, Elihu calls Job to remembrance of his first reaction to suffering, the words his heart inclined him to speak before the combination of suffering and frustration at the faulty reasoning of his companions led him to declare his righteousness. This is the beginning of Job's final humiliation, which will climax in his complete surrender before God:

> "I know that you can do all things,
>   and that no purpose of yours can be thwarted.
> 'Who is this that hides counsel without knowledge?'
> Therefore I have uttered what I did not understand,
>   things too wonderful for me, which I did not know.
> 'Hear, and I will speak;
>   I will question you, and you make it known to me.'
> I had heard of you by the hearing of the ear,
>   but now my eye sees you;
> therefore I despise myself,
>   and repent in dust and ashes."[12]

This is the lesson of the book of Job, the state of consciousness before God in which we should all stand. Job acknowledges the absolute power of God—"no purpose of yours can be thwarted"—and his own finitude and fallen nature. This realization of the Lord's righteous power and our humble reliance upon it is an essential part of the Christian perspective.

[v]

"Mystery is the vital element in Dogmatics." Thus begins the first chapter of Herman Bavinck's *The Doctrine of God*.[13] The sentiment might rightly be extended to include every discipline and all of creation. Mystery is the vital element in everything. When we forget the mystery, when we assume that all of reality shines fluorescent and free of shadow, the bottom drops

---

[12]Job 42:2–6.
[13]Herman Bavinck, *The Doctrine of God*, trans. William Hendriksen (London: Banner of Truth, 1997), 13.

from our perception. There are things out there we do not know, things we cannot know by virtue of who and what we are. We can pretend that the unknowable does not exist, but we will suffer for it.

Even so, no matter how vital mystery is, it is only a part of the whole. While there are things we cannot know, there are also things we can and do know, things we can have confidence in. Epistemology is the study of how we know what we know, but it is probably more precise to say that it is the study of how we explain or justify what we know. Knowing is a given. We possess knowledge. The argument, really, is how to explain our ability to know.

As we have already seen, the third worldview assumption Daniel Estes identified in the first nine chapters of Proverbs was the idea that "Yahweh's world is knowable, but also mysterious." This balance between knowledge and mystery is essential to understanding the Christian world-view. Man was created as a finite being, so he is necessarily limited in his ability to know. Even in perfection, Adam was not omniscient. Since the fall, our ability to know and reason has been corrupted, along with everything else, by sin. So when it comes to knowledge, even the best of us starts with two strikes against him.

The greater we appreciate man's limits, the more exalted our concept of God's perfection becomes. He is so high above us, so transcendent, that it seems nothing could bridge the gap. And if it had not been for God's own condescension, nothing would have. Christians believe that knowledge is possible because God made it so. We believe we can know some things with certainty (even if we do not know them exhaustively) because God has revealed them. Because of this revelation, the scope of our knowledge extends beyond our own ability to discover truth. It shines light into some of the mysterious places, though many remain. We trust the evidence of our senses and our faculty to reason because God has revealed himself in creation, which is comprehended by the senses, and in Scripture, which is comprehended by reason. In addition, we believe in the companionship and illumination of the Holy Spirit, whose mysterious action involves the revelation of knowledge and insight.

The genius of Christian epistemology is that it acknowledges the many ways we have of knowing and provides for knowledge of some things that go beyond them. It does not take up an ideological bias against one faculty or another. It embraces reason, the senses, intuition, experience, and revelation, predicating each one of them on God's decision to make us in his image and to reveal himself to us in limited, analogical, but intelligible ways.

Power Is Knowledge

Rationality is a fundamental assumption, not only of the Christian worldview, but of just about every other conception of reality, too. One might argue that only Christianity can adequately justify a belief in rationality, but whether we can justify it or not, *everyone* relies on it. Ideological movements that seek to undermine rationality or redefine it as a cultural construct might meet with academic success, but even their advocates do not live and work as if these critiques are valid (although there are times when one is tempted to think that certain obscure French philosophers at least *write* as if they do).

When I was in graduate school, I was surprised to discover that the truth is something invented by the powerful and imposed on the rest of us to gain some sort of vague political advantage. Apparently all of history and literature were perpetrated in the interests of a wealthy few with the goal of marginalizing groups of people. Once you realize this, you are free from the notion of "absolute" truth. Your mission in life is then to determine which marginal group you identify with and then work, through the rewriting of history and literature, to impose its truth on everyone else.

There is not enough room in this chapter to bemoan the excesses of postmodernism, and plenty of books have already been written on the subject. In this context, it is enough to note that even a bedrock assumption like rationality is open to question once the Christian worldview is jettisoned. Nietzsche understood that in the absence of the Christian God morality must be invented anew. The same impulse that leads philosophers beyond good and evil can push them past reason, too.

Today, society is splintered and factional. The public square, to remain public, must be purged of all content and value. While the multicultural landscape is held together in America by the soporific effects of affluence, people are, rhetorically speaking, at each other's throats. If we no longer believe in truth, then the idea that opponents are engaged in a mutual search for truth doesn't make sense. Instead, disputes are about power, and the only effective tactic is to talk longer and louder and loftier than your opponent. Yesterday's logical fallacies are today's talking points. While this is nothing new—Socrates had his sophists, after all—the prevalent doctrine that truth is a construct of power gives legitimacy to what would once have been (and ought now to be) laughed to scorn.

Rationality is fundamental to a coherent view of reality. Those who challenge it seem to do so because they reject the possibility of a coherent view of reality—on what other basis could they challenge it? Christians have not always understood that part of their duty in defending the faith is making the case for rationality itself. For a long time, this didn't matter, but today we have a fight on our hands, and it is a war that we should be ready and able to wage.

An Idiosyncratic Aside about Knowledge

Having said this, let's take a moment to consider just how complicated the question of knowledge really is. Now that evangelical Christians are catching up to the various trends that coexist under the heading "postmodernism," there's a lot of talk about epistemology. How we know what we know and how certain our knowledge can be are hot topics, and like most hot topics they're hotly debated by nonspecialists, people who have just enough command of the concepts and terms to generate confusion. I am one of them. After confusing others and myself, I decided it was time to adopt a new starting point. Rather than championing one *-ism* over another, I was hoping to find a good example of how to think about knowing. I found my model in a passage written by the Apostle Paul in 1 Corinthians 13:8–12. Ordinarily this paragraph is invoked in discussions about the so-called "charismatic gifts," but it struck me as a profitable attitude toward knowledge in general. Let's look at the passage and then I'll explain why:

> Love never ends. As for prophecies, they will pass away; as for tongues, they will cease; as for knowledge, it will pass away. For we know in part and we prophesy in part, but when the perfect comes, the partial will pass away. When I was a child, I spoke like a child, I thought like a child, I reasoned like a child. When I became a man, I gave up childish ways. For now we see in a mirror dimly, but then face to face. Now I know in part; then I shall know fully, even as I have been fully known.

The main thing here, of course, is that Paul—a man who had a better claim to knowledge than any of us—characterizes the state of his knowledge as *partial*. Paul, who authored so many epistles taken by Christians as the inspired Word of God, possessed an incomplete knowledge of spiritual things—his specialty, so to speak. His knowledge is partial, but he has no anxiety over that fact because there's an eschatological hope beneath it all. His knowledge strains toward perfection. He isn't eschewing certainty altogether—we do have knowledge—but he compares our state to that of children. Ours is an immature knowledge that looks forward to maturity. It is mediated ("in a mirror dimly") but one day it will be direct ("face to face"). Interestingly, that perfect knowledge will be reciprocal and personal. Paul writes, "Then I shall know fully, even as I am fully known." Christ is the object of our knowledge, and now we know him truly but not fully; but our knowledge of him will be complete even as his knowledge of us is complete. There is, it seems, a relational context to knowledge. No fact is fully known outside that relationship between creature and creator.

Paul is not afraid of "not knowing," because what he seeks is Christ, not facts. There isn't an opposition between Christ and facts, of course. The facts seem to be a means to an end; they are a way of finding real knowledge in Christ.

What does this mean for Christian epistemology? A few tentative observations: First, if we do not share Paul's sense of the partial, incomplete nature of our knowing, then we have a sub-Pauline comprehension of our circumstances. You may want to say, "No, Paul, you're wrong—we've got what's important pretty much figured out," but I don't. Second, if we do not share Paul's sense that our knowledge is true and reliable, we've also slipped into a sub-Pauline mode. We may not have perfect knowledge, but we do know things, and that knowledge comes with obligations. Third, there is a personal aspect to knowledge. When Christ declares in John 8:32 that "you will know the truth, and the truth will set you free," he isn't just saying you will know the *facts* and the *facts* will set you free. Knowing the truth and knowing God are inextricably linked in this discourse. This is more than a tribute to the awareness-raising profit of education. Fourth, while there is a personal aspect to knowledge, knowing does involve the knowledge of facts. It isn't "just" a relationship. So there is no dichotomy between "head knowledge" and "heart knowledge." They constitute an organic whole, or ought to.

Now I don't claim this is a sophisticated, philosophical position. If anything, it strikes me as a kind of commonsense piety, a moderate realism, not skeptical enough to doubt everything but not misguided enough to claim full (or even "essentially full") knowledge. Holding to this view,

I've been mistaken for a modernist, for a postmodernist, and for plenty of things besides. But I would argue that, to the extent this position corresponds to any *ism*, it's merely a case of two streams of thought converging on the truth. This *ism*, I'd like to think, is Paul-ism, or even better, Christ-ism. Everyone is welcome to borrow from it; this is a good stone to build with.

Process and Being

One of the most interesting and frustrating aspects of epistemology, to my mind, is the need to hold two related but rather different ideas together in tension. The first is "knowing as a process" and the second is "knowledge as a state of being." Emphasize the process, and you inevitably end up with an appreciation of the limited, subjective experience of knowing. I know things, but my knowledge is somehow unfinished—over time, I'm coming to know some things better and some things worse; ironically, the more I know about some things, the less I feel I *know* them. I often discover that things I thought I knew, subjects I considered "settled," are actually less certain in my mind than I realized. On the other hand, I sometimes surprise myself with my grasp of things I didn't realize I understood so well. (Admittedly, this seems to happen less and less as time goes on.) If I concentrate on my own process of knowing, then I have to concede a fair amount of uncertainty. I am uncertain about things I believe it's impossible to be certain about, but also uncertain about things that, in theory, I should be able to be certain about. By the same token, I am certain about a lot of things, too—even (I hate to admit) about things it should not be possible, in theory, to be certain about! This, I suppose, is the subjective side of knowledge.

I'm not content to leave it there, though, because I don't think this emphasis gives a full or accurate account of knowledge in the abstract. This is where a sense of knowledge as a state of being comes into play. I have a lot of reasons for supposing that real knowledge is possible and that I actually possess a good bit of it. I do not believe that the things I know are entirely (or even especially) "constructed" by me or my various communities of interpretation, though it is possible to believe in such construction to some extent without giving up on the idea of the "real world." The objects of my knowledge have an existence outside of me, and this, I suppose, is where objectivity comes into play. Now, I've never experienced pure objectivity. I'm content to acknowledge the subjectivity of my knowledge. What I won't do, however, is agree that subjectivity is relativity. In other words, just because I can't get outside of myself doesn't mean that the meaning of everything is settled by me. There is knowledge apart from my experience of knowing.

In other words, there are things to know, and then there's me knowing them. Both sides of the equation are important, and sometimes my experience of one leads me to discount the other. Sometimes, aware of my limitations, I convince myself that I know less than I really do. On other occasions, I let my confidence in objective reality—the object of my perceptions—obliterate all the sensory qualifiers that mediate my knowing. And because I'm a bit of a hypocrite, albeit unintentionally, I take other people to task both for their unwillingness to move beyond relativism and for their reflexive, unqualified certainties. The point, though, is that I try not to project my own inconsistencies onto the world (and knowledge) in general.

From a Christian standpoint, this seems essential. On the one hand, I'm both a fallen and a finite creature. There are some things I can't know because of my built-in limits, and others I'm blinded to by sin. And because I am a creature, it is not possible for me to know what I know exhaustively, as if I were the Creator. I'm derivative, and my knowing is derivative, too. Still, the concept of revelation itself would be nonsense if it weren't possible for finite, fallen creatures to have real knowledge. We perceive things imperfectly through the senses and through reason, but we also have knowledge that comes via revelation—more certain, in theory, than what we sense or reason, but still subject to interpretation. I am held responsible by God for this knowledge, too; so while I may not be absolutely certain, I am at least *culpably* certain.

Binary Oppositions and False Dilemmas

There is a difference between binary oppositions and false dilemmas, but too often the concepts are collapsed. As a result, pointing out a false dichotomy or suggesting a "third way" is often interpreted as a postmodern move. To my mind, it's simply a question of accuracy. If there really are more than two options, one doesn't need a philosophical position to say so. Throughout this book, I have tended toward an inclusive, rather than exclusive, approach to subjects, willing to consider what a variety of perspectives have to offer, and trust them as far as they go. To me, this seems like common sense, but you can label it as you wish.

I've never been uncomfortable with labels. The way I've coped with them is to take on everything that applies, even when they seem incompatible from the outside. A better way of stating this, perhaps, is that I've been willing to own up to my influences. Postmodern thought in its variety of stripes has clearly been an influence, but so have a lot of other strains. I think of myself as a Christian first and foremost, of the neo-Calvinist stripe, with plenty of other qualifiers to get the description right—but even then, I'm reluctant to trumpet these associations because I do not think I always live up to them. I don't boast that my way is necessarily the Christian way, the neo-Calvinist way, or what have you. My way is how I've managed to bring all my influences (and, I'd like to think, a little original elbow grease) to bear.

So while I hate to see binary opposition and false dilemmas confused with one another, I am ready to admit that what I understand about structuralism and post-structuralism (which isn't much, really) has been helpful. Here's a cheap summary: structuralists figured out that thought is structured into binary oppositions—life and death, black and white, right and wrong, saved and damned, reason and emotion; then post-structuralists came along and said, "No, it isn't," but they called it deconstruction. The example I remember (and I don't know if this comes from Derrida or just an interpreter) is the distinction between death and life. You're either dead or alive, right? Well, what about zombies? They're dead . . . but alive. When I heard this, I thought, "But, hey, zombies aren't real!" That didn't seem to matter.

My second thought: Christ would be a better example. It took the cross to deconstruct the dead/alive binary forever.

When I consider my own habits of thought, I see that I'm an organizer. To understand things, I need to arrange them (into categories like worldview, wisdom, and witness, for example). I take all the raw data, my experiences and observations, and I create categories to put them in.

Throughout this book, you will encounter theorizing of this sort—two types of this, three stages of that. In one sense, I made the distinctions up; but in another, I was attempting to hit on real differences. Difference is a key to knowing things. Dictionary definitions focus on distinctions. History does, too. I have always had a knack for history. (I will inflict it on you in chapter 7.) I'm one of those people with a rich mental timeline who can visualize the "look" of various epochs. One reason for this skill, I think, was my early interest in arms and armor, and in costume in general. I studied the way fashions changed, the way technology changed, the way war changed, and now my historical mind functions like a continuity person on a film set. "This goes, this doesn't go."

So establishing categories based on what I perceive to be essential differences has been a fundamental way of knowing for me. That involves the search for binary opposition—because the most telling differences are the starkest ones—but it also requires some skill at sniffing out false dichotomies, since the categories I am working with are typically my own (and therefore problematic on a number of levels). The knowledge I arrive at by this means I would characterize as "working knowledge." It may or may not correspond to absolutes (and probably doesn't absolutely, given what I am), but it was built, first and foremost, in order to function. If I find something that functions better—whether it involves a refinement of my system or a wholesale replacement—I'm open to that. My interest is in the truth, not in my categories.

In a roundabout way, this takes us back to the question of rationality. In affirming its importance to the Christian perspective, we have no need to flatten out the nuances or sweep the subjective component of knowledge under the carpet. We assert not only the possibility of real knowledge, but also the limits of knowledge. That balance is essential to preserve.

[VI]

To bring this chapter to a close, we must consider the last of the four pillars: fear. Whenever the phrase "fear of the Lord" occurs in Scripture, we are often quick to remind ourselves: not that kind of fear. When the Bible says fear, it really means reverence. We are to reverence and respect God, not to be afraid of him.

I do the same thing with guns. Whenever I hear someone say that they are afraid of guns, I cringe. My lifelong interest in weapons meant that, early on, I devoured everything I could read about firearms. I studied how they work and what they are capable of doing. I learned how to fire them safely and accurately, how to take them apart and clean them, and most importantly I learned what you must *never* do with them. One thing I never did was fear them. Although I try to see things from other perspectives, I have never quite understood the genuine, deep-seated fear that some people experience at the sight of a pistol. Reverence and respect? Sure. But fear? No way.

Then again, I have never had a gun pointed *at* me.

It is one thing to know power in the abstract and appreciate it and quite another to be its object, to feel threatened by it. If someone points a gun at you, its power threatens you. You would be foolish not to be afraid. Understanding how the mechanism works (and how unlikely the mechanism is *not* to work) should give your fear a fullness that the fright of the ignorant never achieves. The more you know, the more afraid you should be.

Perhaps the same is true of God. It is easy for us to dismiss the idea of truly fearing him because we do not truly see ourselves as the object of his wrath. And yet, as we have already seen, God's wrath is revealed against *all* unrighteousness, not just the unrighteousness of everybody but you and me. If Elihu could burn with anger toward the righteous Job, how much more can the Creator burn in just indignation at our sin? We are quick to hedge and qualify that word "fear," but I suspect that it captures precisely the attitude that men should have when they approach the Holy One of Israel.

The priests of the Old Testament approached God with literal fear. It was not the same kind of fear that a lone pedestrian feels when he walks down a dark alley; it was much worse—because the approach to the Almighty is brilliantly lit and nothing is hidden from him. All our imperfections, all our craven desires, all the petty indulgences we rationalize—all are open to God's view and the Lord is a righteous judge. Only the innocent need not fear him, and there are none who are without sin.

The fear we ought to have of God includes reverence. It includes awe and wonder, too. It is a magnificent, healthy fear, an open, honest trembling at the power and unfathomable perfection of the Creator. This fear constitutes our right relationship with God. As the Bible says in several places, it is the beginning of wisdom.

What Are You Afraid Of?

Each of the four pillars is under attack. The doctrine of creation is embraced only by a lunatic fringe. Everyone else has known for ages that no one "created" the world. Although some of its defenders claim that the doctrine of evolution is not inconsistent with Christian faith, most adherents act as if it disproves the whole of the Bible. We no longer need God to explain the world, so we no longer need God at all.

If there is no God, then there is no overarching power governing events. There is no *telos*, no transcendent "meaning" behind the things that happen around us. Now, we are beginning to wonder if the force that shapes reality isn't Chaos after all. In a chaotic world, there is nothing to impose on us but chance, and reality is what we make of it.

That means truth is what we make of it, too. The old transcendent morality was something imposed on us not by God but by powerful men who invented God as a way to frighten us into conformity. The same conspiracy that invented morality may have perpetrated logic, too, as a way to enclose and confine our self-expression. Relativity, not rationality, is the fundamental epistemological starting point.

And if all this is true—if there is no creation and no divine order or plan, if there is no absolute truth—then the question is: what are you afraid of? There is no God to fear. There is only freedom—freedom from an imposed obedience; freedom from a metaphysical potter who expects us to be mere clay; freedom from codes of morality and logic; freedom from judgment and condemnation; freedom to be whatever we choose to be; freedom to make the world whatever we want it to be; freedom to be creative; freedom to express ourselves; freedom to make reality in our own image.

Paul says of us: "They exchanged the truth about God for a lie and worshiped and served the creature rather than the Creator." What is behind our Promethean urge to topple the pillars that underlie all of reality if not the desire to twist all of reality into a shape that pleases us, to make it anew in the image of the creature rather than the Creator? Each of the four pillars stands like a bulwark against this human longing, an arch that holds the weight of a worldview that puts God in his place as sovereign creator, Lord of all, and man on his knees as worshiper and servant of the one who made him.

Creation, order, rationality, and fear. These are not the only pillars that underlie the Christian worldview, but they are the principal ones. If they crumble, the whole structure falls, and we beneath it are crushed under the weight.

But there is no danger of that collapse, because the pillars are buttressed by a hand whose grip none on earth have the power to break.

3

God, Man, and the World: Worldview as System

I mistrust all systematizers and avoid them. The will to system is a lack of integrity.

FRIEDRICH NIETZSCHE

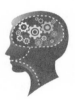

[I]

The question put to Martin Luther at the Diet of Worms, the challenge that provoked the greatest uncertainty and caused more soul-searching than his defenders would like to admit, was the issue of authority. How could one man be right and everyone else wrong? How could the whole of church tradition say one thing and Martin Luther remain confident while teaching something else? Who did he think he was? Surely the consensus of opinion against him should have suggested to a man as intelligent as Luther that his views were in error. That was the substance of the case against him, and it was enough to shake anyone's confidence.

In hindsight, we can take some of the sting out of the rebuke. Luther was not alone. He was not the first to challenge the power of the papacy; in fact, just a century before, the Council of Constance, which had burned Jan Hus at the stake and condemned John Wycliffe posthumously, had deposed a series of pretender popes and put a new pontiff in office, effectively demonstrating the reign of church councils over popes. The church had also seen its share of critics, from Savonarola to Erasmus, so in this Luther was not unique. Many of the debates that would animate the Reformation were not new, either—they were sixteenth-century revivals of arguments that had been ongoing for two millennia.

Even so, Luther was one man standing against the teaching authority of the papacy. He did not lack friends or precedent, but both must have seemed small comfort in comparison to the weight of power marshaled against him. It is never an easy thing to stand against the majority, especially when it has the power to censure and silence you. But Martin Luther decided that he would be ruled, not by the majority, but by his conscience.

Majority Rules

The story of one man's stand against the majority has the power to kindle imagination, especially in a culture that prizes individualism as highly as ours. In fact, it could be argued that the whole of Western civilization—or at least the classical component of the culture—rests on a famous example of such a case: the trial of Socrates. We know Socrates primarily through the dialogues of his student Plato, who also passed down the dramatic record of the master's *Apology*, or defense. Socrates styled himself as a "gadfly," a philosopher who asked inconvenient questions of the men in power. In the dialogues, he presents himself as a bit of a simpleton in search of wisdom, which he proposes to get by questioning people who claim to know the things he wants to discover. What happens, though, is that as Socrates probes their answers with further questions and observations, their certainties are undermined, and we see that it is Socrates who is wise and the so-called wise men who are simple.

It isn't difficult to see how someone like Socrates could become unpopular. On the one hand, you wouldn't want to meet him in the street for fear of being made to look like an idiot. On the other, you wouldn't want to be seen avoiding him, since that would reveal your lack of confidence. To follow along with Socrates' reasoning, a man would also have to consider with skepticism certain beliefs that most people take for granted. That kind of mental exercise can be taxing. Sometimes it is easy to conclude that a man who questions the gods must not believe in them, even if he claims that he wants to know them more.

That's what happened to Socrates. When the people who mattered had finally had enough, they decided to humble him with a trial. He was an atheist, they said, and his teachings were corrupting the youth of Athens. After all this time, it is hard to know whether the charges were serious. Perhaps they were intended merely to shut the man up. But Socrates defended himself with the same principled disregard for the beliefs of the majority that had characterized his entire philosophical project. As Alain de Botton observes, although "the approval of others forms an essential part of our capacity to believe that we are right," Socrates understood that "the validity of an idea or action is determined not by whether it is widely believed or widely reviled but by whether it obeys the rules of logic."[1]

Luther might have said the same thing. He had worked through Paul's epistle to the Romans with a fine-tooth comb and the doctrines he found were not what the majority believed. He was not willing to be persuaded by force alone, though he was willing to concede his error *if it could be shown from Scripture*. His opponents were not about to open their Bibles and debate with him, just as the enemies of Socrates had no intention of being convinced by his arguments. The decision had already been made and the point was that Martin Luther was in no position, as one man, to negotiate points of doctrine with the Roman Catholic Church. It was a collision of truth against power. The support of the majority does not make an idea right. Being a minority view doesn't make it right, either. The real issue is whether the idea corresponds to reality.

Having said that, it is impossible to ignore the fact that something in the plight of the underdog is morally appealing. All of us—believer and unbeliever, idealist and realist—assume that the majority is wrong most of the time. It isn't easy to be right, especially on complex subjects, so it is no surprise that the majority is content to be wrong. This isn't the case, of course, with those truths that are so painfully obvious that everyone grasps them—for example, practically everyone believes the earth moves around the sun, and it does. But it was only ever possible to be *proud* of holding heliocentric notions when the man on the street scoffed at them. Today it is nothing special. The convictions we cherish most are the ones we hold in opposition to the majority.

One against the World

One of the reasons it is profitable for Christians to study the subject of worldviews is that their own worldview stands in radical contrast to every other perspective on reality. This does not, in and of itself, make the Christian viewpoint correct. Christianity is right because it corresponds to the way things really are. But that is a huge claim that can only be justified in eternity. Meanwhile, the fact that Christianity offers a unique understanding of the world around us is, at the very least, intriguing.

---

[1]Alain de Botton, *The Consolations of Philosophy* (New York: Pantheon, 2000), 29, 42.

A student of comparative religion might balk at this claim. Christianity is, after all, one of several "great religions," each of which has a number of things in common. The Christian faith draws heavily on Judaism, even to the point of appropriating its sacred texts in the form of the Old Testament. Its central conceit, the idea that God became a man, died to atone for our sins, and then was resurrected, is (we are told) nothing more than a variation on a theme that would have been familiar to the Hellenic cults. In the early centuries, Christianity borrowed heavily from the Platonist school in developing its theology, and over the centuries it developed in response to threats from paganism and Islam. The Christian faith is one of many, and while it has distinguished itself in minor ways from the pack, there is nothing radically different about the way Christians view the world.

If this were true, it would not invalidate the Christian faith. We must concede that our religion does not have a monopoly on the truth. It is true that we have learned many valuable lessons about the world and ourselves with the aid of non-Christian thinkers. In fact, our worldview demands that we accord these thinkers respect as people made in God's image, recipients of the common grace he showers on all creation, in spite of the fall.

Anyone can be right, but not everything can be true. There can be a thousand different theories, but only one of them proves correct. We would expect the many wrong answers all to have something in common, a shared element not present in the truth. So if we can defend the claim that Christianity stands in complete contrast to every other worldview, if we can demonstrate that Christianity says one thing and everyone else says something else, then we create a compelling case that our faith (while not "proven" by this observation) bears an unmistakable hallmark of truth.

[II]

Abraham Kuyper was the quintessential public intellectual, the kind of multi-talented figure we look back upon in awe. A Reformed theologian, journalist, and statesman, Kuyper fought in the front lines of the late-nineteenth-century culture wars. He established the Free University of Amsterdam, founded a political party, and served from 1901–1905 as the prime minister of the Netherlands. In the early twenty-first century, we are inclined to despise politicians as men manufactured by their parties, afraid to speak in anything but the most banal sound bites for fear of taking a position. Kuyper was not that kind of man. He left behind a remarkable legacy, including the concept of "sphere sovereignty." He was also largely responsible for introducing the concept of worldview to evangelical theology.

This introduction occurred by means of the Stone Lectures, a series of six lectures delivered at Princeton University in 1898 and popular today under the title *Lectures on Calvinism*. Instead of confining it to the private realm, Kuyper applied the thought system of his own Reformed faith to every aspect of life, as the titles of the lectures demonstrate: "Calvinism as a Life-system," "Calvinism and Religion," "Calvinism and Politics," "Calvinism and Science," "Calvinism and Art," and "Calvinism and the Future." Religion, politics, science, art, the future—in other words, the whole of life—were considered from the perspective of the Reformed faith. In the lectures, Kuyper introduces the terms *life system* and *life and world view,* approximations of the German philosophical term *Weltanschauung,* marking the introduction to American theology of the worldview concept. A year prior to the Stone Lectures, James Orr, another Reformed theologian, published his own lectures under the title *The Christian View of God and the World* in Edinburgh. Between them, Kuyper and Orr opened up a new approach to theology and apologetics. Instead of defending particular doctrines, the worldview concept made it possible to put Christianity forward as a whole and to defend it on the basis of internal coherence and the necessity of Christian first principles to understanding the world correctly.

Kuyper understood Calvinism as the purest expression of Christianity, but even those who disagreed could see the value of his message. The Christian faith offered a unique and valuable perspective from which to interpret life. Many of the great achievements of the past could be directly or indirectly traced to the Christian worldview of the men and women who performed them. At a time when modernist assumptions had infiltrated and undermined theology, here was a robust counterattack along intellectual lines. What Kuyper labeled the Calvinist worldview was for all practical purposes the worldview of evangelical Christians in general, as evidenced by the later acceptance of Kuyper's concept across broad denominational lines when it was popularized by the mid-twentieth-century apologist Francis Schaeffer.

God, Man, and the World

According to Kuyper, a belief system must speak to three points before it can be considered a worldview: man's relation to God, man's relation to other men, and man's relation to the world. In the late nineteenth century, Kuyper could point to five major worldviews that had shaped contemporary thought: Paganism, Islamism, Romanism, Calvinism, and the emerging Modernism. Today we can point to many more. But the nexus of God, man, and the world remains the same.

Kuyper describes the relationship with God, with man, and with the world as the "three fundamental relations of all human existence." To know who and what we are, we must orient ourselves according to these three landmarks. By describing these relationships, we locate ourselves, but we also define the relation between the three things themselves—how God relates to man and the world, and how the world relates to God and man. The Christian worldview outlines the three relations this way:

> For our relation to God: an immediate fellowship of man with the Eternal, independently of priest or church. For the relation of man to man: the recognition in each person of human worth, which is his by virtue of his creation after the Divine likeness, and therefore of the equality of all men before God and his magistrate. And for our relation to the world: the recognition that in the whole world the curse is restrained by grace, that the life of the world is to be honored in its independence, and that we must, in every domain, discover the treasures and develop the potencies hidden by God in nature and in human life.[2]

Kuyper's view of the relation between man and God is quintessentially Protestant. Man enjoys an unmediated relationship with his Creator. The only intercessor he needs is Christ. We are directly responsible to God both for worship and for service. The object of our faith is a person, not a proposition. First, we believe in someone, and only consequently in something. We put our faith in the person of Christ, not in the teaching of the church. (Does this mean that doctrine has no value? Of course not. But we are not saved by being right; we are saved by being his.) The relationship of man with his fellow creature recognizes that we all bear God's image, and, therefore, we are worthy of respect and dignity. To show contempt to man is, in fact, to treat God with contempt, just as Jesus said—a man who hates his brother hates God and that charity performed on behalf of the least of men is, in reality, done to him. From this principle, Kuyper derives the concept of equality before God and before the law. Scripture tells us

---

[2]Abraham Kuyper, *Lectures on Calvinism* (Grand Rapids, MI: Eerdmans, 1931), 31. The Stone Lectures were delivered at Princeton Seminary in 1898.

that God does not esteem some men more highly than others. Likewise magistrates, who hold their authority from God, are bound to exercise it with similar impartiality.

As an aside, it is interesting to see how such fundamental doctrines lead immediately to concepts like social justice. If there is no God and therefore no absolute truth and no transcendent morality, then on what basis could we defend the idea of human dignity? The lesson of nature, interpreted through a Darwinian lens, seems to be that those are worthy of respect who earn it. If you want to be treated with human dignity, then demonstrate that you deserve to be. This, of course, is the language and logic of bigots, and there is a stream in Darwinist thought notorious for its bigotry. But why should bigotry be wrong, if nature values only the beings that prove themselves through strength and cunning? Because of our doctrine of man's creation in God's image, Christians believe that men are inherently worthy of dignity, whether they have "earned" it or not. We treat with respect even those who do not seem worthy in our eyes, because we believe that in so doing we honor the image of God in them. That is why the words "I will respect him once he has *earned* it" are particularly abhorrent on the lips of a believer.

Man is made in God's image but fallen. As a consequence of the fall, creation itself is cursed. But Kuyper's third point acknowledges the presence of God's grace in creation, restraining the evil effects of the curse. Another contribution for which Kuyper is remembered is the impetus he gave to the doctrine of "common grace." This grace, denoted as common to distinguish it from God's special or saving grace, comprises the many benefits that God bestows on creation. He prevents fallen men from reaching the depths of depravity. He allows the sun to shine, rain to fall, and crops to grow. He blesses the work of believer and unbeliever alike with success. While there are blessings he reserves for his own, God is not stingy with his riches. The very fact that we can shake our fists at him and live is evidence of his mercy. We have already touched on this point in our discussion of providence, and here we see that God's attitude toward the world opens up avenues that we can explore. Kuyper refers to them as the treasures and potencies that God has secreted in nature and life. As scientists, artists, politicians, executives, and people of every profession and pursuit, we are called to enter into the world and to discover the richness with which God has endowed it.

This is by no means an exhaustive vision, but these three fundamental relations constitute the core of the Christian perspective. Resting on the pillars of creation, order, rationality, and fear, the Christian worldview puts forward a vision of direct communion between God and man. We live in a world bursting with knowledge, wealth, and wonder, all of it placed there by the Creator. While the effects of the fall are still evident in wars and disease, famine and mendacity, God puts a restraining hand on evil, by his mercy preserving us from the just consequence of our error, through his goodness leading us to repentance. We find ourselves in a world populated by fallen, imperfect people, but each of them—believer and unbeliever alike—is made in the image of God and therefore demands our respect.

The obedience we owe to God includes benevolence and love toward other people and careful stewardship of the world around us.

[III]

There is no such thing as the Christian worldview.

On the one hand, there are too many divisions within Christianity to speak of a single, monolithic view of reality. On the other, Christians are too imperfect to see the world around them in a consistent and consistently biblical way.

So while the Christian worldview is theoretically possible, the only example of it we can point to is Christ himself, and it seems a bit anachronistic to say that Jesus had a "Christian worldview." Of course, in spite of the anachronism, it does at least demonstrate how high the standard of a Christian worldview, if it existed, would be: nothing short of perfection would be required. When we speak of a Christian worldview, we mean seeing the world as it truly is, down to the smallest detail. This is something none of us have done.

So we must admit at the outset that the Christian worldview does not exist.

There are as many Christian *worldviews* as there are Christians, but if we were to examine these belief systems in detail, we would likely find that they are not purely, or even particularly, Christian. We are promiscuous thinkers, sampling the pleasures of whatever philosophies turn our heads. We are also inattentive thinkers, unlikely to puzzle over contradictions until some crisis brings them to the forefront. We are not all equally devout, and among those who are faithful we are more, not less, likely to find disagreement. The community of faith is riddled with factions and strife. It is not of one mind.

If it is true that there are many Christian worldviews, then it is also true, as I have said, that in another sense there is none. Paul admonishes us to have the "mind of Christ." Jesus himself tells us that the way the world will know that we are his followers is by the love we have for one another. After two millennia, this visible, distinguishing love is not much in evidence. And if we have not managed to get this right, imagine how great are our omissions in the finer points of faith.

What We Have, What We Wish We Had, and the Difference between the Two

So when we speak of a Christian worldview, we should be aware of the difficulties and ambiguities of such language. There are, in fact, three different (but sometimes overlapping) connotations that surround the term. The "Christian worldview" sometimes refers to the *ideal,* how Christians ought to see the world. Sometimes it refers instead to the *actuality,* the way individual Christians really do see things, and what their various worldviews have in common. At other times, though, the "Christian worldview" is invoked to make a *distinction,* to identify the things that set Christian perspectives apart from other worldviews.

The four pillars discussed in chapter 2 and the three fundamental relations we have just looked at are both examples of the Ideal. Derived from Scripture, they are principles and outlooks that are necessary to the biblical perspective. A Christian *ought* to embrace them. The Ideal is much broader than four concepts and three relationships; it includes the entire teaching of the Bible. It is, in essence, the mind of Christ, the perspective a person would have if he perfectly embraced the whole of Scripture and lived life accordingly.

In this lifetime, we have no hope of measuring up to the Ideal. That is what I mean when I say that there is no such thing as the Christian worldview. No one can demonstrate it to us in its entirety; in fact, no one can adequately explain it. All of our pillars and relationships are sad substitutes for the glorious reality, but we hope that they serve a didactic value. Through the process of sanctification believers are constantly striving to become like Christ. To possess a Christian worldview is, in that sense, what it means to follow Christ with the mind.

Not only does no Christian perfectly embody the Ideal, but many disagree over its very substance. Believers may be united in Christ but they are divided in doctrine, and some of the disputes center on fundamental issues. Is grace imputed through justification or is it infused through sacrament? What are the sacraments, and how (and to whom and by whom) are they to be administered? What must a man do to be saved? Can he do it? If he does it, can he undo it? There is some consensus: the early church struggled over the nature of God, and out of that struggle emerged our orthodox Trinitarian and christological creeds. But within orthodoxy, there remain many unsettled issues, which is why the Christian world is splintered into denominations, and denominations themselves are divided into factions. This is what I mean when I say that there are many Christian worldviews. Since worldview is an interpretive scheme that affects every aspect of reality, even minor disagreements can result in major worldview shifts.

This is the actuality. In light of this situation, we sometimes speak of the Christian worldview as the consensus of the various traditions, the common ground they all share. Although its expression and emphasis is characteristically Reformed, Kuyper's three fundamental relations are conceived in broad enough terms that you don't have to be a Calvinist to see your faith reflected in them. All of the doctrines central to the Christian worldview are contained in the Apostles' Creed and the Nicene Creed, so it is possible to speak of a perspective that is shared by Christians of very different persuasions. For example, a Southern Baptist and a Roman Catholic will disagree on the veneration of saints, but both confess that God is three in one, and that Christ in his incarnation was fully God and fully man. By the same token, a Christian who believes that God created the world in six literal days will disagree profoundly with another who says God created the world over a period of ages, but if they both confess God as the Creator, there is common ground.

These are all examples of the way that actual Christian worldviews differ from the ideal. Because of our fallen condition, it seems inevitable that they do. This is not an excuse, however. We should all be striving toward a better understanding, and part of that struggle is to weigh various interpretations and test them in light of what the Bible teaches. By distinguishing between the actual and ideal, we acknowledge the fact that there are a variety of Christian worldviews among which there remains significant common ground, and that every individual Christian should be working to bring his worldview into closer conformity to the ideal.

The third category is one that I alluded to at the beginning of the chapter: how do Christian worldviews differ from every other perspective on reality? Is there a stark contrast between Christianity on the one hand, and every rival worldview on the other? That is the question we will consider now.

Anthropology: Hyde vs. Frankenstein

Saturday mornings when I was a boy were devoted to the films of Ray Harryhausen. I didn't know who he was back then, but Harryhausen was the master of stop-motion animation who brought to life such mythical monsters as the Cyclops, Medusa, and the Kraken, in addition to a host of dinosaurs and aliens. In the days before cable and satellite television, geography was the key to entertainment. I lived near the border of Texas and Louisiana, just close enough to Houston to catch Channel 39's weekly Harryhausen broadcasts. I saw *The Golden Voyage of Sinbad* so many times that Sinbad's fight against the six-armed statue of Kali (each hand clasping a menacing scimitar) is burned into my subconscious. Looking back after thirty years, Kali's stuttering movements seem entirely laughable, but my childhood imagination "rendered" the scene in the same way computers do today, transforming the clay model into a frightening reality. And who can forget Jason and the Argonauts with its climactic struggle between Greeks and reanimated skeletons? In addition to Harryhausen, Channel 39 aired its fair share of Godzilla movies. These were billed like boxing matches: *Godzilla vs. Mothra, Godzilla vs. Gigan, Godzilla vs. Megalon.* Somehow as a ten-year-old I found it possible to sympathize with Godzilla as he battled his monstrous foes.[3] I certainly rooted for him against King Kong.

The point of this embarrassing confession is to note that monsters make for great movies. Is it any wonder that *Dracula, Frankenstein,* and *Dr. Jekyll and Mr. Hyde* have been brought to the silver screen time and time again, while other classics languish? What is it about bloodsuckers with electrodes sticking out of their necks that drink foul potions to unlock their dark side? I don't know, but I have to admit that I share the fascination with monsters.

But I never expected to learn theology from them!

That's why Jeff Baldwin's *The Deadliest Monster: A Christian Introduction to Worldviews* came as a surprise. Jeff is one of my colleagues at Worldview Academy, and he'll come up again at the end of this

---

[3] We all have to start somewhere, and when you're in elementary school it doesn't have to be very high. As an online reviewer said of one of these films: "This is a movie I really wish I had seen when I was 8 years old, still filled with awe and wonder, and not concerned with little things such as plot, acting, and production values."

chapter and in the next. In his excellent book, Frankenstein's monster goes toe-to-toe with Mr. Hyde to find out which of them personifies the correct view of man. There is no doubt that Frankenstein is the more likeable of the monsters. He is bewildered and shy, but friendly enough and eager to learn about the world around him. The lesson he is taught, though, is one of cruelty and persecution. Attacked by society and labeled a monster, Frankenstein retaliates in kind. His revenge is bloody and made all the more ironic by the fact that it need never have happened. If the world had treated him with respect, he would have followed his benign impulses and remained good.

Hyde, on the other hand, is the very personification of corruption. He is the good Dr. Jekyll's corrupt and depraved side. When he is set loose, he seeks nothing but self-interested debauchery and is willing to trample anyone who gets in his way—literally! Once Hyde is released, it is more and more difficult to hold him back. He is a force for evil who desires to perpetrate infamies, if only society did not stand in his way.

The monsters we invent are projections of ourselves, so it makes sense to see in Frankenstein and Hyde the embodiment of two rival views of man. Frankenstein is basically good, but society has compelled him to do evil. Hyde, on the other hand, is essentially bad. In one case, the source of evil is outside of man; in the other it is within him.

The Deadliest Monster reveals one of the fundamental differences between Christianity and every rival worldview: anthropology. The Christian doctrine of man teaches that although he is made in God's image, man is fallen. In other words, he is a sinner and his will is in bondage to sin. The grip of sin is so powerful that one theologian writes, "Sin is not a peripheral defect; it is not an unfortunate but subsidiary feature of our lives. Sin determines our identities."[4] Sin is central to who man is. He desires to do wrong and by God's grace those desires are restrained, but if he had his own way, man would be bad.

Soteriology: Who Saves?

As a consequence, we discover the second radical distinction between Christianity and its competitors: soteriology. According to the Christian doctrine of salvation, man is in need of salvation but in no position to obtain it. He cannot change his heart, his nature, and yet it is his heart, his nature, that must change. Because of his sin, he owes a debt greater than

---

[4]R. R. Reno, "Fear of Redemption," in *First Things*, June/July 2004, 31.

he can pay. If he is to be saved, he must look outside himself and behind his own abilities. In the Christian worldview, God saves sinners.

Every competing worldview disagrees. However the language is nuanced, it amounts to the same thing: man is "basically good."[5] No, he is not perfect, but his imperfection is not central to his identity. Depending on the rival worldview, man may not be in need of salvation at all, but if he is, it is a salvation he is capable of achieving through hard work, enlightenment, or some form of cooperation with (or ascension to) the divine. According to Christianity's critics, man saves himself.

To prove this point, Baldwin surveys a series of rival worldviews including atheism, Buddhism, Hinduism, Islam, Jehovah's Witnesses, Marxism, Mormonism, and the New Age movement. In each case, complex anthropologies and soteriologies are summed up in the idea that man is basically good and is capable of achieving his own salvation. Admittedly, these are all very different perspectives, some of them sharing more common ground with Christianity than others, but isn't it significant that they all ultimately agree on these two points?

Herman Bavinck, whose thoughts on mystery we discussed in the last chapter, wrote that "all religions except the Christian are autosoteric. . . . [They all] come in the end to an appeal to the will, the wisdom and the power of man."[6] In the Christian view, man's will, wisdom, and power are not equal to the task of salvation. Only the grace of God will suffice. The Princeton theologian B. B. Warfield undertook a study of soteriology in which he classified a wide spectrum of views—the supernatural and the naturalistic, the evangelical and the sacerdotal, the particularistic and the universalist, the supralapsarian, infralapsarian, and Amyraldian—according to how closely they aligned with the opposing principles that "God saves sinners" and "man saves himself." Warfield sees in the distinction an echo of the fifth-century battle between the followers of Augustine and Pelagius:

> The opposition between the two systems was thus absolute. In [Pelagianism], everything was attributed to man; in [Augustinianism], everything was ascribed to God. In them, two religions, the only two possible religions at bottom, met in mortal combat: the religion of faith

---

[5] We should note that, while rival anthropologies imagine man to be "basically good," this is not the antithesis of the Christian view. Christians do not believe that man is "basically evil." The two truths—that he is made in God's image but fallen—are maintained in tension. A view that characterized man as nothing more than a demon might do justice to his depravity but would not sufficiently account for his status as image bearer or the restraining force of God's grace.

[6] Herman Bavinck, in B. B. Warfield, *The Plan of Salvation* (Eugene, OR: Wipf & Stock: 2000), 27.

and the religion of works; the religion which despairs of self and casts all its hope on God the Saviour, and the religion which puts complete trust in self; or since religion is in its very name utter dependence on God, religion in the purity of its conception and a mere quasi-religious moralism.[7]

Anthropology and soteriology are intertwined. If men are not so bad, their salvation need not be too difficult. It is at least within their grasp. If, however, men have committed a terrible wrong—and against a God who is perfectly holy (theology proper enters the picture)—then their salvation becomes a difficult thing indeed, something of which they are rendered incapable by sin.

Warfield's distinction between a religion of grace and one of moralism may seem surprising. After all, isn't Christianity that quintessential moralizing religion? As a matter of fact, no. In Christianity, God's law is a perfect standard that man has broken. As a consequence, no morality can save man. The moral standard in Christianity is a component not of salvation but sanctification. Once a man is saved by grace, he responds with obedience. Obedience apart from faith is meaningless.

If you remain unconvinced, ask yourself who the moralizers of the twenty-first century are. Who tells you what you can wear, what you can eat and drink, what you can drive, whom you must condemn, and whom you must tolerate? The emerging moral consensus is decidedly non-Christian. It is beyond doubt that there is within Christianity a moralizing stain, but I would argue that it is the result of a deficiency in our appreciation of God's grace and not a sign of our fidelity to the Christian worldview. According to Christ, salvation comes before sanctification, not afterward.

It is not enough to be different from everyone else. Just because Christianity claims that man is fallen and salvation is God's work alone doesn't mean that everyone else isn't right about man being basically good and capable of earning his own salvation (assuming he needs it). What matters is which view corresponds to reality, which is just another way of asking which one is true. Obviously, this is a matter we cannot easily prove one way or the other. No laboratory tests have yet been developed to determine the basic goodness or corruption of human nature, and the precise nature of salvation is one of the things to be revealed on the last day. But in the meantime it is still possible to draw conclusions based on experience.

---

[7]Ibid., 30.

Christian Coherence

I was raised as a Christian, but like many young people in similar circumstances, I did not come to appreciate Christian theology until later in life. When I discovered it, I found that it was a better explanation of the way the world worked than the philosophical systems that had fascinated me up until then. The Christian view of man seemed to account for the way people actually behave without ignoring key aspects of human experience. It did not reduce us to a jumble of chemical reactions, but it did not treat us naïvely as autonomous agents driven only by choice. Christianity did justice to the complexity of the world. It accounted for both the good and the evil in human behavior without having to redefine or ignore either one. It explained why we have an ineradicable consciousness of something we have never experienced—perfection—and why we tremble in the presence of both the beautiful and horrible.

None of this would have mattered, obviously, if I had not already been a convert to Christ. As we have noted, faith is placed in him, not in something as abstract as a philosophy or a worldview. But having found that faith in myself, I discovered that it was no longer necessary to turn a blind eye to anything in reality. The Christian faith did not give me all the answers, but it did help me to make peace with the unknown.

The "Will To" System

A few years ago, I discovered that the quickest way to get under the skin of my friend Jeff Baldwin was to use phrases like "the system of truth revealed in Scripture." He doesn't have a problem with Scripture, revelation, or truth, though. His *bête noire* is the idea of "system"—as in systematic theology, confessions of faith, interconnected universal abstractions worked out through a combination of exegesis and logic. For him, as for many contemporary believers—though he won't want to be subsumed in that category—there is something suspicious about the will to systematize. It strikes them as an urge akin to "putting God in a box." Exponents of systematic theology are seen as arrogant know-it-alls who think they have the mysteries of the divine neatly quantified. When Jeff and I first commenced our friendly sparring on the topic, I conceived of myself as holding the majority position, standing very much in line with the Christian tradition (at least in the West). Now, though, I have come to realize how rarified my perspective is. Most people alive and kicking today, whose minds are still active and not confined to an inadequate mapping on the dusty page, share Jeff's desire to dodge systematics, a discipline that seems as necessary and viable to them as metaphysics seemed to Derrida.

How to account for this shift? Centuries of rival systematics, competing and endlessly revised confessions, convince me that suspicion toward the idea that Scripture reveals a coherent, interconnected set of truths is relatively recent. It surely has existed throughout time, but in the West it wasn't dominant until the nineteenth and twentieth centuries. Before then, a believer was more likely to take issue with the particular tenets of a confession (doubting their accuracy, questioning how they were derived) than to dismiss the whole project as impossible, a product of Emersonian "foolish consistency." Today, the average believer has no qualms about rejecting systematic theology as a whole, even if he or she is in ignorance of what it contains. In fact, that ignorance is treasured as a kind of spiritual virtue, the way the fundamentalists of my youth valued the absence of book learning.

Now all of this is a little strange to me. As ready as I am to concede the limitations of their thought, I do not feel the need to sweep out the habits of thought that characterized my forbears in the faith. I do not conceive of systematic theology as a perfect revelation of the divine—or a perfect anything, for that matter—but I have found the study of it more helpful to me as a thinking Christian than a whole host of warm devotional essays or fashionably disjointed spiritual riffs. Maybe I'm just strange.

In my little war with Jeff, I eventually came across a gem of a quotation. In *Twilight of the Idols,* Nietzsche writes: "I mistrust all systematizers and avoid them. The will to system is a lack of integrity." I fired this line off to Jeff in an e-mail, adding, "Sounds like somebody I know."

The more I learn about Friedrich Nietzsche, the more I am convinced that we are living in his shadow. Whitehead famously said that the whole of philosophy consists of footnotes to Plato, but it strikes me that when it comes to the popular mind, we're dealing with annotations to Nietzsche. The indebtedness of poststructuralism and the postmodern in general to Nietzsche is well established. (I remember how surprised I was in grad school that my modern thought class began with a long immersion in his work—which I then considered a quaint artifact of the fin de siècle. Now it makes perfect sense.)

I'm going to suggest tentatively that the knee-jerk evangelical and post-evangelical skepticism toward systematics is an example (one of many, perhaps) of the internalization of a critique of Christianity put forward by Nietzsche and those he influenced, and that—noble as it can be made to sound—it is as much a capitulation as a caution.

Systematic theology is not perfect, and there are many examples of excess we could point to, tendencies toward mind-numbing scholasticism and false orthodoxies. But the same could be said for any endeavor of the human intellect. A general pessimism might be warranted, but I do not think the fruit of theological thought deserves to be singled out for a particularly fierce suspicion. I suppose Christians are always afraid that someone will build a seemingly airtight system on the basis of Scripture and bind their consciences accordingly. I sympathize with that concern, but it seems that, these days, such binding is accomplished perfectly well without the aid of any theology whatsoever. Perhaps it is time to be as skeptical of our suspicions as we are of anything else.

Worldview functions on the level of system, and there's no reason to be afraid of that fact. Where we must be careful, though, is in not allowing our systems to become closed systems—or in mistaking our conclusions with God's. To strike the right balance, we will turn from this consideration of worldview as system to a new perspective: the way in which worldview functions on the level of story.

4

Creation, Fall, and Redemption: Worldview as Story

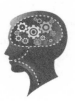

It was the first time I'd ever cried in front of an audience. So unfamiliar was the experience that I didn't recognize it at first. The words stopped coming. I tried to speak and couldn't. I was trembling and my face was wet. *What's going on?* My mind raced, and then it dawned on me. I was in tears. Two hundred high school students and their parents sat in the auditorium in front of me, here on the final morning of our weeklong odyssey. Some of them looked shocked—my speaking style is more ironically comic than painfully sincere—but I could see some heads nodding on the periphery, encouraging me to let it all out.

Painful sincerity hadn't been my goal for this lecture. There are people, I know, who see a speaker's tears as a sign of authenticity, but if a man gives the same talk again and again to various audiences and cries at the same cues, you really have to wonder. By nature, I'm emotionally reserved, and that tendency has been reinforced by seeing too many television preachers back their plays with crocodile tears. From the time I started teaching, I eschewed any tactic that suggested emotional manipulation.

So these tears were real, and they surprised me more than anyone.

To explain where they came from, I have to go back to the beginning of the week. I was in Flagstaff, Arizona, about to begin another Worldview Academy leadership camp. During the summer, our team travels from one college campus to another, leading up to two hundred students through a weeklong academic program focusing on worldview, leadership, and apologetics. Each week, I was responsible for delivering a series of lectures based on chapters for this book. But in Flagstaff the plan changed. My friend Jeff Baldwin, who I mentioned in the last chapter, one of the founders of Worldview Academy and our team's anchor, received news that his father had passed away. He had to leave right away to be with his family.

As we grieved along with our friend, we were faced with a challenge. Jeff taught more classes than anyone during the week, so his absence would be felt in more ways than one. The three remaining faculty members would have to pick up the slack, adding new material to fill the gaps. The big question was, who would teach the two-hour wrap-up session on Friday morning? Answer: yours truly.

I had filled this slot once before, back in North Carolina, at the end of a miserable week at Wake Forest—miserable because I'd suffered from the worst cold of my life, with a head so congested I could barely keep my balance on stage. It's a testament to the power of NyQuil that I made it through that lecture and remember nothing whatsoever about it. This time I was determined to do a better job.

My lecture was about the power of story as it relates to our understanding of worldviews, so it was only natural to begin by telling a story. Thinking about Jeff's loss during the week, I kept remembering a circumstance of my own. I'd been at another Worldview Academy camp in Seattle the summer my grandfather died. My wife and I flew to Louisiana for the funeral, then returned to the Northwest for our final camp of the summer. The more I thought about my grandfather and the special bond we'd had, the more I wanted to talk about him in this lecture, to share some of the stories he'd passed along to me.

My Grandfather's Stories

My grandfather worked at a chemical plant in Louisiana for most of his life. We lived just a block away, so I spent a lot of time at his house. To me, he looked a lot like John Wayne: tall and ruggedly handsome, with a bit of a swagger. When Pearl Harbor was bombed at the beginning of the Second World War, he was a boy of sixteen. All of his older brothers enlisted, but he was too young. In a move that has always reminded me of young David during the reign of King Saul, my grandfather nevertheless found his way to the battle. He lied about his age and joined the Navy. (Ironically enough, his brothers all failed their physicals and didn't get to fight.)

He served on the battleship *New Jersey* in the Pacific, and since I'd grown up playing with toy soldiers and reading comics about World War II, he always seemed larger than life to me. One afternoon, we sat together at the kitchen counter and he started telling me stories about his experience during the war. He was a radio operator, and he remembered the long hours spent monitoring Japanese telegraph traffic. Once, when they were supposed to be listening for enemy code, he and his buddies had tuned in a baseball game being broadcast back home. When they were feeling particularly mischievous, they would add extra keystrokes to the Japanese telegraphy.

"If you were really good," he said, "you could do it without anyone knowing. When they tried to decipher the code at the other end, everything would be garbled."

Before leaving for the war, he'd married my grandmother, and one day she decided too much time had passed since she last saw him. So she filed papers with the Navy for a compassionate leave on the grounds that his grandmother was dying. The leave was approved, but he was a little confused: his grandmother had been "dying" for years! Still, when you have an opportunity to take a break from combat and visit home, you don't ask too many questions. While he was gone, a lone Japanese plane happened upon the battleship and dropped a single bomb, which slid down a stack and exploded near the radio room, killing my grandfather's replacement.

"Your grandmother saved my life," he joked. "After that, I always listened to her."

When the war ended, for example, the Navy tried to keep him on because of his signals training. They wanted him to do some kind of intelligence work. But my grandmother put a stop to that. She said no, and he listened.

He told his stories and I listened avidly. Later, I wanted to know more about this intelligence work, so I asked my grandmother a question about it. She was shocked.

"Who told you about that?"

She called my mother in, and the two of them interrogated me, making me repeat all the stories I'd been told.

"Well, I'll be," my grandmother said. "You must be pretty special. He's never told anybody else these stories."

The Power of Stories

I did feel special. By passing on his stories, my grandfather had given me a way to identify with him, to know him better. Whenever I think about him, I remember that afternoon when it was just the two of us, a war veteran and a wide-eyed boy. It wasn't the facts or the history that captivated me—as important as they are—but the personal connection. He had been privy to great experiences, and this was his way of letting me in on them.

That was the point I was trying to make in Flagstaff, in front of that audience of expectant students. Simple enough, I would have thought. On the screen behind me, some footage of Pearl Harbor played, and then a photo of the *U.S.S. New Jersey* followed by a picture of my grandfather as a young man wearing his naval uniform, his white cap at a jaunty angle.

But when the picture came up and I tried to explain his role, my throat closed and the tears welled up. I'd talked about the moment many times before in private, so why was it so difficult now? Maybe it was the atmosphere, the fact that I was standing in for Jeff, who'd just lost his father. Maybe it was the sadness I still felt about my grandfather's death, that I'd been across the country instead of at his bedside. Whatever it was, I found myself mute and vulnerable for a moment on stage.

I managed to continue, but the rest of the lecture was a little rushed, a little scattered. The thing about real emotion is that it's difficult to work around. You can't incorporate it easily into a slick presentation—at least, *I* can't. And I wouldn't want it any other way. That lecture may not have been memorable to the audience, but for me it was a milestone. I'd spoken before in the abstract about the power of story, but here was a concrete example. A man cold-blooded enough to give Mr. Spock a run for his money had choked up over the telling of a simple story. To say that moment taught me something would be an understatement.

Starting Points, Systems, and Stories

The worldview concept functions on many levels, but for convenience I have divided them into three: starting points, systems, and stories. Many people talk about worldviews as if they function exclusively in one of these ways, and not in the others. For example, there are some who insist that worldviews are, strictly speaking, underlying assumptions, beliefs the individual accepts as given or perhaps isn't even aware of. Christians are then admonished to be sure they are not attempting to live a godly life with ungodly assumptions.

Others, though, worry that this emphasis on basic assumptions results in a minimalist conception of the Christian worldview, stripped of all its rich particulars. They insist on a fuller definition, encompassing the specific teachings of Scripture and their logical consequences, a systematized perspective usually expressed through creeds and confessions.

Still others worry that the "starting points and systems" approach is too rational and takes us too far from the kernel of the gospel story. Christians are people who follow Jesus, not adherents to a philosophical (or even a theological) system. We need to strip away the accumulated tradition and speculation to find ourselves united by the story of redemption.

My tendency in such disputes is to be inclusive rather than exclusive. The worldview concept is complicated, and we are not faced with an either/or proposition. In the preceding chapters, I have attempted to show how worldviews function both as starting points and as systems. Both approaches are valid—right up until the moment they attempt to edge out the other. The same is true in the case of story. Looking at worldview through the lens of narrative is extraordinarily valuable—right up to the moment you oppose story to starting point or story to system.

The Rise of Story

Jesus Christ is the way, the truth, and the life. Worldviews are interpretative schemes. As a Christian, my faith is in the person of Christ, not in an abstract intellectual concept. Too often, though, we forget this distinction and allow interpretative tools to take center stage. We argue for one method over another instead of acknowledging the good in each and using other tools to qualify the inevitable bad. That, in a nutshell, is what has happened with the idea of story.

As we are constantly being reminded, we live in a "postmodern" age, and the defining characteristic of this period is its skepticism toward what are supposed to have been the unqualified assumptions of modernism—the belief in science, progress, reason, and what not. In the modern age, people were always trying to pin down objective reality, to define truth on behalf of everyone else in a kind of idealistic power play. Now, we are rightly skeptical of such attempts. If the modern world strived toward a kind of unity, the postmodern seeks to guard itself from the horrors of modernism by cultivating diversity.

This shift has cast doubt on rational, systematic attempts to describe reality. When we look out at the universe, postmodern people tend to find possibilities instead of rules. Instead of systems, we make stories.

The theological emphasis on story does not begin with postmodernism, however. In a sense, it has always been with us. The belief system expressed in the Nicene Creed, for example, has a definite narrative thrust. It is an abstract statement of faith, but it is based on and incorporates specific elements of the gospel story. If postliberal theology in the twentieth century has given us narrative theology, conservative theology has its parallel interest in redemptive history. What is new is not the focus on story, but the conviction that story cannot coexist with a more systematic understanding of faith. In other words, tools that should be complementary are treated as if they are incompatible, in competition with each other.

I applaud the rising interest in story as a tool for understanding the Christian worldview. After all, I studied fiction in graduate school, not theology. But I have waited to treat worldview as story last because, while I want the narrative approach to bestow all its benefits, I do not want to lose anything in the transaction. Story works best when understood in context.

We are often reminded that Jesus taught in parables, which is true. But he did not teach exclusively in parables. In fact, he was more than willing to demonstrate to his disciples how his stories had abstract doctrine behind them. The same mixture of starting point, system, and story can be found in the epistles of Paul. A narrative emphasis offers valuable insight that an abstract systematic approach does not, but the opposite is also true.

Not long ago, I found myself at a coffee shop in a small college town, overhearing a deep conversation between two students. They were explaining to each other how abstractions were dead and story was everything. It sounded good. I imagined this was something a professor had said in class and the two men were trying the perspective on for size. What didn't occur to them, though, was the irony of having a rational, abstract conversation about the death of abstraction. They were crowning story king without engaging in one whit of storytelling. These were bright young men, but they managed, as so many of us do, to miss the forest for the trees. Things are rarely as simple as exchanging a bad paradigm for a perfect replacement.

The Glue of Community

With that proviso in place, let us affirm in no uncertain terms that the rise of story is a good thing. One of its benefits for the Christian community has been an emphasis on our shared identity in spite of our differences. My experience with Worldview Academy is a great example. The faculty I work with there are united by a broad orthodoxy—what's been dubbed, following C. S. Lewis, "mere Christianity"—but when it comes to the specifics of our belief systems, we are not in accord. Some of us are Reformed, some are Lutheran. Some are low church, others liturgical. We have Southern Baptists teaching side-by-side with nondenominational Bible church men, Presbyterians with Evangelical Free Churchers, and plenty more besides. We are Protestant and evangelical, but beyond that all bets are off.

With all these differences, when we come together to teach about the Christian worldview, there is still an uncanny overlap in what we say. Our different approaches complement each other much more often than they conflict. As much as we value our various belief systems and confessions, they are not the glue that holds our community together. What we have in common is the story of the Bible, a narrative each of us has located himself within. We have a common identity that goes beyond the strength of our personal relationships, because we share in the same story of redemption.

Think of it this way. Little children in church, no matter what their denomination, share a similar understanding of Scripture, because their parents and Sunday school teachers tend to emphasize the stories: Noah's Ark, David and Goliath, Daniel and the Lion's Den, the Nativity, the Passion and Resurrection, the Missionary Journeys of Paul. I have friends who have taught their children the Westminster Shorter Catechism, but the vast majority of kids have only a miniscule conception of the theological framework that becomes so important later on. When I was a boy, the Bible was a book of stories that I could enter into imaginatively. A minority of us are gifted with the parallel ability to enter into abstract thought imaginatively, but all of us share this skill when it comes to stories.

To grasp the radical difference between stories and abstract principles, consider the most basic of all syllogisms:

All men are mortal.
Socrates is a man.
Therefore, Socrates is mortal.

This is the stuff of Logic 101. It's a given that all men are mortal. We assume this to be true without even examining the matter, because we know of no exceptions. Socrates, the celebrated ancient philosopher we looked at in the last chapter, is a stand-in here for the average man, which is appropriate considering the persona he cultivated. Working logically from the underlying assumption, we establish that Socrates, because he is a man, is mortal. But Socrates here isn't really a man. His name is invoked as a kind of algebraic equivalent. Replace him with an X and the logic holds up. The truth of the syllogism is evident, but who will it inspire? No one.

But when we set the syllogism aside and read an account of Socrates' death, the matter changes. He is brought to trial before the men of Athens for asking hard questions, defends himself nobly, but is nevertheless condemned. His enemies assume that he will flee from the sentence, so they do not take the injustice of their verdict too seriously. But Socrates does not run, despite the urging of his friends. He chooses to stay and die on principle.

In my book, the example of Socrates, his willingness to make a noble sacrifice, is more inspiring than the principle for which he died. Hearing this story, we are more likely to make a similar sacrifice than if we were only acquainted with the principle in the abstract. Story makes a more visceral impact. That doesn't mean the logic is meaningless, or that the example of the story, no matter what its moral, ought to be followed. But it does point to the reason why poets (or, in our age, filmmakers) are the unacknowledged legislators. They work in the most powerful medium. Everyone is influenced by story.

This is why communities of every kind, no matter how dearly they may cherish their abstract organizing principles, are held together largely by relationships and stories. A group of people develops a history over time, and it transmits those tales to newcomers.

When I joined the faculty of Worldview Academy, the organization already had a long history, a chronicle of milestones and misadventures that made my head spin. Before I joined this group, I had always fancied myself a storyteller, but these guys spin yarns of Homeric proportions. In the early years, the fact that I'd never heard the stories and couldn't tell them to others marked me as a newcomer. In time, I learned the history and even became a part of it, so that new faculty members are now regaled with a few exploits of mine. Worldview Academy is a parachurch organization, but churches work the same way—all communities do. Metaphorically speaking, we're all hunched around the campfire telling tales.

There's a flip-side to this. Conflict within communities, though it often cloaks itself in abstraction, is usually personal.

I have seen more than my share of church splits, a few of them too close for comfort. In each case, the conflicting parties justified themselves on doctrinal grounds, but it was clear to an outside observer that the reasons were personal. After all, in spite of their differences, these people had gotten along until now. Pride and alienation are much bigger factors in these situations than principle, so they are better understood by the novelist than the theologian.

The stories of the Bible, taken together with the stories of the church, of various denominations and congregations and even cliques, constitute a kind of individual worldview perspective. The stories we've been told and the weight we've given them go a long way to shaping the outlook we adopt. So if you want to come to grips with your own worldview and interrogate it in light of Scripture, you have to be self-conscious about your stories.

Story and Tradition

When stories are handed down from the past, they form a personal history. The tales my grandfather shared, for example, are now family lore. They belong to me in a way that the history of World War II as a whole does not. The stories of Worldview Academy are the same. They create a tradition within the community, a way of seeing ourselves collectively, and there's a certain amount of positive pressure to live up to expectations. We want to fit within the tradition, to add new but consistent chapters to the history.

These are positive influences, but the power of story can be negative, too. Because we identify with stories in a way that we rarely can with abstract principles, it is sometimes difficult to abandon a faulty belief enshrined by tradition. The fundamentalist tradition in which I grew up identified many things as sin that were not condemned in Scripture—in fact, I would go so far as to say that the *definitive* sins, the ones we thought most important to condemn, fell into this category. As a result, I found myself embroiled in a strange conflict between the teaching of Scripture and the tradition I'd inherited from people who believed they had no tradition but Scripture! To rely on what I found in the Bible (or what I didn't find) would mean rejecting a history with which I had identified deeply. Eventually, I managed to do it, but part of the process involved identifying with new stories, a new tradition.

I have had friends who could not cross the chasm. "I believe that *intellectually*," one of them said, "but my heart is still here."

Once upon a time, I thought the distinction between head and heart was spurious, just a slack-minded excuse for turning a blind eye to truth. Now I'm not so sure. This little network of personal histories carries the same weight in life as precedent does in law. Operate outside of them and you find yourself at sea, set adrift, not exactly sure who you are anymore. Again, it is a testament to the power of story, the narratives that pin us down but give us just enough wiggle room to feel free.

If stories play such a profound role in shaping one's idea of self, it follows that they can be both stifling and liberating. If the gospel, which is communicated to us primarily through four witness narratives, is true, then it ought to be the most liberating story of all. To enjoy that place of privilege, though, Christians must think of it not as one of many stories that have been told, but rather as the best and highest story, the one that puts the rest in context and makes sense of the world. If we find our identity through stories, then the most important thing to discover about ourselves will be found in the story of Christ, who died for us.

The Story of Christ, Who Died for Us

When I was a child, as I have already said, the Bible seemed to me to be a collection of stories. Some of them were interesting and some not so much. When the book of Judges related the story of Ehud, who plunged his hidden sword into fat King Eglon and buried it to the hilt, I was all ears. The three Hebrew boys choosing to eat vegetables at the beginning of the book of Daniel didn't pique my curiosity, but when the same lads were thrown into the fiery furnace, I perked up. As a prepubescent boy,

I didn't exactly choose my favorite Bible stories on the basis of moral edification. Blood and guts was the order of the day.

Over time, I came to see that in addition to the stories, the Bible offered a collection of moral teachings. The book of Proverbs, for example, had a lot of advice about what to do and what not to do, and so did the Old Testament law and the Pauline epistles. Eventually, I could identify specific doctrines connected with famous passages. This, combined with a fair amount of memorization and a solid memory, helped me pass for a reasonably good student of Scripture—so much so that, when my Christian high school attended a statewide academic competition, my teachers entered me in the "preaching competition." I ended up with the blue ribbon, in spite of the fact that I'd never claimed any calling to ministry, and the only criticism my first sermon received from the panel of ministers who judged the competition was that it was "too intellectual" and needed more of an emotional appeal at the end.

I was not, however, a good student of Scripture. What I possessed was a mass of knowledge, a collection of dates, facts, and maxims which I believed fervently without grasping either their simplicity or their interrelation. That changed in early adulthood, when I was introduced to a new way of seeing the story of Scripture, a trajectory with three points: creation, fall, and redemption. Like many churchgoers, I was accustomed to thinking of these as doctrines, not chapters in a story, but a subtle shift in thinking made all the difference.

The Bible opens with a story about the creation of the world. Unlike the account that opens John's Gospel, this one is fairly stark and uninterpreted—a plain retelling of the event. That story is followed closely by a narrative about the fall. Immediately, the Bible establishes a status quo and then relates a conflict. God made Adam and Eve a certain way, and through disobedience they brought about a catastrophe that condemned all humanity. The first intimation of what will follow comes in Genesis 3:15—the so-called *proto-evangelion*—where God says to the serpent, "I will put enmity between you and the woman, and between your offspring and her offspring; he shall bruise your head, and you shall bruise his heel." The rest of the Bible recounts the unfolding of that elliptical promise, the coming of a Messiah who will restore what was broken in the fall. Redemption, planned from eternity, enters time in the person of Jesus Christ.

All history before the cross looks forward to it, just as all history since looks back upon it. Creation, fall, and redemption are the story of the Bible, but they are also the story of the world in which we live. It is our story. The gospel is a proclamation that God has made good on his promise, that the old enemy, Death, has been defeated by Christ, and if we are in Christ we live in hope of resurrection. This is a starting point, a belief system and a story all at once. It tells us who made us, what's become of us, and what's in store for us. It is a testament to the sacrificial love God has for us.

We sometimes speak of our lives as books we write with our choices. It's a hopeful metaphor, suggesting that whatever has gone before, we have the power to turn the page and make something beautiful. But suppose that, just once, you glimpse the notion that all of life, all of existence and history, is in fact a book that God is writing through his choices? Suppose that God is moving in the world around us to bring about some good end? This intuition of providence, this conception of God as author, has the power to vitalize a dusty, bookish faith. That's how it was for me. Suddenly, looking at Scripture through the lens of God's history, his plan of redemption, even the notoriously boring genealogies took on a new significance. I remember reading the genealogy of Christ found in Luke 3 and trembling by the end. It starts in verses 23–24 calmly enough: "Jesus, when he began his ministry, was about thirty years of age, being the son (as was supposed) of Joseph, the son of Heli, the son of Matthat, the son of Levi, the son of Melchi, the son of Jannai, the son of Joseph. . . ." It continues like this for several verses, tracing the line back to King David (v. 31) and then further back into antiquity. Then, in verses 36–38, come the familiar names from the book of Genesis: "the son of Noah, the son of Lamech, the son of Methuselah, the son of Enoch, the son of Jared, the son of Mahalaleel, the son of Cainan, the son of Enos, the son of Seth, the son of Adam, the son of God."

That final name—the son of God—comes so unexpectedly, representing such an ontological jump from creature to creator, that it always strikes with the force of a thunderclap. It brings the list full circle, too, given the fact that "son of God" is one of the titles ascribed to Christ, and Paul refers to Christ in the famous passage on the resurrection found in 1 Corinthians 15 as "the last Adam" (v. 45). The continuity in all this is striking. After creation and fall comes redemption, a feat accomplished at the cross and applied to us now by the Spirit, looking forward to the second coming and the resurrection of the dead. Instead of a disconnected anthology of useful arcana, Scripture moves with all the determination of an arrow's flight, a shaft already on target that has not yet landed.

This vitality is all too often lost in the minutiae of theological (and philosophical) talk. As interesting as I find such things, I am reminded of a phrase used by a seminary professor of mine: "Truly, this is theology which leads us to doxology." In other words, proper theological contemplation ought to lead, as it does for the apostle Paul at the close of Romans 8, to religious ecstasy, to worship.

Two Pitfalls

The gospel is indeed, in the words of the nineteenth-century hymn, the "old, old story," and we move away from that burning narrative at our peril. Systematic theology has always been at risk of coming untethered, departing from its source material into philosophical speculation and rational argumentation. As a result, some Christians are suspicious of the whole project. But again, this is one of those instances where an inclusive rather than an exclusive approach is best. Systematic thought has its place. In his inaugural address at Princeton Seminary, theologian Geerhardus Vos emphasized the proper relationship between biblical theology, derived from exegesis, and systematic theology:

> The line of revelation is like the stem of those trees that grow in rings. Each successive ring has grown out of the preceding one. But out of the sap and vigor that is in this stem there springs a crown with branches and leaves and flowers and fruit. Such is the true relation between Biblical and Systematic Theology. Dogmatics is the crown which grows out of all the work that Biblical Theology can accomplish.[1]

Thus Vos, the father of Reformed biblical theology, rather than perceiving systematic theology as a rival, celebrates it—when it flows organically from the source in Scripture. Instead of thinking in binary terms (either system or story), we have a model here for the inclusive approach, everything in its proper place. This is a corrective that cuts both ways, admonishing us against belief systems that stray fancifully from the text, but also guarding against the wholesale rejection of systematic thought. If the former is a pitfall, so is the latter.

But there is another blind alley to consider. In this chapter I've spoken for the most part of story in the abstract, though I've told a few stories along the way. But the Christian brief isn't for story in general; it's for a particular story. If it is true that in this postmodern moment we relate bet-

---

[1] "The Idea of Biblical Theology as a Science and as a Theological Discipline," in *Redemptive History and Biblical Interpretation: The Shorter Writings of Geerhardus Vos* (Phillipsburg, NJ: P&R, 1980), 24.

ter to stories than systems, it's also a fact that there are lots of stories out there competing for attention. It is all too easy to be in thrall to them.

We have a story to tell, and it's the best story, one with power that people need to hear. The better we know it, the better we know ourselves. The gospel story delivers us from the power of other tales, other conceptions of ourselves. Pray that God gives us ears to hear.

Full Circle

The end of this chapter marks the close of the book's first and lengthiest section, where we've looked at the idea of worldview from a variety of perspectives. Although we've moved from starting point to system to story, I want to reverse polarity for a moment. In a sense, story comes first. The gospel comes to us in narrative form, and we first hear and comprehend it in this way. Believing in that story and in its author brings us into the community of faith, where we learn other stories and move, as we mature, to doctrinal, systematic thought. As we do this, however, old ideas persist. We find ourselves professing one thing and doing another, and this prompts scrutiny of our underlying assumptions. In the Christian life, which includes the formation of a biblical worldview, we move from story to system to starting point. Or perhaps we shuffle between the categories all at once in a confusing, organic, Spirit-led way.

All men are mortal. Socrates is a man. Therefore Socrates is mortal. Earlier, I shared the syllogism and the moving story that brings it to life. But there is a problem with the underlying assumption, a fault the Christian story brings to light. Christ was fully God and fully man, but he is not mortal, and through him mortal man finds life everlasting. This may very well be, as Paul says, foolishness to the Greeks, but to us it is Christ the power of God and the wisdom of God. And the wisdom of God is what we will consider in the next section.

PART TWO

WISDOM

5

The Principal Thing: Regaining Wisdom

Show me your faith apart from your works, and I will show you my faith by my works.

JAMES 2:18

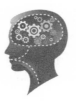

One weekend I was sitting in jail, and the next I was teaching a Sunday school class. If only I could claim that, like the apostles, I was behind bars for obeying God rather than man. But that's not how it happened. My family was flying back from Chicago to Houston, and the ticket agents in the first class line were hassling us about our upgrades. I've never had much patience for bureaucracy, so instead of jumping into the fray, I let my wife and mother do the talking. It was obvious, though, from what I could overhear, that the ticket agents were jerking us around. Finally, one of them printed out my ticket and extended it over my wife's shoulder toward me. I snatched it from her and said, "Thanks."

Although I hadn't touched her, had never even been close enough to, and had only exchanged one word with her throughout the process, a group of security guards arrived on the scene, pulled me out of the line, and handcuffed me. I only discovered the reason later: assault. Absurd as it sounds, the ticket agent claimed I had assaulted her with the ticket.

This was clearly an injustice, and I was confident that once my story was told, the police would laugh at the absurdity of it all. So I responded meekly, even stoically, as they led me to the paddy wagon outside for transport to the detention cell. I'd never been arrested before, so I was naturally curious about the process, and that helped me stay calm. Still, being arrested is never fun, and it is particularly awkward when your mother is there to witness the whole thing. And mine not only witnessed but protested. Vigorously. At one point, a policeman turned to her and said, "If you don't shut up, we'll arrest you, too."

So there I was, being led away in handcuffs, a grown man begging his mother not to embarrass him in front of everyone.

I assumed the police would ask me what happened and release me once they heard the truth, but as far as they were concerned, it was up to the judge to decide. After cooling my heels at the airport detention, I was transferred to a nearby precinct where the jailer, while processing my fingerprints, asked what had happened. After he heard, he laughed and said there was a real problem with people being arrested for nothing at the airport. I didn't see what was so funny about it. One of my fellow detainees was a Turkish exchange student who, according to the conversation I overheard between two detectives, had been arrested for having a thousand dollars in cash and not speaking English well enough to explain why. (And this was before September 11.) I spoke to the guy and found out his family had been caught in the earthquake that had recently shattered Turkey. My problems seemed small in comparison.

There was another complication, though. In addition to my wife and mother, someone else had been standing at the ticket counter in Chicago: my pastor's son. He was working for me as an intern and had accompanied us on the trip. And he had witnessed my arrest just a week before I was scheduled to begin teaching a Sunday school class for college students at my church. "Awkward" didn't begin to cover it!

Needless to say, I had a lot to think about in that jail cell. Sure, I was a victim of injustice, only I couldn't exactly claim the moral high ground. A bad attitude shouldn't get you arrested, but that's no excuse for having one. If I hadn't gotten worked up in the first place, if I'd responded to the ticket agent's provocation with grace, then I wouldn't have opened myself up to what happened next.

The charges, I'm happy to say, were dropped and I was a free man. Everyone who heard the story took my side, and they were too polite to point out that I'd brought the trouble on myself through simple foolishness. But I already knew that. I offered to resign my Sunday school class before starting, but the pastor brushed aside the suggestion. And that's how, just a week after I'd been thrown in jail, I found myself teaching a class of college students. Our first series of lessons was about

wisdom. Needless to say, it was something I needed to hear as much as
they did.

Wise Counsel

A teacher's job does not end in the classroom. Because of his position of
authority, students naturally turn to a teacher for advice in the outside
world. I felt very comfortable standing in front of an easel explicating a
passage of Scripture, but when a young man cornered me in the hallway
and asked for personal counseling, all my comfort disappeared. Who was
I to give advice? My choices, insignificant as they had seemed, led me
to jail. I was afraid that any counsel I gave might lead to similarly catastrophic results in the lives of others.

As more of these requests for counseling popped up, I began to notice
a pattern. People came to me wanting one of two things. Either they hoped
to lay out their circumstances and have me tell them exactly what to do,
or they wanted me to share a technique or method for divining the will of
God. I say *divining,* not discerning, because the requests really did seem
to be aimed more at divination than discernment. The students imagined
there must be a spiritual equivalent to the Magic 8-Ball® that they could
shake via prayer or good works to arrive at God's answer.

Something was wrong about this, but I couldn't put my finger on
precisely what.

In the first instance, the students who wanted me to give them the
answers were looking for a shortcut. Instead of working through their
issues, they wanted to fall back on an authority figure. I should point out
here that they really were looking to me for answers, not just soliciting
my input. Seeking counsel is wise, but it's not the same thing as abrogat-
ing responsibility for one's own decisions. It seemed to me that, for these
students, the pressure of decision making was overwhelming and they'd
grown accustomed to having other people decide for them. As college
students, they couldn't bear the thought of deferring to their own parents,
so they were looking for surrogates to serve the same function. I was
reluctant to play that role.

After some reflection, I decided that the second group of students
had a similar dilemma, only they were hoping to surrender their decision making to God, not me. That was a good impulse, given what an
unreliable guide I was, but there was something strange about the *way*
they wanted God to function. The ideal God to suit their purposes

would have been an all-knowing answer bank who only responded to yes/no and multiple choice questions. But the more I dug into the Bible's wisdom literature, the less convinced I was that God works that way. If knowing God's will was that easy, why bother with all that wisdom literature in the first place?

Fleeces, Green Lights, and Closed Doors

The more you reflect on other people's problems, the more aware you become of your own. The students who wanted me to give them all the answers frustrated me, but that was largely because I could see my own desire for easy answers reflected in them. When the kids looking for the divine 8-Ball made me squirm, I knew it was because I'd sought long and hard for that chimera myself—and if I was honest with myself, I had to admit I still did. As mild as my recent arrest had been, as far as it had been from persecution, there was a part of me sitting in that cell that couldn't help thinking God had dropped the ball. His plan had somehow gone off the rails; otherwise, how could something so bad happen to someone as good as me? If anything, I was worse than the students wanting a heavenly yes/no, because I was expecting God to smooth the path without my even having to consult him.

Once again, I found myself sinking from a sense of superiority to one of humility—or more precisely, humiliation. If my students were looking for shortcuts, instead of condemning them, I should have sympathized, because there was nobody looking for a shorter cut than I was.

Growing up, I'd always been fascinated by the sanctified processes of divination described by the "prayer warriors" in church. They talked about "putting out a fleece" the way Gideon had in Judges 6, looking for a sign from above before making a big decision. Sometimes in prayer they sensed that God was placing a green light in their path signaling them to go forward or a red one signifying a halt. When people pursued what they assumed from the fleeces and green lights must be God's will, only to run into trouble, they spoke of God "closing a door." Sometimes, though, God opened doors, too—and when he did, it was essential to hustle through them right away.

I'm sure that these expressions were sincere and that they gave those godly people great comfort and guidance. But for me, the overall effect was different. A metaphor took shape. I imagined the Christian life as a mysterious, arbitrary maze, where one could never be certain exactly what God wanted or where to take the next step. So pronounced was the effect that I could even imagine God's will turning in ironic or vindictive paths, going against the grain of his words revealed in Scripture.

When I was a teen, a missionary to Africa visited our church. Afterward a girl in my youth group said, "I hope God doesn't send me to Africa."

"Don't say that," somebody warned her, "or he will!"

And the rest of us nodded sagely, not knowing any better.

Perhaps this is an instance where something that starts off good results in unintended consequences, but the result of all this talk of spiritual divination was a group of young people, myself included, who were utterly baffled about the will of God, in spite of having grown up in church and committed a fair portion of Scripture to memory.

Above the Subtext

There's a scene from Whit Stillman's 1994 film *Barcelona* that perfectly illustrates the situation. In the movie, which is set in Spain during the 1980s, a literal-minded young naval officer named Fred Boynton invades the Barcelona pad of his cousin Ted, a Bible-reading businessman who considers himself by far the more savvy of the two. The cousins have a series of quirky cross-cultural adventures with the local population, during the course of which Fred puzzles over the great mysteries of existence, not realizing how obvious the answers he's seeking really are. Here's an exchange Fred and Ted have while ambling down the sidewalk:

> Fred: Clarify something for me. Since I've been waiting for the fleet, I've read a lot.

> Ted: Really?

> Fred: One thing that keeps cropping up is "subtext." Plays, novels, songs, all have a subtext . . . which I take to mean a hidden message or import of some kind. Subtext, we know. But what do you call the message or meaning . . . that's on the surface, open and obvious? They never talk about that. What do you call what's above the subtext?

> Ted: The text.

> Fred: That's right, but they never talk about that.[1]

---

[1] *Barcelona* (1994), directed by Whit Stillman.

The scene always cracks me up, because Fred so obviously feels that he's onto something, that he's pushing the mystery one step further than anyone else has. When Ted bursts his bubble, he recovers immediately: "That's right, but they never talk about that." As they say, it's funny because it is so true.

Chasing after fleeces and green lights and open doors, whatever its virtue, can have the unintended effect of displacing the text in the hunt for a deeper subtext. Far from being mysterious, the will of God is written down, repeated, and even interpreted for us in Scripture. No, not all of our questions are answered, but even where the Bible remains silent, it does not leave us without guidance. We have the Spirit, we have prayer—and we also have an extensive wisdom literature, page after page. Take your Bible and pinch together the books of Job, Psalms, Proverbs, and Ecclesiastes, and then compare the size of that block to the New Testament. There is plenty there to sink your teeth into.

Only we don't. Job and Ecclesiastes are hard books. Proverbs is more popular, because it is perceived as being "practical," but even there I think we focus on the details—specific advice about what to do in particular situations—and less on the implication: that God's answer to life's many dilemmas and uncertainties is to cultivate wisdom and discernment. We are missing what's right in front of us, mainly because "wisdom and discernment" is a long road and we're looking for expressways. Hunting for mysterious subtexts is more glamorous sometimes than merely dwelling on the text itself.

An Apology for Wisdom

This section of the book deals with wisdom, and I'm convinced that it must be prefaced with an apology, or defense, of the subject. I do not propose here to exhaustively unpack the teachings of biblical wisdom literature. That goal is beyond the scope of this book and far beyond the abilities of its author. Also, there is something not quite right about handing you a book about the Bible's teaching rather than insisting that you go directly to the source. I haven't set out here to provide yet another shortcut. The chapters in this section will touch on issues important to the development of discernment, both spiritual and cultural, but they make a sorry substitute indeed for the Bible's wisdom literature.

As I said in the Preface, this book is meant to be read side-by-side with Scripture. Nothing I say about wisdom will obviate the need to go to the source, and there is no insight I can offer that will prepare you better for the experience of reading. As you read Part Two, I urge you to plunge into the book of Job or Ecclesiastes at the same time. It really will make a difference.

One thing I can do is help create a context for thinking about wisdom.

First, I want to reiterate the point I've made so far, that wisdom is God's reply to the question we often attempt to answer through mystical practices of our own invention. If Christ is indeed, as Paul says in 1 Corinthians 1, the "wisdom of God," then it makes sense to see the Old Testament pursuit of wisdom in the New Testament context of sanctification. Part of our duty as believers is to mature, and maturity involves growing in wisdom. The Spirit's guidance and prayer are not God's substitutes for this—they are all part of the same divine process at work in us. So I am not arguing for wisdom *against* spiritual guidance. Far from it. Wisdom is not the application of principles or systems: like sanctification, it is Christ working in us, the consequence of the spiritual change God has wrought. Still, I'm suggesting that the pendulum has swung to an alarming degree in one direction, and (to mix a metaphor) we must regain a place at the table for the difficult process of growing in discernment.

Second, to anticipate a point we will look at in greater detail in the following chapter, let us agree that wisdom should flow organically from worldview. One of the blind spots of much worldview chatter is the failure to connect thinking and living. Worldview formation is not just a means of getting one's intellectual ducks in a row, ensuring that one buys into the official evangelical position on the various hot-button issues of the day.

Instead, worldview thinking should lead inevitably and organically to changed behavior. In worldview we focus on justification, on theology proper, on grace as distinct from works, since every view but ours implies that man, if he is delivered at all, saves himself. In wisdom we focus on sanctification, on the works that flow from grace. We might say worldview is Paul, and wisdom is James. In James 2:18, the apostle offers quite a challenge. "Show me your faith apart from your works," he says, "and I will show you my faith by my works." In other words, you can try demonstrating your faith in the abstract, but I will show mine through concrete action. James also writes, "Religion that is pure and undefiled before God, the Father, is this: to visit orphans and widows in their affliction, and to keep oneself unstained from the world" (1:27). He isn't saying that it doesn't matter whether you believe in Christ or not, so long as you do good deeds, but he is saying that if you do believe in

Christ, you will do good and refrain from evil. God insists that we follow him with our minds, but it is impossible to follow him only in the mind. Right belief is important, but right belief that doesn't lead to right action isn't as right as it seems.

This is the reason why, when I teach worldview, I always follow up by covering wisdom, too. As far as I'm concerned, it should be a one-two punch. Equipping people to think is a noble task, but not a sufficient one. God expects us not just to think, but to live.

God's Wisdom, Man's Wisdom

In the passage from 1 Corinthians I mentioned earlier, where Paul speaks of Christ as "the wisdom of God," he does so in the course of a larger argument that serves as an essential preface to the study of wisdom. He explains in 1 Corinthians 2 that although he imparts wisdom to the mature, it is not the "wisdom of this age" (v. 6), but rather the "secret and hidden wisdom of God, which God decreed before the ages for our glory" (v. 7). Paul also talks (1:20) about God using what men perceive as foolishness to confound those esteemed as wise: "Has not God made foolish the wisdom of the world?"

As a result of these passages, we often draw a stark contrast between the wisdom of God and the wisdom of man. Some people argue that the two are polar opposites. "What seems like wisdom to men," they say, "is actually foolishness, and what seems like foolishness to men is actually wisdom." To pursue wisdom, we must look not to what the world esteems as wise, but to God's wisdom. And what is God's wisdom? It is whatever men think is foolish. As a result of this kind of thinking, many things that might be categorized, in Old Testament terms, as folly, are rechristened spiritual wisdom because the world thinks they are folly, too. Bad stewardship, for example, is excused as a case of trusting God rather than conforming to man's idea of wisdom—in spite of the fact that Scripture clearly enjoins us to be good stewards of what we're given.

To clear the fog, we need to pull our noses out of the subtext and take another look at the text. When Paul speaks of a secret, hidden wisdom from God, is he employing a vague abstraction, or does he have a particular piece of wisdom in mind? If we compare passages where he employs similar language, we find that Paul is not speaking of God's wisdom and man's wisdom in the general, but of a particular mystery God has revealed spiritually, a truth that confounds human expectations. In Ephesians 3, Paul makes the case plainly:

> For this reason I, Paul, a prisoner for Christ Jesus on behalf of you Gentiles—assuming that you have heard of the stewardship of God's grace that was given to me for you, how the mystery was made known to me by revelation, as I have written briefly. When you read this, you can perceive my insight into the mystery of Christ, which was not made known to the sons of men in other generations as it has now been revealed to his holy apostles and prophets by the Spirit. This mystery is that the Gentiles are fellow heirs, members of the same body, and partakers of the promise in Christ Jesus through the gospel. (vv. 1–6)

The gospel itself is the spiritual wisdom that Paul proclaims, and its unexpected twist is that, far from being a racial salvation only for ethnic Jews, Christ's redemption is for Jew and Gentile alike. The death and resurrection of Christ, his divinity and our hope of everlasting life—this is the specific "foolishness" which God has used to confound the wise. Wisdom is not an abstraction at all, but a person, namely Christ.

Why is this important? Because the general condemnation of "man's wisdom" is one of the great barriers to the serious study of the practical insight offered in the Old Testament wisdom literature. It's not that people see the proverbs and precepts as foolish; it's just that there's a certain redundancy to that approach in light of the New Testament's gift of the Holy Spirit. This is, of course, an unspoken bias, showing up not in Christian rhetoric but in Christian practice. We treat the Old Testament wisdom literature as if we no longer have much use for it, and see the pursuit of wisdom through study and experience as something less exalted than spiritual insight, perhaps even a bit suspicious.

Let me illustrate this with a parable. A certain man went to his friend having already decided on a course of action. The friend could see that his mind was made up, but the man presented his choice along with several other options and then attempted to guide the friend into agreement with the course he preferred. But the friend had a problem: of all the options on the table, the one the man leaned toward was clearly not biblical. When the friend said so, the man didn't miss a beat.

"Maybe we should pray about it together," the man suggested.

"We don't need to pray about it," his friend said. "We already know what the Bible says."

"Still, maybe God will give us some insight."

But the friend knew better. Whenever the man looked to God for insight, God always seemed to conveniently endorse his course of action.

"God already gave us insight," the friend replied. "It's the Bible."

Now this parable is based on many encounters I've witnessed and been a part of over the years. The irony is that, afterward, the man looking for approval of his wrong choice goes away feeling peaceful, while the friend is made to feel impious for being unwilling to "pray about it." But there is nothing impious about the conviction that if God has revealed himself in the Bible, it behooves us to study that revelation. Seeking new light where God does not offer it is a fruitless task, but all too often it is the lot of the wise man to see his fellows do precisely this and to find himself all but powerless to prevent them.

The Liberality of God

But what about James? Doesn't that apostle, at the beginning of his epistle, assure us that the path to wisdom is as simple as asking? Let's take a look at the famous passage:

> If any of you lacks wisdom, let him ask God, who gives generously to all without reproach, and it will be given him. But let him ask in faith, with no doubting, for the one who doubts is like a wave of the sea that is driven and tossed by the wind. For that person must not suppose that he will receive anything from the Lord; he is a double-minded man, unstable in all his ways. (1:5–8)

Yes, James tells us that God stands willing to give wisdom to those who ask. He is liberal and indiscriminate in his gifts. But James does not speak to the process by which God gives wisdom. Like sanctification, wisdom is something God accomplishes over time. Asking is not enough; we must ask "in faith, with no doubting," because God cannot be expected to give anything to unstable, double-minded people.

When I discuss this passage with my students at Worldview Academy, I always preface it with a question: "Do we live in an age of wisdom?" Not surprisingly, the students answer in the negative. For all our science and technology, we seem to be just as in thrall, if not more so, to moral immaturity, as any other generation. And yet, if what James says is true, wisdom should be present in abundance. Either James is wrong, or we have not met his criteria. We do not ask in faith. Maybe we do not ask at all.

If we do ask, it's safe to say we don't know what we're asking for. How many people pray to become more Christlike and then protest when adversity is poured on them and they are called upon to make deep, scarring sacrifices? They asked but didn't realize what they were asking for. They did not consider the means by which such a request is granted. The same thing, I believe, applies to wisdom. God is more willing to give than we are to receive.

An Invitation to the Voyage

This isn't an age of wisdom, and looking at the church I think it's safe to say that, by and large, we are not a good example of wisdom, either. There are shining exceptions, for which I am grateful, and my hope is that you and I might follow in their footsteps. If what I have shared in this chapter reveals nothing else, it should at least establish that it is beyond my power to make readers wise. If anything, this section of the book is designed as a blueprint or roadmap, an outline of a journey you should embark on yourself. It won't surprise me if you make it farther than I have thus far—assuming you are not already there.

This journey is not a trek toward greater intelligence, or even knowledge. If anything, it is a movement from knowledge to action. The goal is not to transform yourself into a guru, a font of wisdom for the guidance of others. Think of this as a journey that ends, not with your exaltation, but at the foot of the cross.

6

Not What You Think:
The Reality of Wisdom

*Then I said in my heart, "What happens to the fool will happen to me
also. Why then have I been so very wise?"*
ECCLESIASTES 2:15

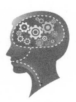

[1]

Suppose you were to find an old bottle washed up on the beach, open
it, and discover a considerate genie inside? What three wishes would you
make?

As unlikely as it is to happen, most of us have given the matter some
thought. I remember one of my school friends explaining that your first
wish, obviously, should be for infinite wishes. (The fact that no one on
television ever thought of this was truly puzzling to us.) He also rec-
ommended that wishes be phrased in great detail, including plenty of
examples of how you do not want the genie to interpret the wish. This is
important because based on what we could tell from TV, genies can be
excessively literal-minded. You don't want to blow your opportunity and
have self-righteous onlookers saying things like: "Be careful what you
wish for—it may come true!"

Isn't it interesting the way we mentally prepare ourselves for events
that will never happen and leave some rather important things to sort
themselves out? You will never get your three wishes, but you are in a
position to ask something from God, who has the power to do more than
we can imagine. What would you say you wanted if it were God who
was asking?

Solomon's Prayer

That opportunity came to Solomon soon after the death of his father, David. He had traveled to Gibeon to make a sacrifice, and that night as he slept, the Lord appeared to him in a dream, saying, in essence, name your request. Ask me for whatever you want, and I will give it to you. Here is Solomon's reply:

> You have shown great and steadfast love to your servant David my father, because he walked before you in faithfulness, in righteousness, and in uprightness of heart toward you. And you have kept for him this great and steadfast love and have given him a son to sit on his throne this day. And now, O LORD my God, you have made your servant king in place of David my father, although I am but a little child. I do not know how to go out or come in. And your servant is in the midst of your people whom you have chosen, a great people, too many to be numbered or counted for multitude. Give your servant therefore an understanding mind to govern your people, that I may discern between good and evil, for who is able to govern this your great people?[1]

This is a humble and devout prayer. It begins by acknowledging the goodness of God to David and then confesses Solomon's fears about the great task before him. He feels unequal to the task of governing well. So instead of the many things he might have asked for, Solomon petitions God for wisdom. He wants "an understanding mind" and the ability to tell right from wrong.

This is the kind of prayer God delights in hearing. In the New Testament, James admonishes believers to pray along similar lines: "If any of you lacks wisdom, let him ask God, who gives generously to all without reproach, and it will be given him."[2] Perhaps he had the example of Solomon in mind.

God's reply to Solomon is as generous as James suggests. He promises Solomon a "wise and discerning mind" and on top of this bestows the riches and honor that Solomon didn't request. Both his wisdom and his wealth will be without precedent. They will be the two things by which Solomon is known to the world and remembered for all time. This promise, of course, is fulfilled; even today, Solomon's reputation on both counts is unmatched.

For the Christian interested in pursuing the path of wisdom, the Bible

---

[1] 1 Kings 3:6–9.
[2] James 1:5.

offers an extensive literature. The books of Job, Proverbs, and Ecclesiastes are packed with both practical and philosophical insight. Together they provide a profoundly stirring picture of the riches (and the limits) of wisdom. The New Testament utterly transforms the topic when Christ is revealed as "the power of God and the wisdom of God," whom God has made the believer's "wisdom . . . righteousness and sanctification and redemption."[3] The person of Christ is the very personification of wisdom. To be like Christ means growing not only in grace but in wisdom.

But what does it mean to be wise?

When I speak on the topic of wisdom, I always invite the audience to put forward some wise role models. Depending on the location, the candidates can be quite interesting. The group usually includes prominent evangelists, leading politicians, and an assortment of characters from literature. Since the release of the *Lord of the Rings* movies, for example, Gandalf has been a popular choice. If we happen to be in the South, Robert E. Lee often makes the list, too. When I ask the audience *why* they have singled these people out as wise, however, they have a hard time answering, particularly if I limit the discussion to real people. The fact is, they have nominated their personal heroes without really considering whether they are paragons of wisdom or not. If I insist on examples of the wisdom of these heroes, the list narrows considerably.

Splitting the Baby

The Bible provides an example of King Solomon's wisdom in the same chapter that includes his famous prayer. It is a curious example, too; one that is worthy of some consideration. Oddly enough, in Solomon's day he was best known for having cleverly threatened to chop a baby in half. Those of us who grew up in Sunday school are so accustomed to the exploit that its fundamental strangeness is lost on us. But it is a very strange incident indeed.

The circumstances are simple enough to relate: two prostitutes who share a room give birth to sons within three days of each other. One of them rolls onto her child while asleep, smothering him, and when she discovers what she has done, she substitutes her dead child for the other woman's living son. The other woman wakes up, and as she readies herself to feed her child, she notices that he is dead—only, when she studies the baby closely in the morning light, she discovers that it is not her son who

---

[3]See 1 Cor. 1:24–30.

is dead, but her companion's. Both women claim the living child as their own, so they are brought before King Solomon to resolve the dispute.

Solomon is both sovereign and judge. He has the power of life and death over the women. After he listens to their arguments, Solomon calls for a sword. He explains with equitable perversity that since each woman claims the remaining child, the boy will be divided in half and distributed between them. It is a cruel pronouncement. The true mother must either renounce her child or see him killed. She breaks down before Solomon. The Bible tells us "her heart yearned for her son." In a moment of grief we can imagine only too well, she relinquishes her claim to the living child.

"Oh, my lord," she pleads, "give her the living child, and by no means put him to death."

"He shall be neither mine nor yours," the other prostitute says. Apparently something in the royal verdict appeals to her warped sense of justice. "Divide him."

This, of course, is what Solomon has been waiting for. By their reactions, it is clear which of the two women is the child's mother. He calls off the mock execution and restores the boy to his mother.

The Bible does not tell us of the false mother's fate. Perhaps she was punished for her crime; perhaps it was excused as the fruit of madness sparked by grief. The story concludes with a note about Solomon's reputation once word of this episode spread through the land: "And all Israel heard of the judgment that the king had rendered, and they stood in awe of the king, because they perceived that the wisdom of God was in him to do justice."[4]

Solomon's Big Risk

Solomon's ploy was not a logical problem with only one solution. Once he had imposed his dilemma on the two women, things might have developed in any number of ways. For the stratagem to succeed, several contingencies had to fall into place. First, the mother of the living child had to be willing to sacrifice her own interests for the sake of the boy, even if it meant enduring injustice. Second, the other woman had to be simpleminded enough (or, at least, sufficiently distraught) to reveal through her callous indifference that the child was not hers. If she had been more cunning, she might have echoed the true mother's plea of renunciation. What

---

[4]1 Kings 3:28.

would Solomon have done if *both* women had surrendered their stake in the child? Even worse, suppose the false mother had been clever enough to give up the child first? Considered in the abstract, the plan was far from foolproof; in fact, it seems downright reckless.

Except for one thing: Solomon had taken the measure of these women.

As they spoke, he appraised their words and weighed each gesture and expression. His experience of life and his God-given wisdom combined to shape an intuition. Before he called for the sword, Solomon had made up his mind which woman was the child's mother. The threat to divide the boy in half was not a trick to determine the truth; it was an experiment to validate what Solomon must have already divined, and to demonstrate it to the witnesses around him. This is speculation, of course; the Bible does not say so much. But when you turn the story over in your mind, it seems like an inevitable conclusion. Why was Solomon prepared to risk a child's life, or at the very least his future, on the reaction of two distressed and traumatized women? He was prepared because he had already discerned the truth of the matter.

Like many biblical narratives, the account in 1 Kings 3 is economical. A few bits of dialogue are preserved, but we are left to imagine most of the scene for ourselves. Our sympathies are with the mother. In spite of her profession, we can identify with the maternal impulse that prompts her to give up her son to save his life. It is hard not to think of the other woman as a treacherous villain. And yet, if she had really been as sly and deceitful as all that, she wouldn't have fallen so easily into Solomon's trap. Consider the circumstances of her life, and the words she speaks before the king, and a different possibility emerges.

She was a mother, too. Her negligence results in the death of her own child. Imagine it: she wakes at midnight to discover that she has killed her own son. It is an abominable, an unthinkable crime. In the darkness, she must ask herself over and over, "Why me?" If only she had not been so exhausted, if only she had not slept through her child's muffled cry, if only it had been her friend's child who died and not her own. The possibility forms in her mind: exchange the babies. It is so simple, the work of just a moment or two. When the sun rises, her friend will mourn her own child's death, and the woman will raise the living son as her own. No one will ever know. These are the actions of a disturbed mind.

Like most midnight plans, this one doesn't work. But once her trick is discovered in the morning, she clings to the stolen child and refuses to acknowledge the truth. This is denial, sheer make-believe. She is pretending that her own child is still alive. Only when Solomon announces his intention to cut the baby in half does she betray the truth.

Why does she go along with the verdict? Perhaps because she knows that it is just that she should not keep the substitute child. Perhaps because she does not want to be alone in her grief. She says to the mother, "He shall be neither mine nor yours," and the words are those of a fatalist, a person hardened to misfortune so long as it befalls everyone alike. To understand her actions, we must construct a complex psychology. We must piece together through inference what wise Solomon saw right away.

The remarkable thing about this story is that Solomon, born into a royal family and raised as a favorite, far removed from the sordid lives of the lowest orders, can see into the hearts of two prostitutes and devise a way to demonstrate which one is the liar and which one tells the truth. The type of wisdom on display here is quite different from the sort of mystical knowledge that is often implied by the term. Remember the words of Solomon's prayer for wisdom: "That I may discern between good and evil." This is the kind of wisdom Solomon is demonstrating. It is practical discernment, the ability to judge, the faculty for distinguishing the truth from lies.

Wisdom Is Not What You Think

There are three lessons embedded in this story. I believe that they are essential to a proper Christian understanding of what wisdom really is.

The First Lesson: WISDOM Is Not What You Think.

Our modern assumptions about wisdom are wrong. We assume that we know what wisdom is, but we don't. We can't even talk about it with a straight face. If you don't believe me, give it a try. Arrange to meet a friend for coffee and find a natural moment in the conversation to insert the topic of wisdom. (That alone will prove difficult.) Your chat might go something like this:

"Who would you say is the wisest person you know?"

"Uh, the wisest?" your friend asks with a puzzled look on her face. "Um, I don't know."

"Come on, who would you say?"

She shrugs. "I guess my pastor."

You'll be thrilled at this, because it will seem to invalidate what I just said. *What do you mean we can't talk meaningfully about wisdom? What do you call this?*

"So tell me, why do you think your pastor is the wisest?"

"Is this a trick question?"

"No."

Your friend blinks. She thinks she is on to your angle. "Am I supposed to say it's you—that you're the wisest?"

"It's not a trick," you protest. "I know, why don't you tell me what wisdom means to you. Go ahead."

Her eyes roll. "This is stupid. Why are we talking about this?"

And your friend is right. It is stupid. It is hard to imagine anything more forced and inauthentic than two twenty-first-century people talking about the nature of wisdom at a coffee shop. It doesn't fit. This is Starbucks, not the Shaolin Temple.

The reason we have a hard time talking about wisdom is that we have a very misguided notion of what it is. For modern people the pursuit of wisdom sounds like something you'd have to travel to Tibet for. To us, wisdom is mystical and esoteric. It conjures up images of cave-dwelling hermits, saffron-robed monks, and, well, Yoda.

Yoda is the tiny green Jedi master from the *Star Wars* movies. He never makes it into the first wave of recommendations because people are too embarrassed to mention him, but once the name is out there, everyone agrees that it fits. Yoda, with his withered body, his sprigs of white ear hair, and his shaky grasp of diction, is the perfect embodiment of our many twisted notions about wisdom. Consider the virtues of Yoda:

1) *He is small and puny.* Yoda's desiccated form is just what you'd expect from a being whose primary strengths are mental. It is almost as if he compensates for physical weakness with psychic power, the way a blind man might develop sensitive hearing. The ultimate expression of wisdom would be a disembodied brain, and Yoda comes pretty close.

2) *He is difficult to understand.* The fact is, most of the time we just have to assume that what Yoda says is wise, because nobody can follow it. When he isn't speaking in riddles, he is swapping his nouns and verbs around like a bad Victorian poet. Wise must he be, for understand him I cannot.

3) *He lives in an out-of-the-way place.* To find Yoda, Luke Skywalker has to travel to a remote and swampy planet. The esoterically wise do

not live with the rest of us. You must undertake an arduous quest for the privilege of sitting at their feet.

4) *He has magic, almost supernatural mental powers.* Yoda can move things with his mind, read thoughts, and scrupulously avoid proper syntax all at the same time. He has reached the plateau of spiritual enlightenment and is no longer bound by the laws of physics and grammar.

All right, so this is clearly an exaggeration. But it is an exaggeration of assumptions we really do have. By and large, we have adopted an Eastern concept of wisdom as enlightenment (which is not without its Western parallels), and as a result wisdom talk seems to belong more to the realm of fantasy than fact. If wisdom requires the life of a hermit, is it any wonder that so few people want anything to do with it?

Biblical wisdom, of course, is nothing like this. It is not reserved for a tiny elite and does not require an austere life of self-mortification. If the example of Solomon shows anything, it is that wisdom is meant to be used in the world. Properly understood, it is very much a part of everyday life. But before we talk about what wisdom is, let's consider another thing that it is not.

The Second Lesson: Wisdom Is Not What YOU Think.

When Solomon asked God for wisdom, he conceded a point that we are often reluctant to admit ourselves: the source of wisdom was outside himself. That may seem painfully obvious, but carried to its logical conclusion, it reveals something modern man would just as soon ignore. Wisdom is about judging between right and wrong, and if it comes from outside of us, then right and wrong find their source outside of us, too. In other words, the biblical conception of wisdom assumes the transcendent origin of morality.

Wisdom is not what *you* think. It's what God thinks.

Even Christians, who are bound to uphold this conclusion in theory, have a hard time with it in practice. The idea that our actions are governed by a set of immutable moral standards is a little frightening. To people who treasure their freedom, it is quite an intrusion. After all, there are some areas of life we would prefer to consider gray.

The situation is even worse outside the community of faith, where there is a wholesale rejection of transcendent morality. When "truth" can only be written in quotation marks to denote irony, the concepts of right and wrong, good and evil, carry very little weight. If terrorist acts, which were once denounced in the strongest terms, are today branded evil, the use of that morally biased term draws down more criticism, it seems, than the crimes themselves. Surely this is not because people approve of terror; rather, it is the confusion that results from feeling moral urges but denying ourselves the language with which to describe them. If we call something "evil," then that implies the existence of good and evil, and it suggests further that these concepts stand above societies and apply to different cultures equally. International law is one thing—it is clearly a construct—but international morality is something else entirely.

In this context, wisdom is distorted. It is no longer seen as the faculty of discerning right and wrong. Instead, wisdom is transformed into pragmatism and we judge a man wise not because he can tell the difference between good and evil but because he can distinguish between what works and what doesn't. Wisdom is not a moral sense; it is a form of cunning.

Sometimes this cunning is couched in moralistic language. For example, the guiding principle of "situation ethics" is that no abstract ethical code applies across the board. Instead, the right choice changes with the circumstances. There is a sense in which this is true. If I invite a man into my house and then blast him with a shotgun, I am a murderer. If he breaks into my house and attempts to kill me, then it is self-defense. The ethical course does depend on the situation. But this is not what situation ethics is about. Instead, the point is to realize that, outside of the situation, there are no right and wrong answers. The situation constructs right and wrong, and then we, interpreting the circumstances, make the appropriate choice. Critics of situation ethics often act as if it is an attempt to evade morality, but it appears instead to be an effort to reinsert provisional ethics once transcendent morality has been done away with. After abolishing God's moral code, we find that there remains a need for ethical guidance.

Biblical wisdom stands in opposition to these subtleties. The wise man discerns what is right and wrong; he does not invent it. We turn to God for wisdom because we recognize that, to be wise, a man's judgments must correspond to the Creator's. If God is the source of reality, then he (and only he) can supply the means by which reality is interpreted.

But wisdom is more than interpreting reality. It involves making decisions and carrying them out. Solomon's wisdom was not demonstrated in contemplation; it manifested itself in action. That leads to a third qualification about what wisdom is not.

The Third Lesson: Wisdom Is Not What You THINK.

Cerebral gymnastics are all good and well, but wisdom is not about brainpower. Sometimes the Bible uses the words *wisdom, knowledge,* and *understanding* interchangeably, and there is certainly a good deal of overlap between the concepts. Discerning people are often quite knowledgeable; knowledgeable people often display a profound understanding of the world. But the difference between a wise man and a fool does not ultimately come down to his brain activity. Action and, at times, restraint separate the two. Wisdom stems not from the intellect, but from the will. It is mental and physical obedience to God.

That means wisdom can be seen. You can observe a person's actions and discover if he is a wise man or a fool. If it were only a matter of the mind, this would not be so. For all you know, the cranky old man who mumbles under his breath and scowls as you pass him on the street could be a rocket scientist. You cannot peer into his inner thoughts and find out whether or not he is a genius. But if you can spend a little time with him and see him in action, you will know very soon whether or not he is wise. Does he discern between right and wrong and then act on his judgment? Then he is wise. Is he indifferent to good and evil and withdrawn from the world of deeds? Then he is not. We are called not only to think the right thing but to do it.

Good intentions are not enough. Sentiment is not enough. It is not heroic to see someone in danger, to have the power to save him, to earnestly hope that he will be saved, but to do nothing. Heroism is measured in action. And so is wisdom.

[II]

The fear of the Lord is the beginning of wisdom.[5] In chapter 2, we saw that fear is one of the four assumptions that underlie the Christian worldview. The fear of the Lord is not, however, a principle; it is an action. It is not something we merely think but something we do. To fear the Lord is to appreciate his power as creator and sovereign, to respond with a heart inclined to worship and service. But in what sense is this the beginning of wisdom?

If you want to see the world for what it truly is, then you must reverence its Creator. Certainly an unbeliever is capable of discerning truth, but as long as he denies the source of truth there is something lacking in

[5]See Ps. 111:10; Prov. 1:7; 9:10.

all his knowledge. If the fear of the Lord is the beginning of wisdom, then the proper starting point for our investigation of reality is our relationship with its Author. If we see, it is by his light.

Also, as we have already noted, the New Testament reveals Christ not only as the promised Messiah but also as the wisdom of God. To fear the Lord is to enter into a right relationship with him, and that relationship is the start of a life that imitates Christ. Fearing God is the beginning of wisdom in the sense that it is the way we come to first enjoy knowledge of Christ. To grow in Christ is to grow in wisdom.

If fearing God means entering into a right relationship with him and seeing the world as he sees it, then it is fair to say that wisdom starts with worldview.

Wisdom Starts with Worldview

Although his thoughts alone do not make a man wise, they are the wellspring of his actions. The things we do flow from what we believe. Human behavior is not random. We act according to patterns, expectations, assumptions, and beliefs; we act in accord with our worldviews. Worldviews shape actions and are in turn shaped by them. That is why I insist that biblical wisdom starts with a biblical worldview.

Think of wisdom as a mighty wall, a fortification bristling with strength. Worldview is the foundation upon which that wall is built. A worldview, as we have already observed, is a load-bearing structure. It is meant to hold things up, to carry weight. But what is the weight it must carry? The weight is a life of discernment, of judgments, and actions that flow from and in turn help to shape worldview. The relationship between wisdom and worldview is organic. Each requires the other.

The book of Proverbs opens with an arresting image: wisdom personified as a woman calling in the streets. There is nothing subtle about her words. Wisdom gets in people's faces and challenges them in decidedly aggressive tones: "How long, O simple ones, will you love being simple? How long will scoffers delight in their scoffing and fools hate knowledge?"[6] This is a rough wooing, entirely lacking in the suggestive flattery that Folly will use to entice her prey in later chapters. The call of Wisdom is laced with contempt for those who scorn her inestimable treasures. Because fools refuse to listen, wisdom will laugh when trouble inevitably finds them. "Then they will call upon me," Wisdom says, "but I will not answer":

---

[6]Prov. 1:22.

> They will seek me diligently but will not find me. Because they hated knowledge and did not choose the fear of the LORD, would have none of my counsel and despised all my reproof.[7]

It is hard to imagine more chilling words than these: *they will seek me diligently but will not find me.* The prophet Hosea prophesied the coming punishment of an unfaithful Israel in similar terms: "With their flocks and herds they shall go to seek the LORD, but they will not find him; he has withdrawn from them."[8] Likewise, the prophet Amos says of Israel: "They shall wander from sea to sea, and from north to east; they shall run to and fro, to seek the word of the LORD, but they shall not find it."[9] When the author of Hebrews recounts the tragedy of Esau, who sold his birthright for a bowl of food, he says, "When [Esau] desired to inherit the blessing, he was rejected, for he found no chance to repent, though he sought it with tears."[10] All of these passages speak in some sense to the rejection of the wisdom of God. The consequence of confirmed folly is ultimately regret, but a regret that perhaps comes too late.

What Wisdom offers, she offers to those who choose the fear of the Lord. This fear is itself a shift in worldview—from rebellion against the Creator to submission—and it is the beginning of a greater shift, as the believer grows in the kind of knowledge that fools hate. If we hope to be wise, we must submit to the Lord of wisdom. We must struggle to see ourselves and our lives through his eyes.

Where Is Wisdom?

To find what is most valuable, it is often necessary to dig beneath the surface. Where do gold and silver come from? What about more practical metals like iron and copper? They are mined from the earth through human ingenuity. The twenty-eighth chapter of Job begins as a paean to this audacious search for treasure:

> Man puts an end to darkness
>   and searches out to the farthest limit
>   the ore in gloom and deep darkness. . . .
>
> Man puts his hand to the flinty rock
>   and overturns mountains by the roots.

---

[7]Prov. 1:28–30.
[8]Hos. 5:6.
[9]Amos 8:12.
[10]Heb. 12:17.

> He cuts out channels in the rocks,
>> and his eye sees every precious thing.[11]

In all his remarkable tunneling, though, there is one thing man cannot find: wisdom. This is an echo of the age-old reminder that, for all our science, there are limits beyond which we cannot probe. Man knows the value of gold, but he does not know the value of wisdom.

Where, Job asks, is wisdom to be found? It cannot be found in the depths of the earth or the sea. It cannot be purchased; no treasure can be traded for such a prize. Even death and the grave do not possess it. Job concludes:

> God understands the way to it,
>> and he knows its place.
> For he looks to the ends of the earth
>> and sees everything under the heavens.
> When he gave to the wind its weight
>> and apportioned the waters by measure,
> when he made a decree for the rain
>> and a way for the lightning of the thunder,
> then he saw it and declared it;
>> he established it, and searched it out.
> And he said to man,
> "Behold, the fear of the Lord, that is wisdom,
>> and to turn away from evil is understanding."[12]

Man may be the steward of creation, but God is its master. God established wisdom as he established the earth's foundation. It is inseparably linked to man's moral condition. Wisdom consists in fearing God and turning away from evil. This is the Christian message: repent and believe. We cannot do justice to the concept of wisdom without remembering that insistent cry in the streets. If you want to be wise, be reconciled to your Maker and turn away from evil.

What Is Wisdom?

Wisdom, then, is the consistent outworking of belief, action, and discernment from worldview. It is the process of sanctification. If we were perfectly wise, we would believe the right things, do the right things, and possess the faculty for discerning what is right. *Orthodoxy* means literally

---

[11]Job 28:3, 9–10.
[12]Job 28:23–28.

"right belief," and *orthopraxy* means "right action." So wisdom consists in discerning orthodoxy and orthopraxy, what we should believe and what we should do.

One of my professors in college had a knack for frustrating her students. She taught a seminar right after lunch, when everyone was a little sleepy, and she spoke in a slow, measured, melodic tone that lulled some of us into a state of mental unguardedness. Then she would launch into profound discussions of very difficult readings, inviting those of us who dared to venture opinions on the subject. After a student spoke, the professor would sum up the comment. Invariably the summation would go much farther than the original comment.

"That's not what I said," the student would protest.

"I'm just taking your point to its logical conclusion," the professor explained.

Round and round the conversation would turn, and each time one of us made a contribution, the professor would gently reduce it to absurdity in her summations. Afterwards, we would complain that she was putting words into our mouths. Once our ideas had been taken to their "logical conclusion," we disowned them. The result was that, by the end of the semester, no one could really be sure what they believed. And those of us who were sure were not about to say anything out loud!

The point of those somnolent seminars, as I later discovered, was to shake our confidence in the casual assumptions we had brought to the classroom. We were eighteen-year-olds who imagined we knew just about everything. We were convinced that every opinion we held was the absolute truth. Because we had never been challenged to think for ourselves, we mistook our default assumptions for earned beliefs. The professor knew that the reactions we gave her came not from our own thought life but from our unexamined assumptions. She never told us what to believe and what to deny; she only forced us to articulate and defend our claims—and when we had to do that, we found that there were fewer certainties in our head than we had imagined. In other words, we discovered our need for education.

Wisdom is sweet, but first we must develop a taste for it. In the book of Proverbs, it is compared to the honeycomb:

> My son, eat honey, for it is good,
> and the drippings of the honeycomb are sweet to your taste.
> Know that wisdom is such to your soul;

> if you find it, there will be a future,
> and your hope will not be cut off.[13]

For all that wisdom promises, we are not naturally inclined to it. We would rather eat junk food. It is hard work to examine your assumptions, to test whether your view of the world corresponds to the mind of Christ. Even harder is to live consistently with your beliefs, to act out your faith in the world around you. But the consistent outworking of those beliefs and actions is what wisdom is all about. It is not a single insight. It is not a bit of knowledge. It is a way of living, a lifestyle of daily obedience.

Minimize Suffering, Maximize Pleasure

The twin principles that tend to govern our daily existence are: *minimize suffering, maximize pleasure*. If you could study an inventory of your behavior over the past week, a log of decisions and actions, you would find that the motivation for most of the things you do is either to avoid pain, discomfort, and awkwardness or to achieve happiness, excitement, or pleasure. These impulses do not require a great deal of introspection. People who lead the "unexamined life" that Socrates thought was not worth living find no difficulty in ordering their lives consistently according to these maxims. They come naturally.

Because of our doctrine of sin, Christians are skeptical about anything that comes naturally. We know that some things are natural to us because we are made in God's image, but everything about us is tainted by the fall. If it comes naturally, we reason, it is probably sinful.

But is there anything sinful about avoiding pain? I don't put my hand in open flames. The only reason I don't is that in my experience of fire it is painful to do so. When I was a boy, my Christian mother observed this tendency of mine to avoid pain, and she seemed to applaud it. So far as I know, she never worried whether my natural inclination to avoid pain might be a sinful impulse. As far as she was concerned it was a relief, especially since my younger brother appeared to have been born without the fear gene and was always happy to expose himself to danger (and still is today).

If it is sensible to avoid being burned, isn't it also sensible to avoid being emotionally traumatized, taken advantage of, or ridiculed?

And what about pleasure? The word *pleasure* invokes, in theological talk, all sorts of sordid associations, but there are surely innocent plea-

---
[13]Prov. 24:13–14.

sures. In fact, if God made us to delight in him and in his creation, then it stands to reason that sinful pleasures are in the minority, an aberration. Take for example the pleasures of smell. I have been known to come indoors after working outside clouded in a miasma of disagreeable scents. At times like this, my wife shows a marked reluctance to be near me. Sometimes she insists that I shower immediately, as if my labors and the accompanying perspiration have made me unfit for civilized company. Does the fact that she would prefer me to smell nice (or, at least, not to smell) point to some fault in her character? I hope not, since I have similar expectations myself.

There is no guilt in the pleasure we take from smelling a rose, is there? If I am forced to choose between roses and burning rubber, is it a sin to choose what will bring me most joy?

These impulses, when they are confined to the subcognitive level, seem innocent enough. But suppose I become conscious of these desires in myself and structure my life in such a way as to avoid whatever is unpleasant and pursue pleasure as an end in itself? While the act of avoiding pain or seeking pleasure may be faultless, the philosophy of seeking pleasure and avoiding pain is not. As a belief system—and I would argue that it is, by and large, *the* belief system of most people, whatever philosophical professions they make—it elevates as ends two experiences we are intended to absorb in passing.

There are times when virtue demands that we experience pain. There are times when doing right means forgoing pleasure. Christian wisdom differs from that of the world in that it treats as means what others seek as ends. The end, for a Christian, is neither pain nor pleasure, but Christ. If to serve him we must suffer, it is good. If in serving him we find pleasure, it is good. But pain or pleasure aside, our lives are dedicated to service.

Suffer for Good

The apostle Peter assures Christians that "it is better to suffer for doing good, if that should be God's will, than for doing evil."[14] This is a remarkably disheartening statement for the pleasure seeker. Can it ever be God's will that we should suffer? To punish wrongdoing is one thing; and since we do not think of ourselves as guilty, we are willing to concede that those who do evil should suffer. But that those who do good should suffer, and that it should be the will of God that they do, is inconceivable. What kind

---

[14]1 Pet. 3:17.

of God, having the power to do all things, would will that the innocent suffer? The apostle's reasoning calls into question the pleasure seeker's own understanding of the loving God.

One evening a group of friends gathered at my house to discuss a short story by Tolstoy. In the tale, a peddler is wrongfully convicted of a crime and sent to prison in Siberia. At each stage of his suffering, the reader sees a new spiritual depth revealed. An expectation builds in our hearts that the innocent man will be set free. But at the end of the story he dies in prison. I found this fascinating, because it seemed that Tolstoy was making a profound point about suffering and justice in this lifetime. The conventions of drama demand that the innocent be set free and that this freedom is the only adequate resolution of the story. But life does not work this way, Tolstoy tells us. The innocent are punished and they are not exonerated. They die in captivity with the guilty. The biblical truth of this resonated in my mind: it was as if Tolstoy had written with the pen of the preacher in the book of Ecclesiastes.

But one of my friends thought the ending ruined the story and I was amazed to discover why. He said that life does *not* work like this.

"Yes," he admitted, "the innocent sometimes suffer, but in the end God always gives them justice."

"In this lifetime?" I asked.

"In this lifetime," he insisted.

I was stunned. Here was an intelligent believer, comparatively well read and no stranger to experience. This was not a naïve pronouncement. And yet, he was completely wrong. I am not the sort of person who can let these things slide (I believe "gracious" is the word for them), so I had to make a point of this.

"There are innocent people," I said, "who suffer and do not get justice in this life. Yes, they get justice ultimately, but not always before they die."

My friend shook his head vigorously. "I disagree," he said. "Look at Job!"

"Job?" I said. Now I was a little angry. Like many people who have been astounded by that book, I take a proprietary interest in it and don't like to see it used against me.

"Job suffered, but when he passed the test, God gave him back everything he lost and then some. I believe that is the way God works."

We had to agree to disagree. Sometimes God does restore to the innocent what is lost through injustice, but the force of Peter's words is inescapable. He was speaking, after all, to early Christians in the midst of terrible persecution. The suffering they faced was not the threat of lifelong imprisonment but humiliating execution. It is to these people that Peter says, "Let those who suffer according to God's will entrust their souls to a faithful Creator while doing good."[15] He promises God's blessing on those who suffer for the sake of righteousness, but he does not promise justice in this life.

Clearly, Peter envisions an obedience that, far from removing the believer from suffering, may very well bring suffering to the believer. The path of wisdom does not lie in minimizing suffering and seeking pleasure. It lies in enduring (and enjoying) whatever God wills, with a spirit of acceptance and obedience. More than that, wisdom demands that we glorify God even in our suffering.

> Whoever desires to love life
>   and see good days,
> let him keep his tongue from evil
>   and his lips from speaking deceit;
> let him turn away from evil and do good;
>   let him seek peace and pursue it.
> For the eyes of the Lord are on the righteous,
>   and his ears are open to their prayer.
> But the face of the Lord is against those who do evil.[16]

Why Is Wisdom a Woman?

A final question merits our investigation: why does the Bible personify wisdom as a woman?[17] To women reading this book the answer may seem obvious: women are prudent and longsuffering, they endure the boyish whims of men and subtly direct our courses, all the while leaving us with the assurance that we are masters of our fate. I don't dare argue with those points.

But it is interesting that in the book of Proverbs, both wisdom and folly are characterized in the feminine, while instruction is addressed to a young man. Is there something about the relationship between young men and women that might help us understand our own relationship to wisdom?

When I ask these questions of an audience, a battle of the sexes

---

[15]1 Pet. 4:19.
[16]1 Pet. 3:10–12.
[17]Like the earlier discussion of the "four pillars," this section on wisdom's personification as a woman owes a debt to Estes's *Hear My Son*.

ensues (and I do my best to fuel the flames while appearing to be a neutral observer). Men who take little interest in abstractions about belief and action suddenly move to the edge of their seats. In a younger group, they sense an opportunity to impress the fairer sex, while older men (and certain despairing youngsters) are inclined to vent their spleen. The ones who want to ingratiate themselves say wisdom is like a woman in the sense that it is more beautiful and valuable than jewels; it helps man to do what is right, and so on. The general idea is that women are smarter than men, so they were the natural comparison for wisdom.

The naysayers, of course, see things differently. Perhaps wisdom is like a woman in that it is always telling men what to do; it is loud and bossy and so on. The more time I give them to speculate, the deeper a hole they dig. The classic, unforgettable moment was the time I asked a group of high school students the question, and a skinny young man in glasses who was flanked by other boys on either side raised his hand.

"Wisdom is like a woman because you want to chase it."

The young men exploded in laughter while the ladies rolled their eyes. The imp of mischief within me could not let this answer go uncommented upon.

"Hmm," I said, stroking my chin in mock contemplation, "so what you're really saying is, you want to chase these girls."

Now the ladies were squealing with displeasure while the men reveled in the humiliation of their comrade. But the boy who had made the suggestion about pursuit sat with a wide grin on his face. He must have been fourteen and I could see at that moment that my humorous summation had been right on the mark. Oh dear!

And yet, how illuminating. It is precisely to these young men who are sorting out their feelings about women at the same time they are trying to take the measure of life that the book of Proverbs is ostensibly addressed. This notion of pursuit was promising. When you are young, temptations are as fresh and appealing as they will ever be, and the notion of risk seems small indeed. The seductive appeals of folly are real, and like the loose woman Proverbs describes in chapter 7, they are undemanding. It is easy to live up to the standard of foolishness.

Wisdom, though, is the woman we must strive to deserve. She will not give herself to us in a moment but must be earned through the course of a life. In a sense, the difference between wisdom and folly is like that between love and lust. The object of lust is a means to an end, but the object of love is an end in itself. We agonize over the question of our worthiness. We long to be more than we are. We aspire to become the man she desires us to be.

So perhaps the young man was right and wisdom is personified as a woman because we must pursue her. We must chase after her as if nothing more valuable can ever be gained and cling to her as we would to a cherished bride. The call of wisdom is a call to commitment and to faithfulness. It is a call that we neglect at our peril.

> Let your heart hold fast my words;
>   keep my commandments, and live.
> Get wisdom; get insight;
>   do not forget, and do not turn away from the words of my mouth.
> Do not forsake her, and she will keep you;
>   love her, and she will guard you.[18]

---

[18]Prov. 4:4–6.

7

A City without Walls:
Five Lessons for Siege Warfare

A city defended by walls has a choice of alternatives: to treat its city as walled, or to treat it as if it were unwalled. But a people without any walls is a people without any choice.

ARISTOTLE

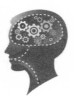

[I]

April 1453. An armada of four ships ends its voyage east with the walls of Constantinople in sight, rising from the sea on the horizon, the battlements dappled with sun. From their place in the rigging, the sailors can see the many palaces and churches crowning the peaks of the city: the outline of the Hippodrome and, magnificent above it all, the dome of St. Sophia, the Church of Holy Wisdom, built a millennium before by the Emperor Justinian. It is a glorious sight!

But there is more. Encamped around the walls is a Turkish army, its banners waving as far as the eye can see. And now, the throaty rumble of cannon reaches the sailors' ears from across the bay, and if they squint they can see columns of smoke and dust ascending from the land walls near the St. Romanus gate. Constantinople is under siege.

Some of the men aboard the four ships are Greek, and for them, this is a bitter homecoming. They had started west with the hope of bringing back a relief force, but instead they have just a handful of men and only enough grain to feed the city for a week. They had hoped against hope to arrive and find the city miraculously saved. But the Ottoman sultan

Mehmet II remains outside, his guns baying like hunting dogs that have caught the scent of blood.

Now the sailors notice what was invisible before: a wave of hundreds of war galleys heading across the waves to intercept them. The city has a naturally defensible harbor, the Golden Horn, and this is defended by a boom that stretches across the inlet to the Genoese colony of Galata on the other side, denying access to all but friendly vessels. Seeing the arrival of the four ships, the entire Turkish naval fleet has come out to meet them. No hope now that the city will be saved; no hope even that the tiny fleet will make it safely into the Golden Horn.

But the wind is with them and the sailors are determined not to give their lives up without a fight. They clear the decks and lash their four ships together to fight as a single floating castle. Because they are sailing ships, they are taller than the Turkish galleys. Men stand ready to receive the Turkish attack, spears and crossbows at the ready. Tubs of burning pitch and the mysterious Greek fire are prepared. A hundred galleys converge at once on the Christian flotilla, and in the unnatural silence before the impact, the sailors notice with despair that the wind that has driven them this far has suddenly abated.

Inside the city, men and women leave what they were doing and stream to the walls by the thousands. The sea battle is too far away for them to help but close enough so they can hear the sound of fighting, the screams of men, and the roar of flames. The entire siege stops for an hour to observe the battle. Then two hours pass and the siege remains still. The odds are so overwhelming that it seems the fight could not last so long—but it has. Galley after galley sheers away in flames, wounded and dead men falling over the sides, while the high-beamed Christian ships remain proudly defiant.

The moment is so dramatic that the young sultan Mehmet, carried away with the action and seething with frustration at seeing his entire navy held at bay by four ships, spurs his horse into the sea and begins to shout orders to his admiral. This spectacle of impotence gives heart to the whole city. What seemed impossible a moment before seems almost in reach. If there were a miracle, the people tell themselves—a miracle could save the men.

In the thick of battle the sailors themselves give no thought to deliverance. They fight with the steady thoughtlessness of machines, only realizing in the lulls, which allow one shredded wave of Turks to retreat while a fresh one replaces it, that something remarkable is taking place. The sea is littered with Turkish dead. The headlong rush to meet the Christian ships has proved a disaster, but in his panic the admiral cannot think to alter his plan. And why should he have to? The math is on his side. The men in the four ships must be overwhelmed. In the closeness of the fight their oars are useless, and their sails hang despondent from their masts. As long as the ships do not move, they will be defeated in time.

The whole city is holding its breath. The whole battle is in the balance. And then, on a thousand upturned faces, they feel it: the wind, the miraculous wind! Sails fill and the four tight-lashed galleons creak forward, their sharp bows shifting the Turkish vessels left and right or crushing them entirely under the weight. Mehmet's saber flashes impotently on the coastline but the ships are free. It is a bloody, hard-fought progress, but every Turkish heart sinks at the realization that the battle is decided. The four ships bully their way through the giant boom that guards the Golden Horn, and the Turks fall back, unwilling to tangle with the line of Venetian galleys that stand behind it.

Night falls and the boom is opened to let the four ragged victors into the city. The celebration that kindled inside the walls when the victory was first realized now reaches a crescendo. The people of Constantinople flock to the shipyards to welcome the sailors home.

Foregone Conclusions

Looking back over the space of more than five hundred years, historians take the fall of Constantinople in May of 1453 as a foregone conclusion. The Turkish army, which included forces from across the Ottoman Empire, including Christian contingents from the occupied Balkan states, numbered between eighty thousand and a hundred thousand. When George Sphrantzes, friend and secretary to the last Byzantine emperor, Constantine XI Palaiologos, conducted a secret census, he found that the defenders inside the wall numbered less than five thousand. The Ottomans were in the ascendance, winners in the cyclical rise and fall of nations, whereas the Byzantines were at the last stage of a disastrous freefall that started at their defeat at Manzikert in 1079 (which would eventually lead to the Crusades), gained momentum after the knights of the Fourth Crusade sacked the city in 1204, and was not about to stop now. All that remained of the once great Eastern Roman Empire was the city of Constantinople and a few tiny principalities in Greece and northern Turkey. Officially, the Greek emperor was a vassal of the sultan and depended on his good will for survival. So it is no surprise that on May 29, 1453, the walls of Constantinople were breached, Constantine XI was killed, and Mehmet entered the city as conqueror and made it the capital of his empire.

The verdict of history is that Constantinople had to fall, but history in this case is wrong. There was nothing inevitable about the city's collapse. Turkish armies had besieged it before, and the ambition of more than one sultan had been crushed against its walls. Even the technological advantage of cannon, an innovation in siege warfare, did not render the fall a foregone conclusion. Every breach the Turkish guns opened during the day was stopped up by the defenders during the night. Even the night of the final battle saw two crushing waves of Turkish soldiers sent packing, and the third assault by the Janissaries nearly teetered, too.

The city withstood the force of Turkish arms for weeks, and there were men in Mehmet's camp who believed he had bitten off more than he could chew. The pressure for the young sultan (who was barely in his twenties) to retire from the field was intense. In fact, the final assault, if it had failed, may have been the last effort before a wholesale retreat. Had the defenders of the city managed to hold on, they might have won the day.

But they didn't, and in their defeat there are lessons for us. Like them, we find ourselves frequently outnumbered and under attack. If we can see where their defense went wrong, it might help to strengthen our own. In this chapter, we're going to make it our business to discover the fate of Constantinople, that once-grand Christian city, the second Rome, which stood as a bulwark against Muslim expansion for eight centuries until it finally succumbed. We will learn from their mistakes in the hope that we will not repeat them.

[II]

In the *Politics*, Aristotle observes that, "a city defended by walls has a choice of alternatives: to treat its city as walled, or to treat it as if it were unwalled. But a people without any walls is a people without any choice."[1] In the immediate context, the walls Aristotle has in mind are literal stone and mortar affairs, the sort that define the boundaries of your city and keep your enemies at bay. But this is the kind of statement that lends itself to metaphor. A people without walls is a people without

---

[1] Aristotle, *Politics*, book 7, chap. 11.

choice. Without barriers and people to defend them, our power to make our own decisions is lost. Without walls, we surrender to the will of the world around us.

The helplessness of a city without walls is a powerful image. In the Bible, it is a picture of the undisciplined life. The book of Proverbs says, "A man without self-control is like a city broken into and left without walls."[2] This image helps us make the leap from a struggling city to a struggling man. The battle for self-control, the battle to think and act in accordance with your faith, is a kind of personal siege in which the forces and pressures of the world blast the barriers that surround your mind. You can respond by building walls and defending them, or you can acquiesce. With walls of discernment, you can judge which influences you will allow in your life. Without them, you are a person without a choice.

We have already seen that your worldview serves as a foundation, and the thoughts and deeds of wisdom are a fortification erected on top of it. This is the wall that needs defending; this is the warfare you must wage. It is not, as the apostle Paul reminds us, a physical fight but a spiritual one. That means the stakes are higher and the enemy more cunning. It means we should take the battle seriously.

Siege Mentality

Strange things happen when you're under siege. Your perception of reality is turned upside down. Whatever was important to you, whatever you cherished before the siege, now seems far off and insignificant. The battle is everything. It is all consuming. Whatever your thoughts were on before, your mind is focused now. Only one thing matters and in the prism of conflict, values and principles are distorted and misshaped.

You are in the grip of siege mentality.

The Bible records a startling example of this affliction in 2 Kings, chapter 6, during the siege of Samaria by Ben-hadad, king of Syria. As a result of the siege, the land was plunged into famine. The situation was so desperate that mules' heads and quarts of doves' dung became valuable commodities. As the siege went on and hope for deliverance waned, the king of Israel went out to survey the defenses:

> Now as the king of Israel was passing by on the wall, a woman cried out to him, saying, "Help, my lord, O king!" And he said, "If the LORD will not help you, how shall I help you? From the threshing

---

[2]Prov. 25:28.

floor, or from the winepress?" And the king asked her, "What is your trouble?" She answered, "This woman said to me, 'Give your son, that we may eat him today, and we will eat my son tomorrow.' So we boiled my son and ate him. And on the next day I said to her, 'Give your son, that we may eat him.' But she has hidden her son." When the king heard the words of the woman, he tore his clothes—now he was passing by on the wall—and the people looked, and behold, he had sackcloth beneath on his body—and he said, "May God do so to me and more also, if the head of Elisha the son of Shaphat remains on his shoulders today."[3]

This is a picture of a world turned upside down by siege mentality. Nothing is as it should be. Mothers eat their children. Justice is perverted. A king of Israel curses the prophet of Israel appointed by God (who has recently delivered another Syrian force into his hands).

Beneath his clothes, the king wore sackcloth, which suggests that he had gone on his knees to God and begged for deliverance. Sackcloth is a sign of piety, just as surveying the defenses of the city is a sign of conscientiousness. When the king sets out that day he is the epitome of all he should be. But when tested by the crisis, he reacts in a wholly unexpected way, his rage brought on by the catalyst of desperation.

And what a crisis! The case brought before him revolves essentially around a breach of contract. Two women have agreed to eat their own children, but one of them has backed out of the arrangement after dining on the other woman's child. The final words of the accusation—*but she has hidden her son*—suggest what? That the woman expects the king to find the hidden child and deliver him up for consumption? It is a monstrous suggestion and the fact that she has gone to the king seeking "justice" demonstrates just how far gone she is. There is an echo here of the two prostitutes who stood before Solomon to be judged, but this king of Israel possesses none of the wisdom of Solomon.

Faced with this confession of cannibalism, the king rips his clothes in a sign of grief. But his wrath is kindled not against the murdering mother but against the prophet Elisha. He vows to have Elisha beheaded and sends a messenger ahead to Elisha with a threat. The messenger's words express the bitterness of the king's heart: "This trouble is from the LORD! Why should I wait for the LORD any longer?"[4] He had asked for deliverance and instead he got trouble. As we have seen, Peter would have

---

[3]2 Kings 6:26–31.
[4]2 Kings 6:33.

admonished to suffer, if it was God's will, for doing good. But the king of Israel was tired of waiting.

Passing the Test

The fact that we must endure a siege is no excuse for siege mentality. If anything, siege mentality is a sign that we have not endured well. Christians view the whole of life as a kind of test—not a quiz, but a trial or proving. We live in the hope that our actions and reactions will bring honor and glory to Christ. Although we do not relish pain, there is a sense in which we welcome suffering for the opportunity it affords to prove ourselves. This explains why so many believers look back seventeen hundred years after the Christian faith became the official religion of the Roman Empire and wonder if it would not have been better to remain persecuted. This is why, in the affluent and comfortable Western democracies, Christians sometimes envy the chances at persecution and even martyrdom their brothers and sisters in Christ enjoy in less hospitable lands.

Enjoy? Is that the word? It seems wrong, and yet joy is the emotion of those who suffer and prove faithful. That feeling is something like what Robert Louis Stevenson ascribed to Admiral Nelson at the Battle of Copenhagen:

> A shot through the mainmast knocked the splinters about; and he observed to one of his officers with a smile, "It is warm work, and this may be the last to any of us at any moment"; and then, stopping short at the gangway, added, with emotion, *"But, mark you—I would not be elsewhere for thousands."*[5]

This must sum up the sober exhilaration of Polycarp or the joy of Hugh Latimer as the flames lapped at his feet and he called out to Ridley, "Be of good comfort, Mr. Ridley, and play the man! We shall this day light such a candle by God's grace, in England, as I trust never shall be put out."

If only our trials were similarly epic. With no hope of martyrdom we find the stakes too low to engage our interest. To die for Christ is not, perhaps, within the realm of our possibilities, and so we envy those who might experience the exaltation of proving faithful to the end, mistaking the joy for what makes the disciple when in fact it is the perseverance.

The purpose of proving is growth. We suffer and are besieged so that

---

[5]Robert Louis Stevenson, "The English Admirals," in *Virginibus Puerisque* (New York: Scribner's, 1916), 182–83 (emphasis in original).

we can endure and conform more closely to the image of Christ. Our attitude toward the threats around us should be free of siege mentality, understanding as we do that all things, even our sorrows, are under God's control.

[III]

Why did Constantinople get the works? That's nobody's business but the Turks. Or so the song goes. But we are going to make it our business to find out what happened to Constantinople and what we can learn from it.

The last ships fought their way into Constantinople just a month before the city's final collapse. What the sailors found when they disembarked was a city in the grip of siege mentality. The people sifted signs and omens, leaving the work of defense to a handful of the population. There was talk of ominous lights above the dome of St. Sophia; there was trouble among the monks who agitated against Constantine's policy of uniting with the Western church; there was unrest among the nobles. The city's defense was in the hands of Italian mercenaries led by Giovanni Giustiniani Longo, who had arrived with a hearty band of men earlier in the year and had so far conducted a spirited defense against the Turks.

As the siege unfolded, five valuable lessons emerged. In this section we will discover those lessons and find out how they apply to our own struggle to think and act in a way that is consistent with our faith.

Lesson One: Take Responsibility for Your Own Walls

Constantinople was encircled by the strongest, most ancient set of walls ever constructed. The city was founded by Constantine, the same Roman emperor who converted to Christianity and presided over the Council of Nicea in A.D. 325. From the beginning it was conceived as a Christian capital for a Christian empire. The city occupies a triangular promontory that juts into the Sea of Marmara with water on two sides and the massive land walls of Emperor Theodosius on the third. Although the city had been sacked by the Crusaders, they had entered through the vulnerable sea walls after being admitted into the Golden Horn. The land walls faced by Mehmet's army had not been breached in over a millennium. Imagine a structure built during the time of the Vikings being successfully defended up to the twenty-first century, and you have an idea of the strength of these walls.

With their age, though, came the inevitable effects of time. As the city grew, its walls were extended, and the work was not always done on the lavish, three-tiered scale of the original structure. There were weak points along the line, places where tight budgets had prevented renovations. When Constantine XI assumed the throne, he knew that trouble with the Turks was a real possibility. Earlier in his career, he had fortified a wall in Greece called the Hexamilion and campaigned unsuccessfully against the Turkish army there. He understood the value of strong walls.

According to some sources, however, the money that was allocated to repairing the walls was misappropriated by men Constantine enlisted to oversee the work:

> Unfortunately the repairs to the walls had been placed in the hands of two monks skilled in engineering but also, it seems, in peculation, so that the repairs were not well done, and after the city fell, the money entrusted to them for this purpose was found where they had buried it.[6]

After the siege, the Turks dug up seventy thousand gold pieces, the money that was supposed to be used to bring the inner walls of the Theodosian line up to standard. Scholars disagree over the incident, but one lesson is clear: take responsibility for your own walls. That work cannot be put in someone else's hands. In the case of Constantinople, the repairs were handed over to men whose religious credentials should have guaranteed their reliability. Sometimes we make the same mistake that Constantine did. Let's consider a virtue that should emerge from this lesson.

Virtue: Personal Responsibility

If the struggle to form right beliefs and express them through right action is the central focus of the Christian life, then it stands to reason that you must assume personal responsibility for your spiritual development and the practice of godliness. Remember the fundamental relation between God and man: an unmediated fellowship. No one stands between you and Christ. Although there are many people who are willing to help—pastors, teachers, mentors—ultimately the responsibility for your spiritual growth is your own.

Specialization is a fact of life. When a difficult situation emerges, our

---

[6]David Dereksen, *The Crescent and the Cross* (New York: Putnam's, 1964), 192. Steven Runciman calls this episode into question, attributing the story to the unreliable archbishop Leonard.

first instinct is to let the experts handle it. The days of the jack-of-all-trades are fast disappearing. It seems negligent to try to do anything for yourself. You don't fix your own car; you go to a mechanic. You don't draw up the plans for your own house; you go to an architect. You don't diagnose your own illness; you go to a doctor. So it is easy to see why, when faced with spiritual concerns, so many of us turn to a minister. There is nothing wrong with this. Ministers are there to minister! But because you must give account for yourself, you cannot rely unthinkingly on someone else. This is an essential lesson in discernment.

Treat spiritual advice and support as you would a movie review. Draw on the wisdom of others to form your own judgments—but form your own judgments. If you never find yourself questioning what other people are saying, then it might be that you simply aren't thinking. To be a discerning thinker, your mind must be switched on. You must be evaluating ideas, comparing notes, and testing conclusions. Paul praised the Berean church for evaluating the things he taught them in light of Scripture. The Bereans took responsibility for their lives before God. We should do the same.

A Note on Discernment

Discernment is a tricky topic. A lot of people in the evangelical community lament that their fellow believers are not discerning enough, and based on my knowledge of human nature, I am compelled to agree. But what the critics put forward as an answer does not always strike me as a real solution. Instead, it looks like the flipside of the problem. Spend some time studying so-called "discernment ministries"—especially on the blogosphere, where they proliferate—and a certain set of assumptions about discernment emerges. For convenience, let me summarize what seems to be the typical mindset: There are two groups of people and things: the good and the bad. Good is, well, good . . . and bad is off-limits. The art of discernment involves examining them and determining which group to categorize them in. Everyone is called to make these category distinctions, but some of us are also appointed by God to make them for others. Because most people are undiscerning, it falls on the discerning few to lead the way, especially when it comes to exposing bad people and things that are generally held (by the undiscerning masses) to be good—the wolves in sheeps' clothing.

Now, as I have already mentioned, one of the things I teach at

Worldview Academy is wisdom, which involves discernment, and the first disclaimer I have to make to students is that I am unqualified to teach the course. I do not hold myself up as a paragon of wisdom. Fortunately, it is not my intention to *be wise for them*. When we talk about discernment, I always make the point that no one can be discerning on their behalf. It seems to me that the whole "discernment ministry" concept is often founded on the opposite assumption. While they often *tell* readers to be more discerning, they provide the answers upfront so that their audience does not have to discern. They hand out their own conclusions instead of equipping others to find answers for themselves, feeding people for a day instead of teaching them to fish.

But the flaw seems more systemic than personal. I believe these folks are operating in good faith, applying the aforementioned model of discernment because they truly believe that is how discernment works. I can relate, because I grew up in a tradition where that is the prevailing view, and for a long time I applied that model without thinking critically—discerningly—about it.

When I did, though, here's what I figured out. There are not two categories of influence, good and bad, that can be discreetly separated. You cannot draw a line between the Christian and the non-Christian, between the evangelical and the non-evangelical, between us and them, and declare everything on one side safe and everything on the other suspect, and then expect the task of discernment to consist of moving people and things like so many checker pieces to one side or the other of that line. For one thing, every person and thing is tainted by the fall, which means there are no pure influences under the sun. For another, God's grace and truth are active throughout creation, which means that not only do we get lies from truth tellers, but we also get the truth from liars.

To be discerning, you have to be critically engaged with a particular influence, sifting it, taking from it what is profitable. So you cannot be discerning about something and ignorant of it at the same time.

Discernment is not about flipping a yes/no switch or pigeonholing other people. It is about individual judgment based on knowledge—knowledge of self, knowledge of the world, knowledge of God, and knowledge of the thing being judged. Given that, you can see that it is as difficult to be discerning for someone else as it is to *think* for another. First and foremost, attend to the beam in your own eye.

Engagers and Discerners

When I consider the various Christians I know who are actively thinking about the surrounding culture, it is tempting to divide them into two groups—I'll call them the Engagers and the Discerners. The Engagers are all about getting involved with what's going on around us, and they typically look for ways to appreciate and understand the world in Christian terms. The Discerners are all about measuring cultural expressions against Christian norms and are usually searching for ways to screen books and films for objectionable or uplifting content.

I see this distinction clearly when I read Christian movie and book reviews. All the critics are, in some sense, both engaging and discerning, but they tend to gravitate toward one pole or the other. Engagers are trying to introduce you to something good, while Discerners are trying to protect you from something bad. Engagers give a lot more space to fiction, while Discerners are more interested in testing the spirits of nonfiction. Engagers are more comfortable with aesthetic language, while Discerners speak in ethical/moral language.

Of course, both trajectories can carry you into uncertain territory. Engagers can try so hard to find redemptive themes in culture that they end up christening some pretty questionable stuff. Discerners, on the other hand, can flip out over bathwater and forget about the baby, calling things unclean that God would not. Some critics guard against these predilections better than others. I think it is safe to say that each pole sees its opposite in the ascendant. Engagers think discerners are calling the shots in the evangelical world, while discerners see themselves as the lone knee that hasn't bowed to Baal in a subculture full of engagers. (These fears, in part, are what draw thinkers to the fringe of either category.)

We will pick up this idea of engagement in the third section of the book. For now, let's turn again to the story of the siege.

Lesson Two: Constantly Repair Your Walls

The moment the first Turkish bombardment commenced on April 6, 1453, it was too late to think about the condition of the walls. Within a few hours, the people of Constantinople learned what cities throughout Europe would soon discover once cannon became commonplace in the siege arsenal: tall stone walls built in the medieval style do not fare well against a cannonade. The effects of the bombardment were devastating:

The cannon-balls, coming from just across the foss, in a cloud of black smoke and with a deafening roar, broke into a thousand pieces as they hit the walls; and the masonry could not stand up to them. The defenders attempted to lessen their impact by hanging sheets of leather and bales of wool over the walls, but with little effect. Within less than a week the outer wall across the Lycus valley had been completely destroyed in many places and the foss in front largely filled up, so that the task of repair was very difficult.[7]

In spite of the difficulty, the people had no choice but to repair the walls. A pattern emerged early in the siege and continued through until the end. During the day, the Turkish cannon hammered the walls into dust, and during the night the defenders of Constantinople filled in the breaches. The new day would dawn and the sultan's gunners would start again.

If there had ever been a time when a defender could tuck himself safely behind the walls and ignore the threat outside, it had ended. The impregnable walls of Constantinople, left unguarded, would have given way the first time they were tested by gunfire. An essential aspect of the defense was to repair them constantly. They could only hold their value in the fight if the daily breaches were closed up again.

A siege is not a single battle. It is a series of skirmishes, a probe here and a test there. Each side maneuvers for advantage, seeking a weakness that can be exploited. If the Christians did not maintain their walls, they would be overwhelmed, and if the Turks came too near the walls they would be cut down in a rain of javelins and crossbow bolts. But because the dangers of a siege are sustained, they eventually become routine. The vigilance provoked by fear subsides as the threat grows familiar.

For this reason, discipline is essential. Inside the city, discipline meant organizing the nightly repair parties, seeing that the soldiers were fed, and keeping a constant guard against unexpected attack. The commanders of the small Christian army knew to keep their men busy at the walls. Allow too many interludes for thought and a soldier might wander off the line to visit his home across town. He might grow weary with the routine and become careless. As long as the integrity of the walls could be maintained, then the only real threat to the city's safety was inside.

If we could prepare for one great battle in life, if we could see it coming and work our way forward, and then throw our whole heart into the struggle and prevail, it would then be over and we could move on

---

[7]Steven Runciman, *The Fall of Constantinople 1453* (Cambridge: Cambridge University Press, 1965), 97.

to other adventures. But a siege offers none of the thrill and none of the finality that our heroic temperaments crave. It is a constant daily struggle over inches of ground, a monotonous and seemingly pointless conflict. There are days when I would rather be strapped to the rack and urged to renounce Christ or die rather than endure the subtle and learned probing of my basic assumptions. That is why the Bible urges us to cultivate the virtue of self-control.

Virtue: Self-Control

If a man without self-control is like a plundered city left without walls, then a man who disciplines himself is a fortified city. Self-control doesn't seem like much of a virtue anymore. Disciplined people are uptight. The rest of us are always urging them to loosen up. *Come on, live a little.* In spite of that perception, self-control is not a nerdy lack of joie de vivre. Instead, it is a stewardship of the passions.

In his study of battle tactics during the Napoleonic Wars, Brent Nosworthy highlights an unusual example of such stewardship: the conduct of British attacks. He sets the stage by describing the boisterous, emotional charges of the French:

> In the French system, all the stakes were placed on the determination, energy and ferocity of the first assault. All the microdynamics underlying this set of tactics worked towards working the men up as soon as the attack had begun in earnest. . . . Whipping soldiers into a frenzy not only guaranteed they would exert themselves to their absolute physical limit, it also created an awesome first impression which naturally tended to demoralize the enemy.

Using such tactics, Napoleon and his marshals were able to defeat the tradition-bound armies of Europe's old regimes. But there was an inherent flaw in the system: because it pushed the men into a state of emotional exaltation, any check in the advance was likely to plunge them into despair. Like any enterprise depending for its success on unbridled enthusiasm, the French army was susceptible to sudden shifts in morale. At one moment, the officers were out in front leading the men; at the next they were behind the ranks pushing the men forward.

The British way was quite different. Known for their celebrated reserve, the British officers husbanded the enthusiasm of their men. They enforced a rule of silence throughout the ranks. As Nosworthy explains,

Everything was done to control the men's emotions, that is, to hold
them back both physically and psychologically. All of the emphasis
was placed on maintaining an emotional reserve which was to be
unleashed only at the critical moment.[8]

When the penultimate moment arrived, when the two armies were so
close that there was no stopping the collision, the British let loose a single
devastating volley and broke into three cheers. All the passion they had
held inside was suddenly released as they rushed forward with bayonets
flashing. The hail of gunfire inevitably took the wind out of the French
sails, and in the ensuing confusion they heard the hitherto silent redcoats
unleash a blood-curdling cry. Before the bayonets descended, the dispir-
ited Gallic warriors were in flight.

Whenever I think of the rigors and boredom of self-control I reflect
on the British line. There are times when I want to be as loud and unruly
as the world around me, times when I want to be whipped into a fury and
ride the mindless wave of enthusiasm, too. In those moments, I remember
the words of the anonymous author of *A Soldier of the Seventy-First,*
who felt trepidation in the face of the enemy's howls: "I looked alongst
the line. It was enough to assure me. The steady, determined scowl of my
companions assured my heart and gave me determination." As much as I
enjoy military history, I was never quite moved by the old song "Onward
Christian Soldiers." Maybe it was because I always envisioned the mighty
host advancing not to the thump of an organ but in awful silence, faces
flashing the same steady, determined scowls that gave the soldier of the
Seventy-First such a sense of encouragement!

Lesson Three: Guard Your Foundations

If Mehmet's artillery park put him in the forefront of military technology, he was not above employing old-fashioned siege tactics, too. On the
same day that the bombardments commenced, the sultan sent his miners to work. Their goal was to dig tunnels under the earth that reached
beneath the Christian fortifications. Once there, they would scoop out
the ground underneath and prop up the weight of the walls with wooden
pillars. These supports would then be doused in pitch and set aflame. As
they burned, they would lose their integrity and the weight above would
be left unsupported. If the miners made their calculations correctly, then

---

[8]Brent Nosworthy, *With Musket, Cannon and Sword: Battle Tactics of Napoleon and His Enemies*
(New York: Sarpedon, 1996), 238–39.

a section of the wall would come crumbling down and soldiers could rush in through the resulting breach. This ancient tactic is the origin of the word *undermine*.

Constantine XI could not match the Turks cannon for cannon. He had a few artillery pieces, but when they were fired from atop the walls they did more damage to the defenses than they did to the Turks. But Constantine was supplied with miners every bit as cunning as the sultan's, and he used them to good effect.

Countermining is difficult and vicious work. It requires the miner to calculate the position of the enemy entrenchment and dig in such a way as to intersect it. Both sides carry on their work as silently as possible, so finding an opponent underground is a daunting task. If there is a break-through, it will happen suddenly and take both sides by surprise, so every man in the mine must be ready to fight for his life. And in the cramped space beneath the earth, the weapons of choice are knife and hands and fire.

The Christian miners managed to pinpoint the sound of spadework beneath their feet and cut an effective countermine into the Turkish shaft. They crawled into the mineshaft, knifed whoever they could sink their blades into, and then torched the tunnel supports and brought the earth down on top of the Turkish miners' heads. Mehmet did not give up on the mines, but while he dominated the battle above ground, the Christian miners ruled the battle for the foundations, stopping every mine in its tracks and bleeding the sultan's mining teams dry.

We have already examined the foundations of the Christian faith, so it is enough to say here that, because they are so vital to the overall structure, they are the object of constant attack. The fight for such pillars as creation, order, rationality, and fear is hot work. Because it goes on beneath the surface, it is not always apparent to the eye—and that means the defense of our foundations is sometimes neglected. That is why it is so important to cultivate a worldview awareness.

Virtue: Worldview Awareness

Worldview awareness is a complicated way of saying that we should be conscious of the foundations that support our faith. The scope of Christianity's foundational doctrines stretches farther than the four pillars we discussed in chapter 2, extending to the doctrine of the Trinity, the incarnation, the resurrection, the second coming, and much more. Sadly, these are the doctrines we tend to assume rather than preach. The average churchgoer hears much more from the pulpit about his marriage, his job, and his feelings of self-worth than about the Trinity, incarnation, resurrection, and the second coming. The apostle Paul predicted to Timothy an age when men would not endure sound doctrine, and it seems clear that we live in such a time. Therefore it is all the more important for believers who take responsibility for themselves and practice the discipline of self-control to develop a worldview awareness.

Such an awareness requires just two things. First, it requires an interest in the doctrines of Scripture and how they fit together. By studying the pieces, you come to a sense of the greater whole. You develop an appreciation for what God has revealed and a respect for what he has not. Second, worldview awareness requires the adoption of a discerning attitude toward other teaching. It means that you read with an eye for the author's worldview assumptions, that you view the movies through a critical lens. You begin to read between the lines and see the messages embedded in the stories people tell.

Above all, worldview awareness means the end of your life as a passive receptor of other men's influences. It means building walls, manning the gates, and giving every thought that enters an appraising glance before you let it pass.

Lesson Four: Plan for Unexpected Attacks

Both on the walls and beneath them, the Christian army had fought the sultan to a standstill. The preliminary Turkish assaults had been routed, and the tiny flotilla of ships with which we began our story had successfully run the gauntlet and entered the city safe. Nicolo Barbaro, a Venetian surgeon who kept a diary of the siege, estimated that at least two hundred Turks had been killed in that naval battle, and not a single Christian had perished.

The inhabitants of the city had reason to be pleased. Although their situation had seemed hopeless, they had held out for more than two weeks against a vastly superior force, defying cannon, mine, and infantry assault. They didn't know it, but the tide was about to turn.

It happened on a Sunday morning, the twenty-second of April. Frustrated with the poor showing of his navy and convinced for the moment that the city's land walls were impregnable, Mehmet had studied the ground looking for an unexpected route of assault. So far, he had been stopped at the Theodosian walls in the Lycus valley and at the boom across the Golden Horn, where the Venetian fleet had proven too strong for his ships time and again. He wanted to apply pressure to the city, and after much thought an idea—an impossible, ridiculous idea—had suddenly come to him. If he could not go through the massive boom that blocked the Horn, he would go around it.

One side of the boom was anchored in the city and the other stretched to the neutral Genoese settlement of Galata across the Horn. Mehmet's idea was to fell a forest of trees and create what amounted to an overland conveyor belt that would carry a portion of his fleet up from the Sea of Marmara and around the back of Galata, then down through the Valley of Springs and into the Golden Horn. The audacity of the plan was breathtaking. Only a man as powerful as the Ottoman sultan could achieve it, with legions at his disposal and time to kill. The work commenced and on the morning of the twenty-second the first ships made the surreal journey over land:

> In every boat the oarsmen sat in their places, moving their oars in the empty air while the officers walked up and down giving the beat. Sails were hoisted exactly as though the vessels were at sea. Flags were flown, drums beaten and fifes and trumpets played while ship after ship was hauled up the hill, as it were in a fantastic carnival. . . . Long before noon the Christian sailors on the Golden Horn and the watchmen on the walls above the harbour saw to their horror this extraordinary movement of ships down the hill opposite them into the waters of the Horn.[9]

Why were the Christians so horrified? There were two reasons. First, it was over the weak sea walls that the Crusaders had advanced back in 1204, and that seemed like an ominous precedent. Second, the disposition of troops had depended on the relative safety of the sea walls. Since they were under little threat, Giustiniani and Constantine could leave a small force to defend them and concentrate the bulk of their small army at the St. Romanus Gate, opposite Mehmet's camp. After this unlikely feat of arms, the Christians would have to shift their strength to compensate, and that would mean spreading the defensive line dangerously thin.

The Christians responded immediately to the new threat by sending fire ships across the Horn at night in search of the Turkish fleet. Unfortunately the Turks were prepared for this old trick and repulsed

---

[9]Steven Runciman, *The Fall of Constantinople*, 106.

the attack with ease. The momentum of the siege had shifted, and now Mehmet, after a string of setbacks, finally had the upper hand.

Expect the unexpected. It seems like worthless advice. The reason the unexpected is such a danger is that you don't expect it. By definition, it wouldn't be unexpected if you did! You might as well say expect *every-thing*, but that's an impossible task.

Studies by the automotive industry suggest that when it comes to safety, drivers focus on the threats that are outside their control to the detriment of those that are. A small, quick, agile car will handle better and help you avoid the most common accidents, but we aren't worried about everyday dangers. What if I am stalled on a train track and broadsided by a locomotive? What if a piece of concrete is knocked off the overpass and lands on top of my vehicle? These are the worries that occupy consumers' minds, so we buy bigger and bigger vehicles, and the manufacturers make them more spacious and soft and rounded inside, all to heighten that sense of security. Never mind that they don't handle well in an emergency and make it more likely, not less, that we will run into trouble. In this case, expecting the unexpected looks a lot like folly.

Mehmet's movement of his fleet overland was a stroke of genius, and there was no way the Christians could have anticipated it. The lesson is not that they were caught unawares but that their response to the new threat was ineffectual.

You can't expect the unexpected, but you can plan for it by cultivating the virtue of flexibility.

Virtue: Flexibility

The problem with a two-thousand-year tradition is that in moments of crisis it looks a lot like a crutch. When faced with an unexpected attack, the Christians at Constantinople replied with the oldest trick in the book. Sometimes those tricks work. A century and a half later, English fireships ripped into the Spanish Armada and caused such panic that Philip II's dream of humbling the upstart island dissolved into vapor. But Mehmet was no Philip. He was a bold tactician who had proven his ingenuity and might have been expected to meet the fireships head on.

Flexibility requires a comprehensive knowledge of first principles and the skill to apply them to new situations. First and foremost it is an attitude toward setbacks that serves to contain their effects and assure us of ultimate success via some unexplored avenue. It is also a recognition that our confidence must be based not on circumstances (which change) but on the Lord of circumstance.

The inflexibility of Roman Catholic apologists during the seventeenth century led them to identify men like Galileo and Kepler as enemies of the faith. Today, a Catholic can embrace both his faith and the heliocentric view of the galaxy without contradiction, but at the time this was unthinkable. If they had been in closer touch with their first principles, it might have occurred to these men that they were defending not God but Ptolemy.

Lesson Five: Remember to Close the Gate

Even once the Golden Horn was breached, the Christians maintained their vigorous defense of the city with great success. The constant fighting took its toll on Christian and Turk alike. While the defenders could not afford the casualties they suffered, they inflicted far worse than they received, and every day that the siege was prolonged made the sultan's ultimate success seem less certain. Keeping such a large army in the field was a difficult task, and after the countless setbacks it was a challenge to maintain morale. Mehmet's oldest councilors wanted to see the siege abandoned, so it was up to the young sultan to make a concerted final push.

The assault was meticulously planned. Mehmet launched it at one in the morning on May 29, 1453, and he threw everything he had into the fight. This was the final battle and a chorus of church bells heralded the moment:

> All along the line of the walls the Turks rushed in to the attack, screaming their battle-cries, while drums and trumpets and fifes urged them on. The Christian troops had been waiting silently; but when the watchmen on the towers gave the alarm the churches near the walls began to ring their bells, and church after church throughout the city took up the warning sound till every belfry was clanging.[10]

With this ethereal soundtrack, the assault commenced in three waves. First the Bashi-bazouks advanced, an irregular force composed of men from throughout the sultan's empire. They were never expected to succeed; instead, their purpose was to inflict casualties and exhaust the defenders in preparation for the next wave. After two hours Mehmet

---

[10]Steven Runciman, *The Fall of Constantinople*, 133.

ordered them to retire, and then he sent in his well-drilled regiments of Anatolian troops.

During the second wave, a cannonball struck the defender's stockade and opened up a breach in the line. A force of some three hundred Anatolians entered the gap, shouting in what they supposed was a victorious assault. But Constantine led his troops to encircle and exterminate the intruders. This blow sent the Anatolians reeling and they were pulled back from the assault.

The last wave consisted of the elite Janissaries, a troop that was actually composed of men born to Christian parents who had been taken away at birth and raised as Muslims in the sultan's service. The Janissaries outnumbered the Christian defenders and they were fresh troops going up against exhausted men who had been fighting for four hours now. When the two armies clashed, the fighting was fierce and bloody, a ruthless hand-to-hand struggle. The defenders could not have known it but this was the last wave in what would probably have been the last assault. Push it back and they would raze the entire siege.

For an hour the Christians held the Janissaries in check. As ferocious as the attack had been, it seemed that its intensity had ebbed. The end of the assault was in sight when two catastrophes struck, one after the other.

First, the kerkoporta, a small gate in the wall near the Blachernae Palace which the Christians had used as a sally port to take the Janissaries in the flank, was accidentally left open by the return troops. It was a minor oversight, forgetting to bolt a door behind you. But one of the Janissaries noticed the error and led a group of men through the gate and up onto the battlements. Realizing their mistake, the Christians turned and fought to retake the gate, but in the confusion a contingent of Turks remained inside.

As this was happening, the Christian general Giustiniani was struck at close range by a culverin shot. Writhing in pain, he ordered his retainers to move him off the battle line. To do this, they had to obtain from Constantine the key to the gate separating the outer wall where they were stationed from the inner wall that led to the city. The emperor tried to persuade Giustiniani to remain, but he would not. Just as his men were evacuating him through the gate, someone spotted the banners of the Turks who had entered through the kerkoporta onto the battlements and mistakenly concluded that the city had fallen. A panic swept through the Genoese mercenaries and before the evacuation gate could be closed they had rushed away from their posts, abandoning Constantine and the depleted Christian ranks.

Although the Greeks fought back tenaciously, their weakened numbers proved no match for the Janissaries, who had taken heart at the confusion and redoubled their efforts. In the desperate fight that followed, Constantine was urged to flee. Instead, he removed his imperial regalia and entered the fray as a common soldier. He died in the fighting, the last of eleven centuries of Christian emperors at Constantinople.

So the city fell and many of its inhabitants were put to the sword. Others were sold into slavery. The riches of Constantinople were looted. Mehmet entered the city in triumph, approached St. Sophia, and spoke the words that converted the ancient church into a mosque. Today it is a museum in Istanbul, the capital of Turkey, still flanked by a brace of minarets. Reflecting on the catastrophe, the Greek chronicler Doukas wrote:

> Alas, the calamity! Alack, the horrendous deed! Woe is me! What has befallen us? Oh! Oh! What have we witnessed? An infidel Turk, standing on the holy altar in whose foundation the relics of Apostles and Martyrs have been deposited! Shudder, O sun! Where is the Lamb of God, and where is the Son and Logos of the Father Who is sacrificed theron, and eaten, and never consumed?[11]

Clearly in the eyes of Doukas, Mehmet had perpetrated the abomination of desecration. The remarkable thing is that such a tragic event should have been precipitated by something as trivial as someone forgetting to close a gate.

Virtue: Care

Such simple oversights stem from a lack of care. When such big events as battles are afoot, something as mundane as locking the door behind you seems quite trivial. But trivial faults are the seed of mighty downfalls.

When we think of the threats leveled against us, the exotic temptations that lurk in the world's darkest corners, it is easy to imagine that it would take such monumental evils to overcome us. Sadly this is not the case. Our greatest sins are born not from prodigious enticement but from simple oversight. We are careless and we fall.

Care for small details is admittedly a mundane virtue. It is not often praised. I include it here because it seems that, of all the virtues, care is

---

[11]Doukas, *Decline and Fall of Byzantium to the Ottoman Turks*, trans. Harry J. Magoulias (Detroit, MI: Wayne State University Press, 1975), 231.

the one that when cultivated offers the best defense against needless over-throw. If someone had taken care of locking the gate in Constantinople, the whole of history might have changed, and there are thousands of examples we could cite where a tiny omission altered the fate of nations. Imagine the disruption such oversights make in our much-less-exalted lives.

The defense of Constantinople was unsuccessful. By cultivating the virtues of personal responsibility, self-control, worldview awareness, flexibility, and care, perhaps the battle for our own minds will yield a far happier result.

8

Learning to Read

Every writer is a moral philosopher.
AYN RAND

[1]

Remember Aesop's fables? You probably heard them as a kid. They were amusing anecdotes about talking animals that always taught a lesson about good behavior. An eagle flying through the air is suddenly pierced through the breast by an arrow. He looks down to see that the arrow is trimmed with one of his own feathers! The moral: "We often give our enemies the means for our own destruction." A runaway slave transforms an angry lion into a friend by removing the thorn from his paw, only to be recaptured and—you guessed it—thrown to the lions. When the lion recognizes the slave, he licks his hands like a pet dog and the emperor, amazed by the scene, pardons the slave. The moral: "Do unto others as you would have them do unto you."

In grade school our teacher used to troop the class down to the library once a week for story time, an exercise calculated to instill a lifelong love of books (in my case, it worked). The librarian would read Aesop's fables and challenge us to guess the moral of the story. I remember wracking my tiny brain in pathetic confusion. The stories were intriguing, but I could never seem to figure out what they were supposed to mean. Even when the moral was revealed I sometimes scratched my head in wonder.

Flash forward to graduate school and I am sitting around a table full of poets. In front of me is a stack of photocopies; we are supposed to be giving feedback on everyone's work. I stare at the lines of verse in mounting desperation as my turn approaches. We are all grown up now and there are no morals to the story. Still, everyone but me seems to have something insightful to say. I feel all alone, the only person in the class whose critical appraisals can be summed up in the words: "I really liked it. Really." After years of education, interpreting the meaning of things hasn't gotten any easier.

Part of the problem is that I suspect everyone else is making things up. When I look at the page in front of me, the things they're observing don't seem to be there. They reference books I haven't heard of and make comparisons with other poems I either haven't read or didn't "get." Time and time again I want to speak up and demand, "What are you talking about? Where did you see that?" But I keep my mouth shut, afraid to look any more foolish than I already do.

The moral: "Reading isn't as easy as it looks."

Stories Are Everywhere

We are surrounded by stories: books, magazines, songs, movies, television, video games, personal conversations, sermons, lectures, radio monologues—all of them packed with narratives and full of meaning. On the subconscious level we absorb it all, and the stories we hear shape the way we think and respond.

Most of the people we admire, the ones we want to be like, all have one thing in common: *they are made up.* Scenes we have imagined from books and witnessed on film make a greater impact on the way we see than the world we live in every day. Beauty and awe and fear and the whole panoply of the great emotions are things we mostly experience within the context of make-believe. We invent ideas of ourselves—and why shouldn't we, when everyone around us is invented too?

Imagination has such power to shape our perceptions! All the dry, analytic systematization pales in the sunlight of a radiant, inventive mind. I have sometimes described our inconsistent (and frankly incoherent) habits of thought as if they are wholly destructive, but this is not the case. Our minds embroider reality, create unlikely and impossible connections, invent and recreate the world around us. And far from being a fault, this creativity is perhaps one of our greatest virtues. It is more evidence that we are made in the likeness of a creator.

The ancient role of storyteller is as central to human society today as it was four millennia ago. Storytellers are, to borrow Shelley's assessment of poets, the "unacknowledged legislators of the world." Alone they may not amount to much, but collectively their stories voice our shared experience. They sculpt the communal mind.

That's why it is essential to learn how to read.

What's Wrong with How I Read?

But you protest: "I can already read!" Of course you can. But that's not the kind of reading we are talking about. The necessary skill is called critical reading, and it's more than knowing what the words mean. It involves knowing *what the author means by the words*. Critical reading also means being able to see the structure inside the text and judge whether the story is told well, whether its embedded messages are true.

Reading is not something you can do only with books. In fact, reading does not even require words. You can read a film just as easily as you can read a story. You can read a painting. You can read a building, too. Critical reading is an act of interpretation. It can be applied to any form of expression. In this chapter, I will use books as a convenient frame of reference, but the same techniques can be used in reading movies, reading songs, and reading architecture as well.

Is there a problem with the way we read? I think there are actually two problems. First, we are *undiscriminating*. We don't make very informed choices about what we read. This is more than saying we read things that we shouldn't. That is no doubt true, but the real problem is not that we are reading the wrong things but that we are not deliberately seeking out the right ones. Our time is limited. When we spend it on certain things—even if they are harmless—we waste it. In fact, your time might be better spent with the harmful books than the innocuous and insipid ones.

The second problem with the way we read is that we are *undemanding*. We don't ask much of the things we read. Instead of examining them through our worldview lens, we submit to the arch nemesis of critical reading: the myth of entertainment. This myth states that we have to choose between discernment and enjoyment, and we will look at it more fully in a moment.

Because we are undiscriminating and undemanding, we do not choose the best stories and we do not get the most from the stories we choose. A demanding reader can sometimes benefit from reading a bad book. But when we choose bad books and make poor use of them, we put ourselves at the mercy of the stories the world is trying to tell (and sell) us—and that is rarely a good place to be.

The best seller lists are full of undemanding books written in the popular, blockbuster style, populated by cardboard characters with unlikely names who run through a series of activities as predictable as they are implausible. You have to suspend more than your disbelief to enjoy these mega-hits. There are exceptions, of course, but by and large, people read to be entertained, not enlightened. We don't choose books because of the ideas inside. We're on the hunt for a "fast read." We are undiscriminating readers who don't ask much of our authors. The less they deliver, the more we seem to love them.

This trend will probably never turn around. It may be hardwired into the rules of society. The best sellers of past ages are not the books we now study as great literature; instead, they have mostly slipped into oblivion, as most of today's leading books will. Taking a wider view, this actually makes sense. Books are written to sell. They are written to entertain. But they are not always written to last. Ironically, a good book costs no more than a bad one. The sad fact is that while everyone can afford a good book, not everyone can appreciate it.

It doesn't have to be that way, of course; otherwise a chapter like this would be worthless. Becoming a critical reader is well within anyone's grasp. It does not require a fancy education or expensive tastes. In the world of ideas, we are all equals, divided only by our willingness to invest ourselves in the cause.

Will Critical Reading Suck the Joy from Life?

When you become a critical reader, the previously mentioned myth of entertainment will rear its ugly head. It will be the excuse your friends will use when you watch the same television programs together but take away entirely different experiences. You will watch an episode of *Survivor* on TV, for example, and marvel that even when people are told to suspend their moral values for the sake of a game, they cannot help making these judgments.

"Does that mean that humans by nature are moral beings?" you will ask. "Does that mean that even when society tells you to set aside the morals it supposedly invented for you, there is something deeper that requires you to judge action in terms of right and wrong?"

And your friends will say that they watch TV for entertainment, not philosophy (they might actually use the term *philosophizing*, in which case, find new friends).

"If we watched something the way you do," they'll say, "it wouldn't be fun anymore. Your critical reading sucks the joy out of life!"

As a critical reader you will face this smoke screen again and again. Don't believe it for a minute. The fact is, critical reading actually enhances your enjoyment of the experience. But like a gourmet, you will find that some fare is no longer palatable. While your friends dine on the buffalo wings of the mind, you will find yourself hungry for more complex and satisfying dishes.

The first thing you'll notice is that critical reading adds depth to the overall experience. This is a point I can illustrate best with a story. Every week for about three years, I taught a Bible study on Friday nights. During that time we covered every line in every epistle of Paul except for 1 and 2 Corinthians. The procedure would go something like this: at the beginning of the study, I divided the chapter for the night into equal sections and each participant would read his or her part aloud. Once that was done, we went around the circle a second time and each person gave a paraphrase of what they had read. Then we discussed the thrust of the argument in the chapter to gain a sense of the "big picture," and after we had done that we turned our attention to specific passages that intrigued or perplexed us. Everything was fair game; there were no "off-limits" questions.

Over time, the weekly participants (myself included) developed an instinctive grasp of the apostle Paul's major themes and style of argument. Passages that might otherwise seem obscure made sense in light of discussions we'd had about other epistles. The more material we covered, the easier it became to digest new ideas and interpret individual points in light of the whole.

But not every participant attended regularly. After all, this was happening on Friday nights! Some people dropped in from time to time, so that the group would grow from ten to thirty and back. I began to notice that as the core group became more sophisticated, the occasional participants had a harder time absorbing their observations. Because they were not privy to the experiences we had shared and the shorthand we had developed along the way, they did not always appreciate where we were coming from.

One night a guy who attended on a semi-regular basis threw up his hands in disgust as I was working through a chapter from Hebrews. The whiteboard was covered in diagrams and the discussion had been buzzing along with intensity. But this guy had had enough.

"That's not what it says!" he protested. "You're all just reading things into it."

That threw a wrench into the works. From the beginning, one of my passions was taking the text at face value. Instead of appropriating a phrase here and a phrase there for proof-texting, I insisted that the students deal with the chapter in its entirety. And I was a stickler for correcting their assumptions when they conflicted with the text—as, for example, when one student insisted that the "weaker brother" in Romans 14 was the one who had fewer convictions, when Paul actually points the finger at the one who has more. So to have a student accuse us of reading into the text was a serious thing. I wanted to hear what he had to say.

His real problem, he explained, was that we were "over interpreting," making things more complicated than they really were. I was reminded of those desperate moments in my poetry workshops when I was convinced that everyone else was pulling things out of the air because I couldn't see them. Now, because I *could* see them, I was in a position not only to answer the objection but to understand my own frustration from years before.

We weren't reading into the text, but we were supplying the larger context and making connections with passages outside the chapter in front of us. Our would-be whistleblower didn't have that larger frame of reference. It wasn't his fault, of course; he simply hadn't been engaged in the study consistently over time. We were coming up with ideas and interpretations without showing where they came from and why they fit. That's what had happened to me in a classroom full of poets whose experiences I had not shared, and now I was inflicting that frustration on someone else!

When you don't have the proper frame of reference, you tend to think that deeper readers are making things up that aren't really there. There's an easy way to diagnose the problem. If you find yourself constantly say-ing, "I don't think the author really thought of that," when someone else raises a point, then your frame of reference might be lacking. One thing you can be fairly sure of is that the author *did* think of it. Writing is a deliberate and thoughtful enterprise, and as one of my fiction professors used to insist, "The author gets credit for everything that's there."

Of course, it is always possible that a text is being misread. The point is, the more experience you have as a critical reader, the deeper you can take the interpretative experience—and this is a legitimate depth. You really will see things that a reader who stays on the surface thinks are not there!

Another benefit of critical reading that will heighten your enjoyment is the development of better taste. Now, taste is a controversial topic because it is such a subjective thing. There are some experiences you can appreciate better than others, and you are likely to rank them higher than the things you don't enjoy. If you insist on seeing these preferences in absolute terms you can fall into a trap. Growing up in a conservative Southern church, I was raised to believe that all contemporary music, including so-called Christian music, was evil, while God took a more lenient view on country music. Some of the people who taught this went so far as to develop theories about good and evil beats! (The fact that Satan and syncopation both start with the same letter is suggestive, isn't it?) These notions, obviously developed by people who liked country music but didn't care for modern tunes, were passed down as if they were biblical doctrines and got more airtime in the pulpit than many fundamentals of the faith. This is what happens when we take our aesthetic judgments out of context.

Still, there are legitimate values at play in aesthetics. Some things are more beautiful than others, and while it is true that the *perception* of beauty is subjective, the thing itself is not. Perhaps the reason we are so passionate about our tastes is that, while we cannot validate them in the acceptable ways, they *feel* so right and important. They come from the part of us that imagines the world and should not be discarded so easily.

The benefit of critical reading is not that you will come to share my tastes, or even some transcendent standard of good taste, but that your own appreciation of things will improve. You will develop tastes of your own and they will help you to be more discriminating and demanding as a reader. And this will give you the tools to be a more discerning reader, too—of books *and* culture.

[II]

The classic guide to reading is *How to Read a Book* by Mortimer J. Adler and Charles Van Doren. I recommend it heartily, even though my own experience with the book has been a little ambivalent. If you find this chapter on how to read somewhat tedious, imagine an extremely methodical and comprehensive four-hundred-page book about it! In spite of my good intentions, I have never managed to read Adler and Van Doren cover to cover. But I have found that every time I take up the book and read over a few pages, they describe things that I have learned through the process of reading. A determined person without a great deal of experience as a critical reader could learn a lot from this book.

What Adler and Van Doren emphasize is the need for "active" reading. The myth of entertainment fosters a passive approach, which is why people who read only for entertainment prefer unchallenging books that are easy to coast through. (I believe the technical term is "page-turner," and it is considered high praise to say that the pages "turn themselves.") An active reader questions the book as he reads it. He interrogates its characters, probes its plot; if it is nonfiction he tries out the arguments and sees if they work. To a sedentary reader, this seems like thankless work, but the active reader delights in it.

When dealing with expository writing, Adler and Van Doren suggest four key questions: *What is the book about as a whole? What is being said in detail, and how? Is the book true, in whole or part?* and *What of it?* These questions are good things to ask about imaginative writing as well, to the extent that you are probing the author's worldview assumptions. But when the active reader tackles imaginative writing, he must also take into account questions of form and execution. Adler and Van Doren sum the process up in a single maxim: "Don't criticize imaginative writing until you fully appreciate what the author has tried to make you experience."[1]

The Author's Agenda

The experience the author wants you to have is part of the problem, though. The "danger" of fiction is that an author creates an entire world, complete with its own moral framework, and within that structure the morality works. What do you do if the moral framework of a story contradicts your own? There are a couple of ways to answer the question. Some people don't think it is an issue. You are constantly dealing with competing moral outlooks in life, so why should the books you read, the movies you watch, or the music you hear be any different? Others are so threatened by the possibility that their values will be subconsciously undermined that they scrupulously avoid contact with rival worldviews.

---

[1]Mortimer J. Adler and Charles Van Doren, *How to Read a Book* (New York: Simon & Schuster, 1972), 213.

Without passing judgment on either extreme, I want to make a case for the middle path.

The mid-twentieth-century novelist and philosopher Ayn Rand said, "Every writer is a moral philosopher." She was in a position to know. Her own novels were clunky pamphlets for her own philosophy, Objectivism, which still enjoys a cult following today. Rand's books pit lone heroes against the evil collective, and while they make for turgid reading it is hard for an American audience raised on rugged individualism not to admire Howard Roark, the iconoclastic architect in *The Fountainhead*. According to Rand, "What is important is not the message a writer projects *explicitly,* but the values and view of life he projects *implicitly.*"[2]

I suspect that these implicit worldviews do exert a negative influence when the reader remains unaware of them. Once he discovers their presence, the threat is largely neutralized.

When a character in a book or film elicits your sympathy, you want her life to work out for the best. The circumstances she finds herself in are a maze of the author's invention, and as she moves forward she is drawn by an invisible filament grasped loosely in the author's hand. But when we place ourselves inside the illusion of the story's reality, we forget that an author has created these contingencies and initiated these actions. We tell ourselves, "This is how life is." Now, if the woman we care about finds that her only option is to divorce her lackluster husband and head to Los Angeles in search of herself, we are inclined to agree. That insufferable bore of a husband deserves what he gets! In real life, we might not condone such a step, but it seems harmless to live out the possibility through the character's experience.

And perhaps it is. The deciding factor is whether we are conscious of the author's worldview manipulation. If I realize that a character's choices are limited by the author's assumptions about reality, then I can probably enjoy the journey without the risk of unknowingly adopting a perverse set of principles. But if, like so many readers, I am unconscious of what happens beneath the surface of a story, seeing bad choices presented in a context that makes them look good can be a very damaging process.

Southern writer Eudora Welty said, "morality as shown through human relationships is the whole heart of fiction, and the serious writer has never lived who dealt with anything else."[3] She had little patience

---

[2]Ayn Rand, *The Art of Fiction: A Guide for Writers and Readers* (New York: Plume, 2000), 15.
[3]Eudora Welty, *On Writing* (New York: Modern Library, 2002), 76.

for what she called crusading novelists, writers whose work aimed at changing society. The novel is not a dramatized editorial. "The writing of a novel is taking life as it already exists, not to report it but to make an object, toward the end that the finished work might contain this life inside it, and offer it to the reader."

When the life the author offers is accepted uncritically, or when a reader's whole conception of life is shaped by a succession of fictions, then the author's depiction of morality (and potentially, his distortion of it) is a subject for concern. But by and large we know when our own ideas are threatened, just as we know when they have changed. The subconscious threat of rival worldviews, like the "backmasking" scare of the 1980s, is mostly exaggerated.

The real challenge is right there on the surface. Just as the discerning Christian did not need to hear the secret messages spinning backwards on a record to know that the tattooed thug bawling into the microphone about worshiping Satan was not producing uplifting art, we do not need to look for subtleties where so many thorns are out in the open. If you read enough books about smart, beautiful young people who wake up one day to realize that God doesn't exist and the only rational response is to party, you just might wake up one day and realize that God doesn't exist and you have an insatiable urge to rave. It won't be because you have been subconsciously programmed to reject your faith. You will have been *consciously* programmed by filling your mind with junk when you ought to have dwelled on "whatever is true, whatever is honorable, whatever is just, whatever is pure, whatever is lovely, whatever is commendable. . . ."[4]

Discovering Worldview

All of us, writers and readers alike, have a perspective, a take on life, and it affects how we interpret life. We experience the same events in very different ways thanks to the unique hermeneutical framework that structures our observations. Once we realize this, it becomes terribly interesting to sift other people's work in search of their fundamental assumptions.

Some authors hit you over the head with their worldviews. In an earlier chapter, I mentioned Thomas Hardy's *Jude the Obscure,* a book that leaves you in no doubt. Another classic in the same category is Jack London's novella *The Call of the Wild.* I didn't need any special tools to

---

[4]Phil. 4:8.

uncover the worldview of this book, a curious blend of Darwinism and paganism. The protagonist is a dog named Buck who is kidnapped in the midst of a complacent life in civilized California and transported to the ruthless landscape of the Klondike during the gold rush. The demand for sled dogs is intense. Buck finds himself strapped to a sled team and plunged into the age-old survival of the fittest as he battles to become the leader of the pack. The morality of the civilized world is left behind for a new but somehow older and more authentic code. London's observations about this put the reader in mind of Friedrich Nietzsche. At the same time, Buck begins to hear the primal "call of the wild." He experiences bizarre recollections of a collective wolf past, which include glimpses of a Neanderthal cave dweller equally at home in the trees and on land.

How do you discover the worldview embedded in a work of fiction? Leland Ryken offers a series of tips in *Windows to the World: Literature in Christian Perspective*. Every story, he points out, implies some comment on what is real, what is right, and what has value. For example, in *The Call of the Wild*, the brutal reality of the Klondike makes the civilized world seem far off and somehow imaginary. The cruel life of a sled dog is what is real; the call of the primal wolf is real. And that changes what is right. Buck learns to abandon the old rules and submit to the "law of the club and fang." He learns to value severe discipline and the will to power, going on to rule over the wolves. Probing these questions of reality, morality, and value will uncover the story's worldview.

Ryken also suggests that the story be viewed as an experiment in life, an exploration of a particular problem. If the reader can find the problem of the story, its answer will lead to the story's belief system. And note that I am referring specifically to the *story's* worldview. Sometimes the ideas you find in the book are not the author's own, and sometimes an author's view changes over the course of several books. Each story has its own set of rules.

If you want to develop skill at discerning the underlying philosophy of a novel, perhaps the best advice I can give is to read a few books like *Jude the Obscure* and *The Call of the Wild*. Since Hardy and London both telegraph their worldviews, it will be easy to find the didactic passages and form a clear idea of how moral perspectives and stories inhabit the page together. There is no substitute for this kind of experience if you want to develop a keen awareness of how worldview assumptions are built into fiction.

More Than Abstractions

After discussing ways to discover the worldview that informs a work of fiction, Ryken notes that at the end of the day literature is more than a worldview, and it should not be reduced to a set of abstractions.

It might be useful to think of a story as the incarnation of ideas. There are certainly ideas imbedded in fiction, and we can think of many examples where authors are clearly out to influence our thinking. But the ideas in fiction are generally simple and poorly argued in comparison with philosophical texts, because the goal of literature is not argumentation but representation, the production of a convincing illusion. We can isolate the ideas in a story and examine them, but to consider the story *as a whole* requires more than this. A Marxist can talk about class issues in Dickens's *Bleak House*, but if the discussion never moves beyond class, then the rest of us will feel that it hasn't done justice to the whole of the book's achievement.

The same thing is true of *The Call of the Wild*. There is a sense in which, as a Christian, I can't help but reject what London is saying. But if my disagreement with his ideas blinds me to the book's many virtues—the rich prose, the narrative drive, the very audacity of writing a novella with a sled dog for protagonist—then the best that can be said of me is that I have a tin ear.

The reason we develop a worldview sensitivity is so that we can use discernment in evaluating the influences around us. Our own worldview, however, includes the notion of God's common grace poured out to believer and unbeliever alike, resulting in (among other things) the presence of truth and beauty even in the work of those who reject their Author. The goal of critical reading, then, is not to install a spiritual V-chip in the Christian's mind, but to help the believer embrace all the truth that unbelievers know, and much more besides.

PART THREE

WITNESS

9

Engagement and Beyond

"God has granted you all those who sail with you."
ACTS 27:24

The inner door opened and an elderly Hispanic woman in a flowery house dress gazed at us through the screen door, eyebrows raised. We were the last thing she'd expected to find on her doorstep: my youth pastor, clad in a white, short-sleeved shirt and knit tie, and yours truly, sweating in the humid Houston afternoon. I smiled silently, an awkward teen, waiting for Al to go into action. I was there to observe, to learn the ropes. Normally, Al was reserved, but during door-to-door visitation, he adopted a bright, almost boisterous persona.

"Hello, ma'am, how are you doing today?"

"Okay," she said cautiously.

"Nice weather we've been having, isn't it?"

She peered sideways down the street, then nodded. "I guess."

The conversation went on like this, the youth pastor making banal observations and the old lady offering tentative agreement, her confusion gradually diminishing as she noticed the wad of gospel tracts in Al's breast pocket and the church brochures clutched, along with his Bible, in his right hand. She relaxed a little, and I realized we probably weren't the first church visitors to intrude on her Saturday afternoons.

We'd been at this for a couple of hours now, trekking through the neighborhoods around our church, knocking on doors and trying to find a natural way to slip our killer question into the dialogue: "If you were to die right now, do you know where you would go?" Officially, we weren't doing evangelism; we were just inviting people to church. But if the opportunity presented itself, our instructions were to share the plan of salvation—and if it didn't present itself, our job was to create an opening, leave a tract, plant a seed.

Visitation was nothing new to me. My church back in Louisiana sent its youth out into the streets every week, so I was a veteran of sorts. But I'd been away at college for a while, and in the meantime my family had moved to Houston and joined a new church, so my summer vacation was spent getting used to the way things were done in the big city. I'd never been comfortable walking up to a stranger and posing spiritual questions, and I could tell that Al wasn't, either. Like many people, he had developed a way of coping with his reluctance, and one of the ways he overcame it was through this loud, irrelevant chit-chat designed to put his audience (and himself) at ease.

The woman heard us out, opening her screen door just wide enough to accept the church brochure and the tract Al slipped through, but as soon as she could close the door on us without being rude, she did. Afterward, there was a long silence. Then Al let out a sigh, and we continued to the next house.

Just a few weeks before, while I was at college in Tennessee, I had gone door-to-door with another student, Jeff. This time, our mission was sociological, not evangelistic. The sociology department at our university was conducting a massive survey throughout the county, sending students into the highways and byways to ask citizens an assortment of questions about education and their views on local school board initiatives. Ironically, these questions had nothing to do with the goal of the survey, which was to calculate literacy rates. This was a Trojan horse assignment. During the course of the interrogation, we handed participants a short essay to read, then asked them questions based on its content. As Jeff posed the questions, I tried to determine if the person had really read the essay, and then rate how well he seemed to understand it.

Some students enjoyed the deception, but it made me even more uncomfortable than I usually was in these situations. I remember one rural address, a ramshackle house whose occupant came to the door in nothing but a pair of overalls. His ancient skin had the color and texture of a cigar wrapper, and his eyes burned with intelligence. Maybe I was wrong, but when we handed him the blue sheet of paper to read, he glanced at both of us with what looked to me like dawning recognition. He knew what we were up to, and he knew that I knew that he knew. As Jeff asked the questions, the man looked at me the whole time. My hand shook as I made the notes. Who were we, two privileged, immature college boys, to stand in judgment over this man? What right did we have to trick him on his own doorstep and administer our little test?

As I walked along the sidewalk with Al, I remembered those awkward afternoons back in Tennessee. In both cases, we met with more closed doors than open ones—and the people who answered our knocks were invariably older. Young people didn't answer the door to strangers, who would undoubtedly be trying to sell something, any more than they would answer the telephone to telemarketers once Caller ID came along. The only people we encountered going door-to-door were the ones old enough to remember when that's the way the world worked.

Methods Should Change with Time

No one accepted Christ that afternoon, and no one attended church as a result of our visits. Were we discouraged? Not really. God works in mysterious ways, we reminded ourselves, and there was no telling what good would come from the work we'd done. The sociology project was bolstered by similar platitudes, but given my firsthand experience of the subjectivity of it all, the inherent shortcomings, I had my doubts. There was no "trigger," no watershed moment, but I found by the time I graduated college that I was a confirmed skeptic where door-to-door was concerned—not because of the message, but because of the method.

Years later, I had lunch with a pastor interested in attracting more people from the community to his church. To achieve the goal, he was considering instituting an adult visitation program and reviving his church's old bus ministry, which had once ferried neighborhood kids to church.

"Why are you thinking of those methods?" I asked, barely concealing my aforementioned skepticism. "Anything is better than nothing, but will those things actually work?"

He shrugged. "That's what we used to do. Everyone did."

He was right. By the mid-twentieth century, a whole methodology had developed for doing outreach, and in some denominations people measured a church's commitment to the gospel by how many of these programs it supported—even if the methods never achieved the desired result.

Churches tend to be conservative organizations, resistant to change.

In one sense, this is good, since it places a burden of proof on theological innovation. The presumption in favor of tradition helps keep the church from being blown about by every philosophical wind, and where this presumption is absent (as it often is today), the church must constantly reinvent itself in the image of the new. Still, fidelity to the gospel of Jesus Christ and loyalty to mid-century outreach methodologies are two different things. This is one instance where, contra Marshall McLuhan, the medium and the message are two different things.

As we embark on the final section of the book, which focuses on the idea of "witness," it is important to keep this distinction between message and method in mind. In the first section, we considered the problem of thinking in this world, and in the second we teased out the implications for living. Now the question becomes, "Given these thoughts and this life, how do we speak to the world around us?" The answers, traditionally, have come under the headings of evangelism and apologetics, but while we will touch on these things, I want to suggest that they are part of a larger, wider cultural expression. Apologetics and evangelism, instead of being technical specialties modeled on rhetorical, sales, and marketing models imported from the outside, ought to be everyday endeavors, the natural result of thinking and living as we do.

The Wide Angle on Witness

When we talked about worldview, my goal was to move from a simple, univocal understanding of the term to a more complex, nuanced understanding, and that's why we considered the concept from three different but interrelated perspectives. With wisdom, the spotlight moved to matters of practical, twenty-first-century discernment, the place where good choices often depend on cultural sophistication and a critical detachment from the spirit of the times. Now, I want to take witness, which is usually such a narrowly focused concept, and widen the perspective. Instead of thinking of it in terms of method—whether the old approach of door-to-door and printed tracts or the new one of relationship building and church marketing—I want to consider what witness really is, and all the different things that might, in their own small way, contribute to it.

Witness isn't a method or technique. It's the sum total of our expression, what we say and what we don't, what we do, who we help, and who we harm. Our actions and reactions, taken as a whole, constitute a message to the world we live in. There's a difference, too, between what our witness ought to be, and what it really is. That tension will run like a faultline through the rest of the book.

To witness something is simply to be present as it happens, to gain firsthand information of the event. As any policeman will tell you, not every witness bears witness. In some neighborhoods, everybody sees what happens, and nobody talks. They keep silent because of distrust of others, and because they fear the consequences of telling the truth. To be a witness is to have information; to bear witness is to share it.

But we are shaped by the events we witness. Seeing what we see, knowing what we know, changes who we are. Consequently, we live in the shadow of what we've witnessed, and our subsequent actions bear witness even when we ourselves are silent. The difference, of course, is between implicit and explicit expression. The child who witnesses a murder might never speak of it, but his whole life afterward becomes a testament to the knowledge. Still, it's usually not a testimony the outside world can comprehend. Based on the behavior of people in adulthood, the pop psychologist in us is sometimes tempted to speculate about childhood traumas, but speculation is a far cry from knowledge. The way we live our lives may indeed be a form of silent witness, but can the world make sense of it if we do not testify to the facts? I don't think so.

The question becomes, how do we testify? If you'd asked the young college student sweating it out on the streets of Houston, he would probably have listed a handful of options: door-to-door, sharing tracts, preaching sermons. Now he takes a wider view of the possibilities. Every form of cultural expression, from the songs we sing to the stories we tell, is a small fleck in the overall mosaic that is our witness to the world. Witness is not, as is sometimes supposed, the province of professionals, nor does it require special training. All it takes to be a witness is a willingness to come forward and reveal what you know, and that honesty can take many forms.

You Are What You Consume

When Hurricane Rita threatened to hit the coast of Texas in 2005, just weeks after Katrina had devastated New Orleans and the surrounding areas, the news prompted the biggest evacuation in modern memory. Highways leading out of Houston were packed with bumper-to-bumper traffic that went on for miles, and the jams lasted for several days. My wife and I packed a few things and hit the road in our tiny hatchback, leaving the city at two in the morning. For some reason, we decided that instead of fighting traffic all the way to Dallas, which would be overwhelmed by evacuees, we would drive a few hours more and spend a pleasant weekend in Tulsa, making a virtue of necessity.

What should have been an eight-hour drive ended up lasting twenty-eight hours, and I spent most of that behind the wheel. We left with half a tank of gas, which didn't last long, and throughout the journey one of our greatest challenges was finding more fuel. Gas stations along the route were either closed or swarmed with dozens (in some cases, hundreds) of waiting vehicles. Around midnight, somewhere in East Texas, I had just put the gas nozzle into the car after waiting half an hour in line, only to have the station owner switch off the lights and declare that all the gas was gone.

"I'll go in and ask if we can at least *try*," my wife said, and before I could voice my pessimism, she was inside the station talking to the attendant. People around me were leaving in disgust, and I was ready to pack it in, but after a few moments my wife returned with news. "He says there's no gas left, but we're welcome to try."

Try we did, and in spite of the attendant's prediction, I managed to fill the tank before the supply ran out. I'm not given to ecstatic expression, but I was ready at that moment to drop to my knees and give thanks to Almighty God.

Throughout the trip, I kept saying that once this was over, we would buy some gasoline cans and keep them filled in case of emergency. I've run out of gas before in the middle of nowhere, but the Rita evacuation brought home a fact that I'd only known in theory before: we are consumers, wholly dependent on our means of supply for survival.

Apart from extraordinary circumstances like this, our consumption is largely unconscious. We depend on the Middle East, that notably hostile and unstable region, for oil, but until gas prices go through the roof, we forget just how fragile that supply line can be. Our need shapes us. In the case of oil, for example, it imposes policy imperatives that would not make sense anywhere else in the world. Ordinarily, we take these necessities for granted, not even making the connection between the need to placate despots and the need for oil.

Consumption's unconscious impact is felt on the personal level, too. Thanks to innovations in marketing, we identify now more than ever with the brands we buy. Companies used to sell us products; now they sell us identity. We are encouraged to think that what we buy declares something to the world about who we are. If I buy a Mercedes Benz, people will think differently about me than if I buy a Ford. If people at Starbucks see me working on an Apple computer, they will form a different impression than if I have a PC. The clothes I wear, the music I listen to, the video games I play, the blogs I read, the television shows I watch—all of these seemingly innocuous choices are presented to me in terms of identity.

Rarely, though, does this manipulation take place out in the open. The campaigns are sophisticated and subtle. All it takes to overcome our postmodern skepticism is a dose of postmodern irony. Advertisers can engage in the most absurd hyperbole without setting off our alarms, as long as they do it with a wink and a nod. As a result, we are divided into clans and tribes that split along the lines of brand loyalty, and we don't stop and question the process.

Some people in the church have responded to this new reality by saying, in essence, if you can't beat them, join them. As a result, many churches are hard at work developing their "brand," exploiting the insights of contemporary marketing the way their predecessors raided the door-to-door sales manuals of a generation gone by. As a result, pastors are just as likely to turn to *Fast Company* for inspiration as they are to *Christianity Today*. I have seen churches planted as if they were simply spiritual corporations, complete with business plans, venture capital, and soft launches—without the people involved betraying any awareness of how strange, even surreal, this approach really is. I cannot say for certain that this is wrong, but it is definitely odd, and I suspect the corporate approach to church, which places the power in the hands of management teams rather than congregations, will stand out to future generations as one of the defining blind spots of our time.

Regardless of what we think of consumerism and the various Christian responses, one thing is clear. If we are to be consumers, it is better to be self-conscious ones, scrutinizing our choices and seeing them for what they are.

From Consumer to Witness

One lesson of self-conscious consumption is that messages are communicated through a variety of means, and those means have the power to distort what is said. To that extent, Marshall McLuhan was right to speak of the medium as the message. Some means are not appropriate to the spreading of certain messages.

To give an extreme example, the gospel cannot be spread at the edge of a sword or the barrel of a gun. History is replete with cases where force has been brought to bear on the question of kingdom building, and the results are never good. Even when the force involved is little more than social pressure, the outcome can never be trusted. Christians want people to profess faith because they actually possess it, not because they feel obligated to say the right thing. As a result, one of the perpetual questions in ministry is how best to share the gospel. On the one hand, I can't help thinking that any means is better than none. God can use even the worst presentation to bring people to him. On the other, I've seen up close how improper means can distort the message of grace and turn it into something else.

If the method should be suited to the message, it is equally true that the means must fit the audience. You wouldn't hand a person who only speaks Spanish an English translation of the Bible and expect God to mysteriously reveal to the reader the significance of the words. God works through ordinary means as well as extraordinary, so we take the sensible precaution of translating the message into the language of its audience. To do otherwise would be to champion obscurantism at the expense of understanding.

By the same token, we should not let the conservative impulse lead us to label everything new as suspect and everything old as effective. Our speech has a cultural context, and that context changes. Preserving outmoded methodologies may keep us within our comfort zones, but it also helps ensure that those zones continue to shrink. For all my skepticism toward flashy, trendy ways of "doing church," I am grateful for the willingness to risk, to test new ideas through trial and error, even at the expense of making mistakes. It suggests a desire to speak to the surrounding world that is sometimes absent where methodologies are given more priority than the gospel message itself.

To move from consumer to witness, first we recognize that other people are consumers, too. They inhabit a cultural context and that culture is shaped by a relatively small group of people. Traditionally, Christians have adopted a critical stance toward these elites, warning others about the evils of Hollywood, liberal politicians, and atheistic academics. In fact, one of the great achievements within evangelicalism in the past thirty years has been the development of a sophisticated, informed cultural criticism. By opting out of the mainstream, we became conscious consumers, and from consumers we matured into critics.

Unfortunately, culture isn't shaped through criticism. Grasp this point and you have a key to understanding what's underneath many of the current culture-related controversies in the church. The development from consumer to witness moves through four stages:

1. Consumer	2. Self-Conscious	3. Critic	4. Contributor
Someone the culture acts upon and shapes, usually without his conscious knowledge.	Someone aware of culture's shaping influence, making deliberate choices.	Someone engaged in a discerning, systematic critique of the culture's shaping process.	Someone making truthful, positive attempts to shape the culture.

We begin as consumers being unconsciously shaped, then mature to self-consciousness, where the important thing is making discerning choices about the influences we give weight to in our lives. Over time, that discernment results in a more systematic critique of the culture, a specific perspective on what's wrong and what needs to change. If the self-conscious consumer is asserting control over his fundamental formation, the critic is working out the implications, taking the process to the next level.

Self-conscious consumption is organically linked to the critical stance; the two states are interdependent. The two ought also to lead naturally into the next stage, that of the contributor. In addition to being shaped, the contributor is actively shaping others through cultural influence, an activity which draws on self-conscious consumption and criticism for strength and direction.

In other words, the chart above parallels the structure of this book:

Worldview: Self-Conscious Consumer	Wisdom: Critic	Witness: Contributor
Someone aware of culture's shaping influence, making deliberate choices.	Someone engaged in a discerning, systematic critique of the culture's shaping process.	Someone making truthful, positive attempts to shape the culture.

Worldview flows into wisdom which flows into witness. Witness draws strength from wisdom and worldview. Instead of discreet stages we enter into and move beyond, these categories are essential parts of a single whole. Ideally, you can't have one without the other, which means that any time you see an emphasis on worldview that doesn't lead to a critical maturity, or criticism that doesn't lead to cultural contribution, something must be wrong.

The Engine Is Stalled and Flooded

Here's where I feel compelled to wear my heart on my sleeve. Too often, rather than developing critical perspectives that empower expression, evangelicals evolve systems that restrain and channel it into tightly prescribed outlets. But what is witness if not unrestrained expression, a desire to share what one knows without regard to setting or propriety?

Bearing witness has more in common with creativity than criticism. While criticism delights in analysis, creativity is, first and foremost, an urge to tell. I have engaged in some cultural criticism in this book, but on the whole, I've approached it as a creative project, an opportunity to take what I've learned (for what it's worth) and pass it on in the most compelling way I can. This expression is part of my movement from critic to contributor, and I hope it bears witness to the strength creativity draws from criticism. If I had relied on my critical instinct alone, though, the thing would never have been written. I'm an artist more than an intellectual, more comfortable with fiction than nonfiction, and every word I write reveals the gaps in my knowledge—or, more precisely, the vast empty deserts of ignorance that connect the occasional oases of understanding. When you bear witness, you expose yourself in a way that the careful critic never does.

I shouldn't be too hard on the critical perspective, though, because I'm a big believer in that kind of detached, measured thinking. But we must draw a distinction between healthy and unhealthy criticism, and the difference is in their fruit. Criticism is healthy when it supports creativity, wisdom leading to witness. It is unhealthy when it inhibits cultural contribution, either by stigmatizing it or by failing to equip us with the necessary tools and mind-set.

Here is what I have seen in the evangelical community. On the one hand, there are groups that still harbor the old suspicions about any form of cultural contribution. A young person in such a church who expresses the desire to write novels or make movies will be rebuffed and redirected into safer, more conventional avenues. In other places, the same young person will be shunted into the appropriate niche of the Christian subculture. "If you want to makes movies," they're told, "make Christian movies." This may benefit the subculture, but it doesn't do much for the world we're trying to help.

Where creativity is encouraged, it is often not accompanied by the kind of rigor necessary to make a successful contribution to the larger culture. We still have a hard time matching the message to the appropriate medium. The weighty grace of the gospel is channeled into the worldview of a sanctified after-school special, an artistic product sufficiently blind to the grit of reality, so that unbelievers, looking at the stories we tell, come away convinced that Christians, in order to hold onto their beliefs, dare not look at the world with both eyes open.

In other words, creative expression is stifled and starved in the sections of the church that have developed an unhealthy critical perspective, and it flourishes in those quarters where there is no critical perspective of any kind to feed on. Where there is criticism, there is no expression; and where there is expression, there is no criticism. We have a socket on the one hand and a plug on the other, and we are left to imagine in frustration what might happen on the glorious day one is introduced to the other.

What we need, both personally and corporately, is a healthy critical outlook that organically blends into creative contribution. We will look at the contours of this contribution in chapter 12; we need to think about the nature of apologetics and the ironies of unbelief.

An Artifact of Truth

Recasting witness, which is ordinarily seen only in terms of evangelism and (sometimes) apologetics, so that it embraces a whole variety of creative expressions, might seem like a dangerous thing. Should we paint pictures instead of sharing the gospel with others? Of course not. But is there any reason not to do both? Our narrow view of witness has resulted in a Christianity that is easily compartmentalized and relegated to the realm of the personal. In many ways, we have gone silent, believing that there are just one or two legitimate means of telling the truth, and then leaving those means to ministerial professionals. We sit and complain about how we are misconstrued by the elites, but our response then is to develop a withering critique of the media, rather than skillfully putting the truth out there for people to experience for themselves.

Our focus was not always so narrow, a fact that was impressed on me not so long ago while teaching at Worldview Academy. For a week's time, our program was hosted by an exceptionally radical university, a campus that showed nothing but hostility to our mission. That did not bother us, of course. One of the reasons we teach on college campuses rather than in cloistered retreat facilities is to create these opportunities for "apologetic encounters." This was a particularly tough week, though, and our faculty and staff felt pretty tense about the situation.

The main classroom was a beautiful old concert hall. Judging from the style of masonry and decoration, I guessed the building had been erected in the late nineteenth century and the interior was redecorated in the 1920s. Bright, anachronistic murals covered the walls, including what seemed to be an allegory of the garden of Eden transposed into early America, complete with plenty of abstract nudes—always exciting at a Christian camp for teens. During one of the lectures, I sat at the back of the hall, thinking about all the friction we had experienced with the university staff over the past couple of days. They made no secret of their hostility toward our faith, and we made every effort to respond in a loving, if baffled, way.

As I mused on this, I noticed that the murals on the wall changed as they neared the top of the stage, where the dancing nudes gave way to illustrations of sheet music, lines from Gregorian chant in blackface type. Curious, I transcribed the fragments into my notebook and went in search of someone with a little better knowledge of Latin. The words turned out to be about the honor and glory of God Almighty.

How strange, I thought, to find an artifact of the truth in a place so hostile to its proclamation. Similar things have happened when I've attended choral concerts, where religious music is regularly performed with great skill and passion by people who revere it for the beauty of its art, overlooking what they take to be the ugliness of the message. Whenever this happens, I am always struck by the quirky course of God's providence, the way he is glorified even from the lips of unbelievers.

And then I reflect on the fact that this beautiful music, this great legacy of past Christian cultural contribution, is so absent from the church. The people who have the most to benefit from it do the least to preserve it. Ah, well.

The sermons of the past, much as I love them, have not aged so well. Believers of the past, through their creative contributions, minister to me today in ways that the ministers of the past rarely can. This is not to discount the ministers or the sermons. They are vital, and if anything I would place them on a pedestal. But they should have their echo elsewhere, rippling through the whole of culture in a way they never can now, because the people they influence contribute nothing—or if they do, they contribute to a needy subculture while leaving the far needier culture at large to fend for itself.

What artifacts will we leave to the faith entrusted to us? What monuments will the truth we've witnessed inspire? These are the questions that keep me up at night. I have no answers. To be more precise, I am still working on the answers for myself, in my own creative life.

The Good News

The good news is that mine is not a lone voice, and I am by no means crying in the wilderness. In fact, it is a testament to my own limitations that I too easily see the trouble and too quickly forget the progress. If anything, the movement from critical to creative is one that the whole church is striving to make. More people are alive now to the need than ever before, and I can hardly claim to be a prophetic loner on this point. To those who wish to make the transition, to witness powerfully and unconventionally to the truth they have seen, there is more critical support and creative fellowship now than I suppose there has been in a long time. The evangelical subculture, which in some ways has turned our attention away from speaking to the world, is now striving (with mixed results) to be an influence for good.

As much hope and ambition as I have for myself, when I discuss these matters with students I cannot help investing much more expectation in them. In many ways, though they've had challenges of their own, these young Christians have not grown up with some of the misconceptions that dogged my early steps. They have a head start, in other words, and I think they will make the most of it. Whenever I am too cynical, I remember the hundreds of bright eyes shining in the audience, contributors who will take my conclusions as mere starting points. It is an encouraging thought.

In the meantime, the following chapters seek to expand and deepen our understanding of witness as a way of speaking to the world. We turn first to the question of what worldview thinking might have to offer when it comes to defending the faith.

10

Three in One:
Worldview Apologetics

Without the high order of personal unity and diversity as given in the
Trinity, there are no answers.
FRANCIS SCHAEFFER

Festus wasn't sure how the charges should read. He was a Roman official after all, new to his post as governor of Judea, and unfamiliar with the internecine struggles of the Jews. He had inherited this troublesome prisoner from his predecessor Felix and all he could tell was that the man had powerful enemies. Just three days after his arrival, Festus had traveled to Jerusalem from his headquarters in Caesarea where the accused, a Jew named Paul, who possessed Roman citizenship, was being held. The chief priests and leaders had gathered to meet him, urging that Paul be summoned to Jerusalem—but Festus was no fool and he could smell a trap. No, the prisoner would stay in safekeeping back at the base. He had appealed his case to Caesar and to Caesar he would go. But in the meantime, what should Festus write in the letter to accompany Paul on his extradition to Rome?

Considering the controversy that surrounded the man, Festus had expected Paul to be charged with some great evil. Instead, it turned out to be a dispute over obscure theological points that were well beyond the Roman's grasp. In his confusion, the new governor turned to King Herod Agrippa II. Although Agrippa was a client king educated at Rome, he possessed a great interest in Jewish culture and religion. He was the ideal go-between. After hearing Paul's case he would be able to suggest to Festus how the charges should be written up. So, Festus arranged a hearing for Paul before Agrippa.

Paul's Apology

When the king gave the apostle permission to speak, the Bible says Paul "stretched out his hand and made his defense."[1] It is an interesting phrase. The way the gesture is described implies a formality in Paul's behavior; he has assumed the posture of an orator. Indeed, the speech he gives is marked by the formality of its tone, which approaches that of classical Greek (in this sense it parallels Paul's earlier speech at the Areopagus in Athens). The word translated "made his defense" is απελογειτο (*apelogeito*), from the root of which we derive *apology* and *apologetics*. Paul is about to engage in apologetics.

The situation is unique. Although Paul stands in shackles before his royal audience, Agrippa has given him leave to speak freely. True to form, he takes it! What follows is a classic presentation of the gospel of Christ.

Paul gives an outline of his upbringing as a devout Pharisee, reminding Agrippa that the resurrection of the dead is a doctrine the Pharisees believe. He recounts the time he spent persecuting the early Christians, and then shares the testimony of his startling conversion, when a light brighter than the sun poured down from heaven and Christ revealed himself. There, Paul was given his charge to minister to the Gentiles—and all that he has done since that moment has been in obedience to that calling. His message of repentance has consisted of declaring nothing but what Moses and the prophets had already predicted: the coming of the Messiah, his death, and resurrection.

The continuity of the Christian message with that of the Old Testament is one of the key themes in Paul's address. Because Agrippa is familiar with the teaching of the prophets, it is an ideal starting point. In fact, it *is* the starting point. Christ is the fulfillment of the promise the Jews had looked forward to for generations.

The speech affects its hearers in different ways. Agrippa is moved to the edge of his seat. He seems to hang on every word. But Festus scoffs. "Paul, you are out of your mind," he says. "Your great learning is driving you out of your mind."

Paul shakes his head. "I am not out of my mind, most excellent Festus,

---

[1] The account on which this narrative is based is found in Acts 26:1–32.

but I am speaking true and rational words." He is speaking to Festus but his eyes are on the stricken Agrippa. "For the king knows about these things, and to him I speak boldly. For I am persuaded that none of these things has escaped his notice, for this has not been done in a corner."

The apostle is right. None of these things *has* escaped Agrippa's notice. Festus settles back in his chair, a little shaken, himself, after seeing the king's reaction. As Paul speaks, Agrippa is drawn forward, as if he might speak, as if he and Paul were alone in the room.

"King Agrippa," Paul continues, his voice trembling, "do you believe the prophets?" The king's eyebrows raise, his lips part. Paul leans forward. "I *know* that you believe."

A pause. Silence. A stillness so profound that only the sound of Paul's breathing can be heard. Festus is startled by the flash in the apostle's eyes.

Then, Agrippa sinks back and exhales. He coughs and manages to turn the coughing at the last moment into laughter. He tries to make light of the moment: "In a short time would you persuade me to be a Christian?"

But Paul holds his gaze with unwavering intensity. "Whether short or long," he says, "I would to God that not only you but also all who hear me this day might become such as I am—except for these chains."

With a final sweep of the hand he indicates the shackles that bind him; then his hand falls. The defense rests. Agrippa and Festus retire to a private chamber, and as they pass through the door, the king says fervently: "This man is doing nothing to deserve death or imprisonment."

Festus shrugs. "This man could have been set free if he had not appealed to Caesar."

Christian Witness

At Mars Hill, Paul had demonstrated to the Athenians where Christ fit into their conception of the world—and how, entering into it, he transformed it. Before King Agrippa, Paul achieves a similar triumph. Agrippa was not involved in priestly politics. He had no reason to blind himself to the ways in which the life, death, and resurrection of Christ corresponded to what the prophets had foretold. And now, a converted Pharisee stood before him, a man who shared his knowledge of the Old Testament, testifying that he had *seen* the Christ, who was the fulfillment of the promise. Paul showed Agrippa where Christ fit into his worldview and how, entering it, he transformed it.

The twenty-sixth chapter of Acts is one of my favorite passages in Scripture, perhaps because I cannot read it without visualizing the scene. I can almost hear Paul's voice. I can almost feel the emotion of Agrippa, overwhelmed by what he hears to the point of exclamation. When Paul concludes with that audacious challenge—"I know that you believe"—I can feel it in my chest. Whether Agrippa was persuaded or not, I can't tell. But it persuades me.

For Paul, the story of the gospel is also the story of his life. He can share the good news about Christ by simply telling what happened to him. It is the same for every believer. Each of us is a firsthand witness to Christ's power. We can point, just like Paul, to the place where Jesus entered in, and entering transformed everything. There is nothing particularly mystifying about the act of witnessing. It is as simple as telling a story.

Christian witness takes many forms, from door-to-door evangelism and street preaching at one end of the spectrum to personal conversations and lifestyle evangelism at the other. Now that religion has been relegated to the private sphere, people are reluctant to talk about their faith, so a thousand different techniques have emerged to make it easier on the believer. But being a witness really requires no special training. There is no wrong way to share your faith. Most of us are not as bold as Paul, but we all have as good a reason to be bold as he had. Perhaps if we appreciated, as he did, to what a great extent the story of Christ was his story, our faith would flow naturally from our lips and through our lives.

Apologetics is not always thought of as a form of witness. It is too abstract, too philosophical. It is too far removed from everyday concerns and too difficult for a layman to master. For all these reasons and more, we tend to view apologetics and evangelism as two distinct activities. But in this chapter, we will consider them as one. We cannot share the faith without defending it, and we cannot defend it without sharing it. Paul sets the example in the passage we have cited: objections are anticipated and the peculiarity of the audience considered. Paul gives reasons to believe and urges faith in the ones who hear him. The story of the apologist and the evangelist are the same.

The Audacity of Paul

One of the poets Paul quotes at Mars Hill is Aratus, whose poem "Phaenomena" opens with the following lines:

> Let us begin with Zeus, whom we men never leave unspoken. Filled
> with Zeus are all highways and all meeting-places of people, filled are
> the sea and harbours; in all circumstances we are all dependent on
> Zeus. For we are also his children.[2]

That last line should be familiar to readers of Acts 17. Paul, in announcing the identity of "the unknown god" to his Athenian audience, assures them that God "is actually not far from each one of us" (v. 27). He backs up this claim not with an Old Testament quote but with a line attributed to Epimenedes of Crete—"In him we live and move and have our being"—and the aforementioned line from Aratus: "For we are indeed his offspring." The fact that Paul was familiar enough with classical pagan authors to quote lines from their poetry in support of his argument is often cited by teachers today as a mandate for cultural engagement. To speak to our culture, we have to know our culture.

But it seems to me that Paul's behavior is even more striking than this. He doesn't just quote a line from Aratus, he quotes Aratus on *the omnipresence of Zeus*. Think about that for a moment. It's the equivalent of a Christian evangelist supporting his argument with a passage from the Qur'an, applying words originally written about Allah to Yahweh or Christ.

I remember a pastor once expressing his shock that students at a Christian school were assigned readings from the Qur'an in their history class. Is it too much of a stretch to suppose that, in Paul's day, there would have been religious folk equally shocked at the apostle's use of Aratus?

What Paul's action suggests to me is simple enough. A Christian thinker should have no problem reading the work of non-Christian authors, finding the truth there, and putting it in the context of a larger truth. "What has Athens to do with Jerusalem?" It's a first-century question that is still rattling around. To answer, you have to flip the question over. What has Jerusalem to do with Athens? From a Christian perspective, Jerusalem has everything to do with everywhere—there is no place in the world with which Jerusalem has nothing to do. What Paul understood, and what we too often forget, is that the God of Jerusalem is the God of Athens, too. The idols of gold and silver signify nothing. The truth is suppressed everywhere but the truth has a weedy tenacity. It breaks through Achaean marble as easily as it does Judaean sand.

---

[2] *Aratus: Phaenomena*, Cambridge Classical Texts and Commentaries, ed. Douglas Kidd. (Cambridge: Cambridge University Press, 1997), 73.

All Things to All Men

Whenever the gospel story is shared, we should expect questions. The role of the apologist is to give answers. Apologetics is therefore a responsive discipline shaped to a large extent by the kind of questions that are being asked. In 1 Corinthians 9:22, Paul demonstrated the flexibility required to share and defend the faith: "I have become all things to all people, that by all means I might save some." Because the questions change from person to person and generation to generation, the work of the apologist changes, too. The question is whether there are tools and insights to aid the apologist in any situation, answering any kind of question.

Worldview awareness is such a tool. When an unbeliever asks a question, it is tied to other questions, and behind the uncertainties are worldview assumptions. These are not innocent questions. They are not requests for information. Instead, they are intended to kick off a chain of responses that will demonstrate the absurdity of the Christian position. "Tell me," the unbeliever asks, "why should I believe in the Bible?" We educate him about the reliability of texts, the historicity of events, and all the while he is preparing the follow-up. "How do I know it wasn't all made up?" We talk about the improbabilities of such a thing. "But isn't it possible? Isn't it conceivable?" And if we say it isn't, we demonstrate (in his eyes) that we are operating from a position of blind faith and not reason. He has proven his superiority and the ascendancy of his position.

When the average Christian takes up the study of apologetics, he does it in the same spirit and with the same objectives as a person signing up for a class on martial arts. He wants effective fighting techniques. He doesn't want to be educated; he wants to be drilled. When the atheist does this, you respond with that. If he twists this way, you counter that way. The younger the Christian, the greater the expectations. High school students want techniques to take down their future college professors. They want a magic bullet, a *botte secreta*, a special trick to settle this question once and for all.

But the more you grow in grace and wisdom, the more the nature of the problem changes. The mature apologist comes to realize that the real problem isn't a lack of bulletproof arguments; it is the lack of ears to hear. There is no "abstract" apologetic. The faith is always being defended against a specific attack. It is always being presented to a specific people. Apologetics is an incarnational event, an encounter with a decidedly spiritual overtone.

This is where worldview comes into play. Applied to apologetics, worldview awareness emphasizes the interconnectedness of ideas. It probes beneath the questions to the network of assumptions that motivates them. It helps us to see the mental and spiritual state of the person before us.

An apologist with worldview awareness, for example, instinctively knows that the opposition of faith and reason is a false dilemma. When unbelievers talk this way, he probes their epistemological assumptions and starts asking questions of his own. The goal is not to win the argument, but to plant a seed of self-doubt (or, to be more precise, self-knowledge) in the unbeliever's mind. He wants to help the unbeliever test *his own* faith commitments.

Worldview awareness aids the apologist in a number of ways. First, it helps him to appreciate the Christian faith as a whole and orient his special field of interest within the broader context. This is particularly beneficial to scholars seeking to integrate narrowly focused research into an overall picture. Second, worldview awareness promotes understanding of other people's belief systems. In the same way that knowledge of your own grammar helps you acquire other languages, a conceptual map of Christianity helps you identify similarities and differences in the worldviews you encounter. The experience of confronting your own inconsistency also teaches you to be patient with the shortcomings of others.

Perhaps the most significant benefit of worldview awareness to the apologist, though, is that it offers a kind of shortcut to ultimate issues. It is negligent to engage with an unbeliever without communicating the gospel story, but an apologist who gets bogged down in the minutiae of secondary issues might find it difficult to direct the conversation toward Christ. Worldview-conscious Christians become adept at seeing the unbeliever not as an opponent but as a person in need of salvation. They see beyond "healthy skepticism" to the underlying enmity that keeps the unbeliever apart from God.

Worldview Apologetics

We all make worldview assumptions. These assumptions are not things we argue for; they are things we argue *from*. They are premises we treat as axiomatic, not the solutions but the tools that yield solutions. Creation, order, rationality, and fear are all Christian worldview assumptions. Evolution, chaos, irrationality, and autonomy are common assumptions of unbelievers. Although sometimes, for the purposes of debate, we marshal arguments in support of these points, we do not come to believe them as the result of such arguments. Worldview assumptions are faith commitments.

These assumptions often cannot be proven or disproved. No test, no experiment, can demonstrate the existence of God. By the same token, none can demonstrate his nonexistence. This is not to say that arguments cannot be made one way or the other. It's just that each side tends to assume what it is trying to prove and invents epistemologies that favor the assumption. The mid-twentieth-century atheist Antony Flew tried to insist that there was a natural presumption in favor of atheism (as a "neutral" position in contrast to theism, which puts forward a positive claim) and argued that no statement could be meaningful if it could not be proven theoretically to be false.[3] In other words, since no conceivable test could prove that God does not exist, it is meaningless to say that he does. In all of this, Flew was attempting to do in the public square what we all do in the privacy of our minds: stack the deck in favor of our own presuppositions.

Many of the traditional Christian proofs for the existence of God have been criticized on the same count. Anselm's ontological argument, which we will consider more fully in a moment, states that God is the being than which nothing greater can be conceived, and since it is greater to exist than not to exist, God must exist. Today this approach is dismissed as circular reasoning. Anselm's argument works because he has invented a definition of God that makes the conclusion inevitable. If Anselm had been an atheist, he would have come up with a different definition—just as Flew, if he had been a believer, would have considered a presumption of theism to be common sense.

Just because we recognize the role assumptions play in our thinking does not mean that all assumptions are equally valid. Some of us assume that murder is wrong, while others assume that it is not (at least when they do it). These are both assumptions, but they are not equally valid. They are not both "true in their own way." The point is not that everyone has a worldview and all perspectives are valuable. On the contrary, worldviews are only worthwhile to the extent that they are coherent and conform to reality. None of us has a right to our own truth. Worldview thinking actually helps us realize this when it reveals the rock-solid premises we believe

---

[3]Interestingly, Antony Flew has recently modified his position, describing it to Christian apologist Gary Habermas as something akin to deism.

our worldviews are based on to be nothing more than untested assumptions that don't fit together and don't make sense of the world around us. The subjectivity of a perspective does not render it inviolable.

How does worldview apologetics work? The Christian apologist begins with the idea that God created the world. Everything in the world is what God made it to be; what he says about it is true. In other words, God's explanation of things is the best. Whenever a rival worldview contains truth, it will be because the rival has "borrowed" that aspect of its perspective from the biblical worldview. To achieve a semblance of coherence, unbelievers' worldviews will correspond to the biblical worldview on some (usually unacknowledged) points. Because unbelievers do have true beliefs, the apologist knows that if he digs deep enough, he will discover these borrowings. The key is to help the unbeliever see them for what they are, to realize that they do not belong in his perspective, that they are not consistent with his espoused principles. When he is provoked to greater consistency, the unbeliever will have to revise his perspective, either by jettisoning the borrowed truth or by borrowing more.

You can see the three worldview tests—correspondence, coherence, and productivity—at work in this description. The biblical worldview is true; it corresponds perfectly to the way things really are. All truth corresponds to reality and therefore to the biblical perspective. Any time an unbelieving worldview borrows truth, a problem of coherence will develop: the truth doesn't fit within a network of lies. As fallen creatures, we are perfectly capable of holding contradicting ideas in tension (in fact, we can even hold them in the mistaken belief that they are not in tension). But when the contradictions are pointed out to us, we question the validity of the system. Even people who revel in paradox and despise logic don't like to be accused of holding contradictory positions unknowingly. Once a person begins to doubt the fundamental coherence of his perspective, he will test it in terms of observed reality. *Are there better solutions to the problems around me?* If his own beliefs (from which he is already in the process of distancing himself) do not produce solutions, perhaps other, more coherent beliefs would. This is the mind-set the worldview apologist aims to provoke.

The Purpose of Apologetics

There is only one drawback. The description in preceding paragraphs of how apologetics works makes the act of sharing and defending the faith sound like a complex mind game. Christian witness is not a battle of wills. It is not a form of intellectual combat. The kingdom of God is not depending for its triumph on the clever manipulations of an apologetic mastermind. The fishermen of Galilee did not turn the world upside down because they were subtle philosophers; in fact, part of their success lay in the fact they were not.

Like evangelism, apologetics is something we do in the hope that the Holy Spirit will use it to further the divine plan. If we mystify the process—either spiritually or intellectually—we do a disservice to the millions who are called to proclaim and defend the faith with all their heart and with sincerity, though not with the talents of an orator or the intellectual foundations of a theologian. The fact that it is the Spirit and not man who gives witness its edge means that none of us, whatever our qualifications, need hold back from the fray.

A good friend of mine listened to a recording of a celebrated debate between R. C. Sproul and the late Greg Bahnsen. The subject was which apologetic method—the so-called classical method or the presuppositional—was superior. It is a fine and fascinating debate and a worthy question to ponder. My friend found himself siding with Bahnsen's presuppositional arguments, except for one thing: he himself had come to faith with the help of Josh McDowell's book *Evidence That Demands a Verdict*. How could he side against evidentialism when it had been so instrumental in his own conversion?

We discussed the problem in a Starbucks parking lot. It wasn't the first time a theological discussion had lasted later than the shop's closing time and driven the participants onto the pavement. There, among the green metal bistro tables with their umbrellas closed and their chairs strapped down with bicycle chains, my friend made an observation that has survived in my mind as the answer to the question of what apologetics is really good for.

"I didn't get saved by reading McDowell's book," he said. "But reading it made me realize that I didn't have to turn off my brain to become a Christian." The evidence did not so much demand a verdict as justify a verdict that the Spirit was achieving through deeper means.

That's when I realized that apologetics is the task of giving unbelievers a way to justify what the Spirit is doing in their hearts. Like all witnessing, it is a way not to accomplish but to facilitate conversion. It is Paul becoming all things to all men in the hope that some will be saved. The principal virtue in an apologist, then, is the willingness and the flexibility to be used by the Spirit in a variety of situations to help many different kinds of people.

The Value of Arguments

In this context, the traditional proofs for the existence of God are not without value. Perhaps they assume what they need to prove, but now we have seen that to prove anything at all, some things simply *must* be assumed. And these assumptions are not just "taken on faith." They cannot be tested in a laboratory, but there are reasons to believe they are true all the same, as we shall see in a moment.

Anselm's ontological argument is an a priori attempt to prove the existence of God. God can be discovered apart from experience if we contemplate the very concept of God itself. The five ways of Thomas Aquinas work from experience itself toward the existence of God. His first way, the argument from change, is what we more commonly refer to as the cosmological argument. All around us we observe a world in flux, constantly changing, and these changes are effects that must have a cause. The chain of causation cannot go on forever. If we trace everything back, we must find the first cause, the force that set everything in motion. And this force is God. Aquinas relies on the principle that there is no such thing as an effect without a cause; it would be absurd to posit uncaused effects because, by definition, an effect is caused.

Another approach that relies on observation of the world around us—in this case, of human society—is the moral argument. Morality today is typically viewed as an artificial construct. Either it is created by society and imposed on man, or individuals invent it for themselves. Although we persist in viewing certain acts like murder or rape as reprehensible, it is increasingly difficult to justify *why* they are wrong. Somehow, to say that they are wrong because society has determined it does not seem to be enough. Suppose society changed its mind? Would they become right? It seems the answer is yes.

The laws that prohibit homosexual practice, for example, were originally believed to correspond to a higher law. Now that there is no higher law, they are being repealed and the stigma associated with the practice has largely disappeared. I am not comparing murder to homosexuality, but it does raise the question whether a person who believes there is no higher moral code would agree that murder and homosexuality were, in the "old days," wrong in the same way and for the same reasons. That seems unlikely, but to argue that murder was *really* wrong while homo-sexuality *really* wasn't suggests some higher standard from which moral judgments come.

If instead one were to argue that there is no right and wrong in an absolute sense, only the standard imposed by the powerful, then it is hard to account for our moral feelings. Why do we feel that society's condem-nation is *not enough* to damn certain crimes? Why do we feel that some deeds are beyond society's ability to punish if it is society itself that has invented the rules and the corresponding penalties? The fact is, our sense of injustice is grounded in the perception that society's code and what is really just *do not correspond.*

Also, if morality is invented, then why do all men invent it? Shouldn't there be at least one example of a human society without a moral code? (By the same token, if we are not in bondage to sin, then why do all men sin? Shouldn't we be able to point to some examples of people who simply choose not to?) Admittedly, the codes in various societies are not the same. But there is a surprising continuity across borders and cultural boundar-ies. Perhaps it could be explained in a number of ways, but the Christian explanation—that we are created in the image of God, the lawgiver, but fallen—accounts both for the persistence of moral judgment and the warped inconsistency we see in its expression.

This kind of reasoning highlights the value of such abstract argu-ments. It is hard to imagine a situation in which you might find Anselm or Aquinas useful while sharing your faith with the cab driver who's taking you to the airport. Like most people, he is probably not interested. It is also hard to imagine that such arguments would prove useful in talking to your friend the atheist college professor. She will know that for every point you make there is a counter argument. But the ontological, the cosmological, and the moral arguments, along with a host of others, do point to ways in which the Christian worldview coherently accounts for the world around us. Any rival worldview will at least have to come up to that standard—and in attempting it, will find that it is not so easy as it looks.

A Note of Caution

As fascinating as these arguments can be, they ought always to be approached with a certain amount of caution. I quoted Herman Bavinck in chapter 2, but his words are worth repeating here: "Mystery is the vital element of Dogmatics." Forget that and you end up with a closed system that explains nothing but itself and endangers the truth it originally sought to illuminate.

I am reminded of this fact whenever I read "A Visit to Morin," Graham Greene's story about a man who discovers a favorite novelist of his youth and accompanies the writer home after a midnight mass. To his surprise, the man finds that the novelist, Morin, once famous for his Catholic belief, believes no more. And it seems theology is somewhat to blame. Here, Morin explains the dangers of glib theological "answers" to the profound mysteries of faith:

> He said, "A man can accept anything to do with God until scholars begin to go into the details and the implications. A man can accept the Trinity, but the arguments that follow. . . ." He gave a gesture of rejection. "I would never try to determine some point in differential calculus with a two-times-two table. You end by disbelieving the calculus."[4]

The inadequacy of our method leads to the message itself being discarded. Personally, I've never had this experience. For me, the study of theology has increased the mystery, not lessened it. But I know that others, studying the very same things, have had opposite reactions. Perhaps it is necessary to enter into the study with fingers crossed, as it were, so you never lose sight of how tentative our reasoning is, how subject to revision and reform. In the story, Morin singles out the medieval Scholastics for special abuse:

> He said, "Can you find anything more inadequate than the Scholastic arguments for the existence of God?"
> "I'm afraid I don't know them."
> "The arguments from an agent, from a cause?"
> "No."
> "They tell you that in all change there are two elements, that which is changed and that which changes it. Each agent of change is itself determined by some higher agent. Can this go on *ad infinitum*? Oh no, they say, that would not give the finality that thought demands. But does thought demand it? Why shouldn't the chain go on forever? Man has invented the idea of infinity. In any case how trivial any argument based on what human thought demands must be. The thoughts of you and me and Monsieur Dupont. I would prefer the thoughts of an ape.

[4]Graham Greene, "A Visit to Morin," in *Complete Short Stories* (New York: Penguin, 2005), 258.

Its instincts are less corrupted. Show me a gorilla praying and I might believe again."

"But surely there are other arguments?"

"Four. Each more inadequate than the other. It needs a child to say to these theologians, Why? Why not? Why not an infinite series of causes? Why should the existence of a good and a better imply the existence of a best? This is playing with words. We invent words and make arguments from them. The better is not a fact: it is only a word and a human judgement."[5]

I'm grateful that the teachers who introduced me to these arguments always underscored their faults and discouraged me from using them as buttresses for faith. Instead, taken collectively, such arguments were used to demonstrate the internal consistency of the Christian perspective. Yes, they made certain assumptions that could not be proven, but those assumptions were the givens of the faith, and what the various arguments suggested was that these foundations were fit to build upon.

The challenge, I think, for the theologically minded is to be aware of the effect speculation has on faith—our own and that of others. It is one thing to say "God's ways are past finding out" and another to behave as if you actually believe it. If all that's left of mystery in our theology is the word itself, then perhaps we've gone astray.

Trinitarian Arguments

In his book *He Is There and He Is Not Silent*, the conclusion of a celebrated apologetic trilogy, Francis Schaeffer makes a rather remarkable claim. He says that when people ask him how he can believe in the Christian doctrine of the Trinity, he replies: "I would still be an agnostic if there was no Trinity, because there would be no answers. Without the high order of personal unity and diversity as given in the Trinity, *there are no answers*."[6]

Before we consider what Schaeffer is getting at, we need to feel the full force of his words. Although the doctrine of the Trinity is one of the defining tenets of orthodoxy, Christians often treat it as an impenetrable (and inconvenient) mystery. From an apologetic point of view, it is considered a liability. We do *not* want to get into the whole "one God in three persons" issue with an unbeliever, who is prone to give up in confusion. No doubt

---

[5]Graham Greene, "A Visit to Morin," 259.
[6]Francis Schaeffer, *Trilogy* (Wheaton: Crossway, 1990), 287 (emphasis in original). This volume includes *The God Who Is There*, *Escape from Reason*, and *He Is There and He Is Not Silent*.

the reason so many people challenged Schaeffer about the Trinity is that they saw it as Christianity's weak link. Schaeffer, however, treats it as if it is the principal strength of our faith.

Apart from the Trinity there would be no answers. The first time I read this, I was profoundly intrigued. One of the weaknesses of the traditional proofs for God's existence, of course, is that even if they are successful, they establish that there is *a* God. A Christian is more than simply a theist. He wants to prove much more than the existence of some God or another. It is the God revealed in Scripture he wants to proclaim and exalt, not the Prime Mover or the Lawgiver. Francis Schaeffer seemed to be saying that there was a reason to believe not just in a God, but in *the* God—the Father, Son, and Holy Spirit of orthodox Christianity. If Schaeffer was right, it would be something of a breakthrough.

Is Schaeffer Right?

Before I could figure out if he was right, though, I had to determine what he was talking about. For me, that wasn't going to be easy. I am not a philosopher. In fact, I am not particularly well suited to rigorous intellectual exercises by virtue of my inborn lack of discipline. My imagination is always captured by the big picture. This is not to say that I don't get enthusiastic about the details; I do. But my enthusiasm sometimes outstrips my comprehension. That is what happened the first time I read Schaeffer's explanation.

It all had to do, apparently, with the problem of man. Man is a personal being, but also a finite one. To account for his existence we require a God who is personal but also infinite. If we assumed instead an impersonal source of origin, then "everything, including man, must be explained in terms of the impersonal plus time plus chance," and this would (in addition to generating a host of other problems) not adequately account for man's personality. If we assumed a personal but finite God, then we would encounter the same problem that plagued Plato, who "understood that you have to have absolutes, or nothing has meaning." The Greek gods were too limited, too small to meet this requirement, "so although [Plato] knew the need, the need fell to the ground because his gods were not big enough to be the point of reference or place of residence for his absolutes, for his ideals." To bear the weight of this need for absolutes, then, "a personal-infinite God" is required. He must also, according to Schaeffer, possess "a personal unity and diversity."

Well, that left me utterly convinced—but I wasn't sure of what.

I could appreciate the idea that nothing short of a personal begin-ning would account for human intelligence and personality. To require anything less would be to reduce the wonder of man to something unrec-ognizable. This, of course, is what many people do. They start thinking of human beings as a kind of animal (if they are naturally inclined to cyni-cism, a lower order of animal). To do this it is necessary not to see what is evident all around them, the full reality of what it means to be human. To do justice to all that man truly is, we must posit a personal God as our source of origin.

I could also relate to Schaeffer's reference to Plato. I remembered reading *Euthypro*, one of the Socratic dialogues, in which Plato poses the question of whether something is holy because the gods love it, or if the gods love it because it is holy. As a Christian, I chose the former option, but given the finite nature of his gods, Plato had to choose the latter. Holiness was too exalted a concept to be defined by such gods as he knew. They could not bear the weight. So the concept of a personal-infinite God made perfect sense.

There is a radical distinction between God the Creator and all that he has made, expressed in his infinitude and our finitude. So when infinity is taken into account, God stands on one side and everything else, including man, on the other. But man is God's image bearer, so there is something we share with him. When his personality is taken into account, God and man stand together and everything else is on the other side. That much seemed clear.

But why does God's existence necessarily entail both unity and diver-sity? That wasn't so clear to me, but Schaeffer was emphatic:

> We need a personal unity and diversity in God—not just an abstract concept of unity and diversity, because we have seen we need a per-sonal God. We need a personal unity and diversity. Without this we have no answer. Christianity has this in the Trinity.[7]

There it was again, the Trinity. I could understand why the Trinity would be described as personal unity and diversity within God. The doctrine states that there is one God, but within the Godhead there are three per-sons: Father, Son, and Holy Spirit. Neither of the three *is* the other—the Father is not the Son, the Son is not the Spirit, and so on—but each of

---

[7]Francis Schaeffer, *Trilogy*, 286.

them *is* God. They are not each a separate God. They are the three persons of the one God. Thus, within the Christian concept of God there is unity (God is one) and diversity (Father, Son, and Holy Spirit).

But why was this a *necessary* condition? Why did this world in general and man in particular *have* to be created by a God with personal unity and diversity? Schaeffer was saying that it could not have been made by nothing, or by an impersonal force, or by the monotheistic god of (for example) Islam. The first two points I could understand, but the third needed some clarification. If I could only grasp the argument! By faith I believed that the Trinity was the answer, but I wanted to know how Schaeffer could make such unqualified claims:

> There is no other sufficient philosophical answer than the one I have outlined. You can search through university philosophy, underground philosophy, filling-station philosophy—it does not matter—there is no other sufficient philosophical answer to existence, to Being, than the one I have outlined. There is only one philosophy, one religion, that fills this need in all the world's thought, whether the East, the West, the ancient, the modern, the new, the old. Only one fills the philosophical need of existence, of Being, and it is the Judeo-Christian God—not just an abstract concept, but rather that this God is really there. He exists. There is no other answer, and orthodox Christians ought to be ashamed of having been so defensive for so long. It is not a time to be defensive. There is no other answer.[8]

Orthodox Christians should be ashamed? I *did* feel shame. What was this great reality that I had failed to take into account? I was determined to find out.

The One and the Many

From the dawn of Western philosophy, men have sought the unifying principle of all reality. We see so many different things around us, so many manifestations. What is it that brings them all together? What is the fundamental reality? Is everything ultimately One? Some thinkers have believed this. Others, though, have argued that the basic principle of existence is change, metamorphosis, diversity. You can never step into the same river twice.

Over the millennia the debate has taken many forms. It is most familiar, perhaps, as the struggle between universals and particulars. When I

---

[8]Ibid.

explain this dilemma I like to use my two cats as examples. Hugo and Clive are both cats, both from a species called Tonkinese, which is a blend of Siamese and Burman. In spite of the exotic name, Tonkinese cats were originally bred in the United States by owners who wanted the sleek beauty of the Siamese cat without the well-known propensity of those beasts for condescension. *We are Siamese, if you please. We are Siamese if you don't please.* The experiment worked. It is hard to imagine more emotionally needy, less aloof animals than Hugo and Clive. They are the quintessential hedonists, living only to eat, sleep in the sun, and be stroked by humans. They are particularly insistent on the last point, and to see the goal fulfilled they will climb into a stranger's lap, run under his feet, and even upend themselves in his path, belly up, to indicate what is expected. Most people have a hard time, when they first encounter these lords of the house, telling the two of them apart. They are very similar to one another—and to all the other Tonkinese, too. In that sense, they might as well be the same: representatives of the universal Cat.

Catness is an idea that distinguishes both Hugo and Clive from other animals, such as the neighbor's dog. If one of them were to run away to the circus, his Catness would be the most important, the most essential thing about him, distinguishing him from the lion, the monkey, and the elephant. But Hugo and Clive roam in a suburban kingdom all their own, within which every animal present possesses Catness, and they are distinguished by their personalities. Hugo is older and a bit more reserved; Clive is much more affectionate but terribly shy. Hugo likes to position himself atop bookshelves and make a dash for the front door whenever it is opened. Clive likes to walk along the stairway railing and get himself trapped inside closets and cabinets. In terms of personality, they could not be more different.

I never find myself worrying about the philosophical status of my cats. But if I were inclined to, they might be a perfect example of the problematic relationship between universals and particulars. How do I know that Hugo and Clive are cats and not dogs? They have this quality of Catness that differentiates them. But is it really a quality? Is there really some Platonic feline ideal stored in my mind or out in the universe that gives me access to this notion? Or is it that Hugo and Clive are real, and Catness is just a convenient construct for pigeonholing them?

Some philosophers would say that the universal of Catness is real, and others would say that only the particulars, Hugo and Clive, are real. Some would say that all of reality is ultimately One, and others that all of reality is ultimately Many. The starting principle of the universe is either unity or diversity.

In our own age, with its suspicion of unifying narratives, the tendency has been toward particularism. We emphasize diversity to such an extent that unity seems both impossible and undesirable. With no concept of the transcendent, no tolerance of the absolute, it is difficult to speak in terms of universals. As Greg Bahnsen notes:

> Non-Christians have stumbled badly over [the problem of the one and the many] (and have sometimes wished simply to ignore it), and thus a persistent effort has been made throughout the history of philosophy to reduce all such abstract, general, or universal entities (or talk about them) to concrete or particular things (or talk about them). All such attempts have proved to be unpersuasive or lacking in cogency. We regularly think and speak and reason in terms of general concepts.[9]

Affirming either side seems to negate the other, or at least make it less real. If we have an ultimate unity, then diversity is really an illusion. In the case of ultimate diversity, then the appearance of unity is just that, an appearance. In everyday terms, we operate as if both things are true—as if universals are real and particulars are real and neither is more real than the other. We behave as if unity and diversity are equally ultimate.

Trinitarian Epistemology

When he made the argument that intrigued me so much, Francis Schaeffer was drawing on an insight formulated by Cornelius Van Til, a professor of apologetics Schaeffer had studied under at Westminster Theological Seminary. Van Til had made the claim that there is no way to account for knowledge without assuming the ontological Trinity revealed in Scripture, and he based the claim at least in part on the doctrine's resolution of the problem of the one and the many:

> As Christians, we hold that in this universe we deal with a derivative one and many, which can be brought into fruitful relation with one another because, back of both, we have in God the original One and Many. If we are to have coherence in our experience, there must be a correspondence of our experience to the eternally coherent experience of God. Human knowledge ultimately rests upon the internal coher-

---

[9]Greg L. Bahnsen, *Van Til's Apologetic: Readings & Analysis* (Phillipsburg, NJ: P&R, 1998), 238.

ence within the Godhead; our knowledge rests upon the ontological Trinity as a presupposition.[10]

Both universals and particulars are essential to knowledge. Whatever our ideological convictions, we make use of both on a daily basis. So the question really isn't which one is superior to the other, which is real and the other false. The issue is how we justify the fact that they exist and we make use of them. Van Til and Schaeffer are saying that we can't justify the existence of universals and particulars in any other way than with the doctrine of the Trinity.

Because God is triune, the world he made possesses unity and diversity, universals and particulars. In fact, you would expect a God with unity and diversity in his person to create precisely the sort of world in which we live. The unity and diversity we see around us are derived, as Van Til said, from the unity and diversity in the personality of God. That is why Schaeffer says only such a God can account for the world as it is. When we possess knowledge, we assume the existence of such a God, whether we believe in him or not.

Although it resolves a fundamental philosophical problem, the doctrine of the Trinity was not formulated for that purpose. Instead, it emerged as the early church affirmed and defended truths about God revealed in Scripture. The divinity of the Son and the personality of the Spirit: as heretical sects denied these doctrines, the church defended them and in the process expressed the doctrine of the Trinity, an ingenious example of how theology ought to be done.

The doctrine affirms what Scripture requires—that Father, Son, and Spirit are all God, and that they are all distinct persons—but does not go on to speculate about how this all works. The reason the Trinity is approached as a mystery is that the precise nature of God is not fully explained in Scripture. The orthodox doctrine includes what is expressly taught and excludes what is clearly not, but it stops short of a complete explanation because where Scripture is silent, we must be silent.

If the doctrine was not formulated to address the problem of the one and many, then how does it happen to achieve just that? The truth is coherent. Because God made the world, and the world (or rather, the philosophers' inadequate concept of the God who made the world) gave rise

---

[10]Cornelius Van Til, *An Introduction to Systematic Theology*, Vol. 5, In Defense of Biblical Christianity (Phillipsburg, NJ: P&R, 1974), 23.

to the problem, it is to be expected that a proper concept of God would resolve it. As Schaeffer explains:

> [The Council of Nicaea] did not invent the Trinity to meet the need; the Trinity was already there and it met the need. They realized that in the Trinity we have what all these people are arguing about and defining, but for which they have no answer.[11]

This is an example of the kind of productivity that characterizes truth. The biblical worldview, at the heart of which lies the doctrine of God, solves problems that other worldviews leave unresolved, because it corresponds to truth in a way that they do not.

Problem Solved?

Van Til's argument is transcendental. In other words, it operates not on the basis of reason or evidence, but on the impossibility of the contrary. When Van Til insisted that all predication presupposes the Trinity, he meant that it was necessary to presuppose the Trinity (with its implicit unity and diversity) in order to make a proposition intelligible. The person making the statement may not believe in the God of Scripture, but the statement itself assumes his existence. To assume the contrary would reduce the proposition to incoherence.

Of course, no argument is without its critics, and there are thinkers both inside and outside the church who find this line of reason unsatisfying. If I were proposing it as a magic bullet, a failsafe apologetic technique, I would be obliged to interact with their arguments and come to some conclusion. But all this philosophical rigor is sadly far beyond me, and my goal is only to suggest that Van Til and Schaeffer have put forward an argument to join the classical proofs—and surpass them, since it is the God of the Bible and not a generic theism that the argument puts forward. And this is an example, I suggest, of what worldview awareness can achieve in apologetics.

One of the things that makes the transcendental argument so compelling is that it goes to the heart of things. It really raises the stakes. This is not the kind of apologetic that contents itself to quibble over minor points. It is a massive retaliation against unbelief, the theological equivalent of a hydrogen bomb.

Why? Because it moves from the defensive to the attack, justifying the faith by challenging the unbeliever to justify himself apart from it.

---

[11]Francis Schaeffer, *Trilogy*, 289.

11

The Enigma of Unbelief

If God himself had appeared to me, it would have changed nothing. In fact, I have only to hear the word God and a curtain comes down in my head.

BINX BOLLING, IN WALKER PERCY'S *THE MOVIEGOER*

[1]

It was one of my infamous trick questions. The regular students knew by now to approach them cautiously or not at all. In fact, they had come to treat every question I asked as if it were designed to elicit a theologically deficient response for me to pounce on. But Andre was new. He didn't know the teacher was out to get him. I posed the question, and when everyone else maintained a stony, measured silence, Andre decided to take a crack at it.

Here was the question. You and your unbelieving friend both hear the gospel. You respond by repenting of your sins and believing in Christ. Your friend remains indifferent. Now, what is the difference between the two of you? What is it about you that made you accept the gospel while your friend didn't?

Andre looked around the table before raising his hand. "Well," he said, "It's not that I was better than him."

"Okay, then what was it?"

I could tell by his expression that he was giving it some thought, looking not for the answer I wanted to hear but for the truth. I liked Andre already, but that made me really warm to him. He was more interested in speaking the truth than avoiding embarrassment.

"I guess I would say this," he began. "I've always been the kind of person to hear things out. A lot of people have already made up their minds, so they don't really listen. Maybe the difference was that I give things the benefit of the doubt and my friend is close-minded."

I nodded. That wasn't a bad answer at all. "So, the difference between you and the person who rejected the gospel is that you're the kind of person who pays attention. You're a better listener."

Andre demurred, a little bashful. "I guess so," he said.

Now the other hands went up. It is interesting how, even in a Bible study, people guard against exposing their weakness but jump at the chance to take advantage of someone else's. I decided not to open up the floor.

"So what you're saying is, you are saved because you are a better listener than your friend?"

Now Andre saw the trap. "I'm not saying *that*. I was saved by God's grace, not because I was a better listener."

"All right," I said. "Then what's the difference between the two of you?"

He wasn't certain. He said, "God's grace?"

Now I opened up the floor and a flood of commentary filled the room. The conversation bounced back and forth around the table leaving both Andre and me in silence. He was nodding in my direction; he'd gotten the point, and unlike many people (myself included) he was grateful for the experience. It is God's grace that separates us, and beyond that it is difficult to go. Beyond that there is, frankly, an enigma.

Simple Ignorance

Either you do believe or you don't. What's the enigma in that? The Bible refers to the unbeliever as a fool. Psalm 14 begins, "The fool says in his heart, 'There is no God.'" People are fools to reject Christ and it's as simple as that. What more needs to be said?

There is more, actually. The gospel is not a line in the sand that divides the wise men from the fools. Our salvation leaves us with nothing to boast about apart from Christ. If we are saved, it is not because God approved of our wisdom while rejecting the folly of others. In fact, Psalm 14 makes that abundantly clear:

> The LORD looks down from heaven on the children of man,
> > to see if there are any who understand,
> > who seek after God.

They have all turned aside; together they have become corrupt;
　　there is none who does good,
　　not even one.[1]

Apart from God's mercy, we are all fools. None of us apart from his grace does good. None of us apart from his goodness seeks after him. We are as worthy of condemnation as our unbelieving friends. Only by God's grace do we escape it.

This ought to provoke a sense of compassion toward unbelievers, but all too often Christians are guilty of self-righteousness. That is certainly what happened in my case. I was raised in church, so I enjoyed all the benefits that come from living in a Christian home and being part of a community of faith. But somehow I imagined that my only knowledge of sinners (apart from myself) was through the outrageous anecdotes I heard in sermons. The sermons were not to blame, though. Somehow I came to understand Christianity doctrinally without grasping certain aspects experientially, which is just a complicated way of confessing that I lacked mercy toward unbelievers.

If you had asked me, I would have admitted that I was a sinner and that my salvation was by grace through faith. Theologically, nothing separated me from my agnostic neighbors but God's grace. In practice, though, I had the heart of a self-satisfied Pharisee and looked upon myself as one who had had the wisdom to do what was required when others (*thank you, Lord, that I am not like them!*) chose to neglect the call. In my early teens, this sinful pride manifested itself primarily in taunting my Catholic friends and assuring them that the pope would not make it to heaven. Ironically enough, these friends had accompanied their parents to a Billy Graham meeting and been converted in the evangelical manner, so I would have been justified in treating them as brothers in Christ rather than deceived fools dancing on the precipice of damnation.

When I left home for college, I actually fretted over whether the university—a conservative liberal arts college sponsored by the Tennessee Baptist Convention—would be sufficiently spiritual. For a long time, I would not attend church services at all because the only ones available were Southern Baptist (as independents we were accustomed to thinking of a "convention" as one step removed from prelacy). In terms of spiritual devotion, I really had no reason to be proud. I was less mature in the faith

---
[1]Ps. 14:2–3.

than many of the students I viewed with such condescension. I knew my Bible better than they did, but they seemed to take more joy in it.

And that is what finally taught me to see. While I was generally more knowledgeable than they were, they were much more devout. Their faith meant more to them. They were more open about it, too. I didn't like to talk about Christianity even with other Christians, unless they were from my particular sect. But the people I was surrounded with had no such inhibitions. They would talk about Christ at the drop of a hat—and even though I sometimes cringed at the things they said, I came to realize that there was something I could learn. This was the beginning of a long spiritual thaw.

Perhaps the final step in that process was coming to see unbelievers through the lens not of my pride but of my faith. The care of other Christians less strict but more devout than me for the souls of people to whom I was frankly indifferent moved me more than any sermon could have done. Christian charity must be lived and not merely professed.

Certainly there are times when the Bible addresses unbelievers with scorn. Persistent rejection of the merciful Creator in the face of so many witnesses to his existence, his goodness, and his love is an unforgivable crime. It is not reasonable; it is not even comprehensible. But because I have something in common with those unrepentant rebels, I cannot help but feel for them. The apostle Paul longed for the salvation of sinners. For the rescue of his fellow Jews, he would have given up his own deliverance. The depth of his compassion is something I could never equal. But it is an example to follow.

Christian witness must be based in compassion for the lost. God requires it. Mere obedience to the Great Commission is not enough. As in all things, he demands the service not only of our hands but of our will and of our heart. If we do not long for the spectacle of a saved humanity, we do not wish to see his kingdom come.

Worthy of Grace

My question to Andre was designed to teach the lesson I myself had learned at such a cost: that we are not saved because we deserve it. I am sure that Andre already knew this. But I wonder if he and thousands more like him really *understood* it. It is one thing to confess that we are saved by grace alone through faith alone and quite another to be convinced in the depth of our soul that we were undeserving.

I admit it. I often think of myself as worthy of grace. Worthy of grace? This must be the quintessential oxymoron. And yet, there is a rebellious way in me, a vestige of the old self, that rears up its head more often than I would like to admit and tries to convince the rest of me that there is something in this to boast about. How could there not be? The gospel has gone out to the four corners of the world. Millions upon millions have heard and not believed. But I, I! Given the choice, did I delay? Given the opportunity, did I resist? None of my work, surely, merited this gift, but at least when he knocked, *the Savior found me ready!*

This boasting is sinful. It is painful to admit. But I am afflicted with a pride that, as unfounded in reality as it is, is nothing short of Promethean.

On the topic of the believer's adoption in Christ, the apostle John writes that we are born "not of blood nor of the will of the flesh nor of the will of man, but of God."[2] Paul says this mercy of God "depends not on human will or exertion, but on God, who has mercy."[3] The more we come to know ourselves, the more comfort these passages bring. When our sense of sin abates and we do enough good to satisfy ourselves, it is hard not to imagine that God favors us for some value he finds in us. And if this is so, then it explains the unbeliever's state, too. God withholds favor from him because, searching the fool, he finds nothing in him of comparable worth.

No Excuse for You

Other worldviews do not have this problem. If a man can save himself, either by keeping the balance of good and evil deeds tilted toward the good, or in accumulating grace through obedience and sacraments, then it is clear to him why he is saved and others are not. They have not done what he has done! But when salvation is by grace alone, there is no distinction to make. Ironically enough, the same generation that rediscovered the doctrines of predestination and election also championed the grace of God in salvation, emphasizing that (whatever the mysteries of God's decree of election might be) no man has anything to boast of but Christ. Apart from grace we are all the same, all equals in a fellowship of rebellion.

When Paul describes the guilty knowledge of God that comes through natural revelation, he concludes by addressing the reader: "Therefore you

---

[2]John 1:13.
[3]Rom. 9:16.

have no excuse, O man. . . ."[4] He does not say that they have no excuse before God. *You* have none. *I* have none. If God has mercy on us, it is not because of who we are, but because of who he is.

[II]

In his novel *The Moviegoer*, Walker Percy gives a description of unbelief that goes to the heart of the enigma. It is a passage spoken by Binx Bolling, the novel's existentialist antihero, describing his complete indifference to Christianity:

> My unbelief was invincible from the beginning. I could never make head or tail of God. The proofs of God's existence may have been true for all I know, but it didn't make the slightest difference. If God himself had appeared to me, it would have changed nothing. In fact, I have only to hear the word God and a curtain comes down in my head.[5]

That curtain is what ought to give us, as Christian witnesses, something to ponder. Percy, himself a Christian, has given a sense of the inner life of unbelief that is more observant than that of many theologians. Binx Bolling is not unaware of the gospel. He has grown up with it. He is very much at home in a church service in spite of his unbelief. It is not ignorance that keeps him from faith; it's bafflement.

This passage uncovers four ironies of unbelief. The point of exploring them is not to mock unbelievers, but to give Christians confidence in approaching them boldly. We are too easily intimidated and, as a result, our interactions with unbelievers are sometimes conducted defensively and without consideration. By examining the inconsistencies that underlie "invincible unbelief," we can develop more compassion for those who, like Binx Bolling, can't make head or tail of God.

Irony #1: Unbelief Treats God as the Enigma

The real issue in any evangelistic or apologetic encounter is the unbeliever's lack of repentance and faith. Faced with the testimony of all creation, it is a mystery that anyone would obstinately persist in willful blindness. But more often than not, the unbeliever turns the tables on you, so that the conversation is transformed into one about the very existence of God. As a Christian, you are made to feel that in bringing up God, you have

---

[4]Rom. 2:1.
[5]Walker Percy, *The Moviegoer* (New York: Vintage, 1998), 145.

proposed a somewhat hair-brained and baffling concept. Modern people don't believe in things like that. In modern life, God is the solution to a problem that no longer exists.

Binx Bolling says, "My unbelief was invincible from the beginning. I could never make head or tail of God." There was no question of religious faith. This notion of God was a curiosity, a puzzle, but ultimately it made no sense. To the unbeliever, the mystery is not his own lack of faith but that any right-minded person believes in this notion of God.

From the Christian perspective, this is deeply ironic. That a creature would regard the Creator as a bit of an oddity is perversely stupid. And yet, what believer has not been guilty of the same fault? The difference is, while unbelievers reject the existence of God, we confess it while behaving as if he is as bizarre in his demands and peculiarities as they make him out to be.

The spiritual blindness at the back of unbelief prevents those who lack faith from seeing themselves or God in the proper light. What is it that provokes this blindness? It is sin and our desire to continue in it. It is our passion for autonomy and a refusal to acknowledge even the possibility of a God who might rob us of it.

In the face of such indifference, it is important for the evangelist/apologist to remember that this attitude toward God reflects a crisis of the heart. It is a spiritual problem. It is brought about by suppressing the fundamental truth of existence. When people shrug away the God they cannot make head or tail of, we should neither give up in frustration nor retaliate in kind. Do not be offended. The Spirit needs to work in the life of this person; do everything you can to be a part of that process.

Irony #2: Unbelief Is a Faith Commitment

In the preceding chapter, I mentioned philosopher Antony Flew and his "presumption of atheism." Unbelievers often conceive of themselves as neutral observers in the debate over faith. Their lack of faith is intellectual prudence; until there is convincing evidence for the existence of some higher power, it makes sense to reserve judgment. They don't see God anywhere, so it makes sense to assume that he is not there. The burden of proof is on the Christian. If there is a God, prove it.

As a counterbalance to this view, consider the parable Jesus told about the rich man and Lazarus. When the rich man dies, he finds himself in torment and appeals to Father Abraham. At first, he asks for the impossible: a visit from Lazarus, who will bring soothing water to relieve the rich man's suffering. When this fails, the rich man appeals to Abraham: "Then I beg you, father, to send [Lazarus] to my father's house—for I have five brothers—so that he may warn them, lest they also come into this place of torment." This seems to be a selfless (even evangelical) impulse. It's too late for me, the rich man concedes, but at least my brothers may be spared this!

But Abraham replies, "They have Moses and the Prophets; let them hear them." In other words, like the rich man himself, the brothers have already been warned. They simply have not heeded Moses and the prophets.

"No, father Abraham," the rich man pleads, "but if someone goes to them from the dead, they will repent." Perhaps the prophets might warn them, the rich man implies, but what is needed is something clear, something straightforward, something that sinners cannot help but believe.

Abraham's reply is rich in foreshadowing: "If they do not hear Moses and the Prophets, neither will they be convinced if someone should rise from the dead."[6] The implication is clear: Christ is on the verge of dying and being resurrected—someone will rise from the dead—but if the witness that is already there does not suffice, then neither will this new miracle.

Unbelief is not neutrality awaiting evidence. It is a faith commitment of its own. As Binx Bolling says, "The proofs of God's existence may have been true for all I know, but it didn't make the slightest difference."

Christians have a tendency to believe the lie that if only we had enough evidence, if only we could devise a good enough argument, then fair-minded unbelievers would get off the fence and join us. But there are no fair-minded unbelievers. There are no neutral observers in the battle between good and evil. Unbelief is not so much lack of faith as faith that there is no Creator, no Lord, and no Righteous Judge. It is a wager made in spite of the odds (and the evidence), for no other reason than that a sinful man would prefer that there be no God.

The proofs for God's existence would make no difference to Bolling not because they are circular or because he has other, better arguments at his disposal; they would make no difference because they lead to a conclusion he has already decided against.

Atheism requires faith. In fact, atheism *is* faith—faith that there is no God. To live according to his faith, an atheist must be willing to

---
[6]Luke 16:19–31.

reinterpret the facts to fit his prior assumption that there can be no God. Transcendent morality would support the existence of God, so it cannot be. The law of cause and effect would support it, so the law of cause and effect must sometimes be suspended. If the very existence of universal concepts suggests some divine mind, then universals cannot exist. The assumption of atheism, if it is consistently pursued, requires that every area of life be robbed of transcendence. Fortunately, atheism is only rarely pursued consistently!

Binx Bolling is not a consistent atheist. If anything, he is indifferent. God may exist or not—it is a matter of indifference. In this, he is typical of unbelievers.

Irony #3: Unbelief Will Not Accept Proof

The unbeliever calls your bluff: "I would believe if only there were proof. You say there is a God; well, prove it to me and I will believe." You think at first that this is a breakthrough—finally, he is ready to listen! But then you discover what he means by proof. Scripture is not proof because the disciples might have lied. History is not truth because it is written by the winners. Experience is not proof because it is subjective. Logic is not proof because, in our postmodern world, it is simply a construct. When it comes down to it, the only admissible evidence is for God to put in a personal appearance.

Of course, this is precisely what Christ did, and as far as the unbeliever is concerned it doesn't count. Binx Bolling's words echo those of Abraham to the rich man: "If God himself had appeared to me, it would have changed nothing."

There is a sense in which I do not agree. When God appears to man, even with only a refracted portion of his glory, they fall down and worship. It is not, I suspect, a voluntary action, at least not in the sense that they observe the glory, ponder its significance, and then make a decision to acknowledge it by prostrating themselves. Instead, it is the response to holiness that is built into humanity. If God himself appears to you, expect to be stunned senseless and on the ground in a posture of abject humiliation and selfless worship.

And yet God has appeared to us in Christ and, as John reports, "his own people did not receive him."[7] God appeared in the flesh, he came and dwelled with us, and for some it really did change nothing. This is

---

[7]John 1:11.

an irony—indeed, a horror—of unbelief: it will not accept proof. As a Christian, you sometimes wrestle with doubt. In spite of your own experience of Christ, you entertain "proofs" that there is no God. What if you're wrong? What if it is all a lie? What if you have refrained from sin while all along you could have indulged with impunity? Although we are sometimes accused of being blind to the evidence against our position, if anything I suspect we are too sensitive to it, too concerned to shape our expressions of faith in ways that will not seem too ridiculous to those who think the whole thing is ridiculous to begin with.

Do unbelievers struggle in this same way? To be honest, I don't know. I know many Christians who report that before they came to faith, they struggled with the reality of God, but I have never heard an unbeliever say as much. In fact, I think they sense this difference in us and draw comfort from it: even with all our supposed confidence, we still have doubts, we still cannot be absolutely sure, while they are quite sure and never troubled with doubt in the night. Their faith comes naturally while ours seems so alien to human nature, so contrary to what is (to them) self-evident. When an unbeliever struggles, it is the Spirit working in him to bring him to truth. When we struggle, what is it? The old, crucified self, refusing to stay dead. And this leads to the final irony.

Irony #4: Unbelief Is a Spiritual, Not an Intellectual, Condition

The way it works is this (or so we're told): reason and experience agree that there is no God, but some need (read "weakness") within certain people leads them to make a leap of faith. They close their eyes to certain truths and hope against hope that reality is not what every shred of evidence suggests. These people find comfort in religion, and frankly it doesn't matter which one. To the extent that it soothes the feathers of such folk, religion is actually a good thing. Where it goes wrong, of course, is in attempting to impose on those who know better the spiritual beliefs of those who ought to—i.e., religion has no place in the public square.

What this explanation assumes is that unbelief is an intellectual state, while faith is a spiritual (that is to say, subintellectual, irrational) condition. In fact, there is a spiritual component to life, and the unbeliever is right to say that faith belongs to it. Where he errs, though, is in thinking that the Christian operates in that realm while the unbeliever does not. Man was made to worship the Creator. If he worships the creature instead, it is a subversion of the desire placed within him—but the subversion occupies the same spiritual plane.

Unbelief, as we have seen, is a faith commitment, and that means it is a spiritual, not an intellectual, condition.

Disputation is an intellectual exercise, but witness is spiritual. Sometimes Christians approach it as a game of the intellect, but the unbeliever faced with the gospel *knows* that he is being engaged on the spiritual plane. The challenge is not just to some notions he holds about human origins and morality. These are, for all practical purposes, matters of indifference. The real challenge of the gospel is that it demands from those who hear it a complete surrender, a sacrifice of their autonomy at the foot of the cross. The gospel expects from the unbeliever precisely what he does not wish to give.

Christianity requires much more than intellectual assent. It is a complete spiritual transformation, a rebuilding (even a recreation) of the fallen creature. In salvation Christ begins a work in us that carries through to the last day and our ultimate glorification. No area of life remains untouched, no zone of existence holds on to its independence. We die to self to live in Christ and that is something that goes well beyond the intellectual sphere. When Christ knocks, he intends to enter and take possession. The Savior does not negotiate terms. He does not offer rain checks, either.

Binx Bolling says, "I have only to hear the word God and a curtain comes down in my head." And no wonder. When Christ enters in he transforms everything, and there are people who would rather build a wall between themselves and the truth than cede such power over themselves to a holy God.

[III]

There are questions an unbeliever doesn't want to ask. The Christian witness wants to see them answered. The problem, though, is that they need to come from within. They are questions best asked by the unbeliever himself. Perhaps the whole art of witness—to the extent that there is an art at all—lies in learning the right questions and helping others to ask themselves.

The fact is, unbelief is complex and confusing. While the Spirit, not human persuasion, is responsible for rescuing the lost, it is good for the witness to understand the basic inconsistencies inherent in the unbeliever's mind-set. If nothing else, it will help him to direct the conversation in profitable directions. For insight into the psychological complexities of unbelief, we turn again to Cornelius Van Til:

> [The unbeliever] lives out of two conflicting frameworks of thought or two mind-sets. He works with two antagonistic sets of presuppositions, and that leaves him in a terrible personal and intellectual state of conflict. One set of presuppositions makes his reasoning, convictions, and commitments possible and intelligible; however, his reasoning, convictions, and commitments constitute a conflicting system of thought and presuppositions which would, if followed out consistently, destroy the intelligibility of his thinking and experience.[8]

So far, we have talked about the Christian's worldview and the unbeliever's as if they were two separate things, but in fact they are not. Just as Christians often fail to realize a fully Christian view of reality, unbelievers find it necessary to adopt at least part of the Christian view to make their own perspective work.

The goal of the Christian witness, then, is not so much to refute rival worldviews as to point the unbeliever to the vestiges of the biblical worldview in his own perspective. An example of this might prove helpful. Apologists who specialize in work with Mormons or Jehovah's Witnesses both make use of the fact that these sects, while departing from biblical faith, still consider the Bible as part of their sacred literature. By appropriating Scripture in this way, the founders of each religion have built in a necessary incoherence, and Christian apologists find that one of the most useful ways to provoke a Mormon or Jehovah's Witness to start asking questions about his own perspective is to help him see the inconsistencies between what the Bible teaches and what his religious institution demands.

Every unbelieving worldview suffers from a similar problem. While departing from the biblical faith, each one relies in some way upon the God of the Bible. If we accept the argument by Van Til that predication presupposes the ontological Trinity, then we can go so far as to say that every unbelieving worldview relies upon the most quintessentially Christian doctrine for whatever coherence it can muster.

Of course, all this makes the task of the witness harder, not easier. There is no chance that the unbeliever will submit intellectually to the

---

[8]Cornelius Van Til, *Introduction to Systematic Theology*, in Greg L. Bahnsen, *Van Til's Apologetic: Readings & Analysis* (Phillipsburg, NJ: P&R, 1998), 452.

doctrine of the Trinity as logically necessary to his perspective *without changing his perspective*—i.e., without repenting of his sin and believing in Christ. So while the practically minded apologist, who is also looking for ways to "use this" on an atheist, wants a tool that will convince the unbeliever so that he can be won, the worldview perspective on unbelief is saying, "Win him and then he will be convinced."

As frustrating as this might seem, it is the right answer.

12

Imagining the Truth:
Christians and
Cultural Contribution

No ideology can tolerate a full historical consciousness. Only realism can.
CLIVE JAMES

[I]

Ever since H. Richard Niebuhr wrote *Christ & Culture*, believers have been telling themselves how important it is to "engage" the culture. Originally, Niebuhr cataloged five attitudes toward the relationship between Christ and culture—"Christ against Culture," "The Christ of Culture," "Christ above Culture," "Christ and Culture in Paradox," and "Christ the Transformer of Culture"—but today the spectrum is usually narrowed to three: isolation, assimilation, and engagement.

Christians who believe in isolation retreat from culture. Like the monastic orders of old, they seek to follow Christ by living outside the world. Ideally, they would prefer a hermetically sealed environment, but since that is not possible, they will construct a counterculture that allows them to take shelter from the influences of the world around them. Isolationists are the spiritual equivalent of the Amish, building a safer life for themselves and their children by steering clear of the culture.

On the other end of the spectrum are the assimilationists, Christians who seek to follow Christ by becoming one with the culture. If the isolationist emphasizes *not of the world*, the assimilationist is decidedly *in the world*. His values are largely the ones of the people around him. As a

Christian, he wants to be a responsible member of the larger community, to share its outlook and concerns. Unlike the isolationist, he sees himself as a part of the world rather than an opponent of it.

The third category is engagement, and here the Christian seeks to follow Christ in transforming culture. Where the isolationist runs and the assimilationist joins, the transformer fights. It is a constructive kind of warfare, though, seeking to further the goals of Christ's kingdom on earth. Since it is the third choice on the list, it is obviously the right one, and anyone (myself included) who talks about this topic expects you to go out and "engage" the culture.

But there is a fatal flaw in this line of thought.

Casting the First Stone

The problem is that no single Christian embodies any of these tendencies perfectly. In fact, all three are present in every tradition, every denomination, every church, and every believer. We all isolate ourselves; we all assimilate; we all, in one way or another, engage. Now that everyone realizes engagement is the "right" answer, everything we do is described as engaging the culture, even when it is actually isolation or assimilation. A mega-church can put a gymnasium and a coffee house on its campus and say that it is engaging the culture, when what it is really doing is creating a safe cocoon for its members. A youth pastor can pierce his tongue and host a skateboarding event for the community, calling it engagement, when in fact it looks more like assimilation.

I'm in no position to cast the first stone. An author can write a book about Christian worldview, wisdom, and witness and tell himself he is engaging the culture, when at the very best he is engaging the Christian subculture, and perhaps not doing that very effectively. The point is that we cannot live our lives as normal and rechristen every action as "engagement." Isolation and assimilation are not things other people do. We should be honest about what our efforts really amount to and reserve the language of transformation for the things that really achieve it.

When all is said and done, engagement is Christian witness. Even further, it is an active, working witness present in evangelism and apologetics but also (perhaps especially) in works of compassion that actually *bear witness* to the transforming power of Christ. Because our good works don't save us, we're inclined not to bother, but as the apostle James demanded: "Show me your faith apart from your works, and I will show you my faith by my works."[1] Real engagement is not entertainment and not a sense of personal authenticity; it is work.

Transforming Power

The real transforming power is not our own but Christ's. Evangelism transforms culture by winning people to Christ, apologetics by challenging a culture's assumptions and thereby turning it to Christ. But there is a third work that is remarkably powerful but not often acknowledged. Rather than making use of it, the church has often mistaken it for a threat: the imagination. How can imagination transform culture? It does so by giving it new eyes.

The power of imagination was not lost on men like G. K. Chesterton and C. S. Lewis. Yes, they were men of faith, but first and foremost we remember them as men of story, men of imagination. And today their stories move us as much, if not more, than their apologetics. As a reader, one of the most striking glimpses I have ever had of the divine came at the climax of *The Man Who Was Thursday*, a novel that starts as a thriller about anarchists and ends in a very different place indeed. If there is a lesson to be learned from this, it is that the truth can be proclaimed and it can be defended, but it can also be *imagined*.

An Imaginative Calling

Christians in search of a prototype for this imaginative calling need look no further than the psalmist David. He was a warrior king, a man of action, and yet his principal legacy to us is literary. What was it in this great saint, this friend of God, that could only find its expression in song? Job's suffering moved him to philosophy while David's moved him to poetry. Over the centuries, the church has been uncomfortable with both tendencies but has found it easier to assimilate the analytic than the imaginative.

Surely the imagination is part of our inheritance as God's image bearers. Because we were created, we are creative. I am inclined to think that the imagination is something close to God's heart. Consider this: when Christ taught on earth, he was more a storyteller than a theologian. He was content to wrap meaning in riddles and to sometimes leave them unexplained. He saw no difficulty in making men struggle through words and images to earn truth.

---

[1]James 2:18.

This is not to say that Jesus *only* told stories. There are some today who believe that, thanks to our postmodern enlightenment, the sermon is dead and if we want to speak to unbelievers all that is left is parable. But I do not agree. We should not emphasize story to the exclusion of all else (which is why I have saved it for the end of this book), but we must restore it to an equal footing, to rehabilitate it, and to ask why Christians, with so many exalted examples to draw upon, should not once more become the champions of imagination.

There was a time when many Christians dismissed the novel as dangerous frivolity. Now it is just dangerous. Film was viewed with similar suspicion during the twentieth century (and that is only just beginning to change). Although it was once a patron of the arts, the church's attitude now is a mix of indifference and suspicion. Protestants worry that involving ourselves in these things is too Roman Catholic; one of John Wycliffe's gripes with the medieval church was the way bishops used the people's tithes to set themselves up as generous patrons. Art smacks too much of idolatry!

And so we take an interest in art only when someone has the audacity to plunge a crucifix in urine.

"That's not art!" we protest.

The world replies, "Then what do you say art is?"

And we find ourselves in a bit of a pickle. We don't know. We don't care. It's just not *that*.

This, at least, is the official version in evangelicalism. In fact, the church is full of art, full of imagination. Under the aegis of the church, I have written and directed plays, painted artwork, and done a thousand other aesthetically demanding tasks. If it had not been for the church, I would never have been introduced to storytelling. On the grassroots level, we are constantly finding ways to express the imaginative side of ourselves, even if we do not acknowledge what we're doing on the theological level.

Two trends have helped evangelicals make peace with art. The first has been the emergence of market-driven, consumer-sensitive churches. These enterprises are self-conscious about issues of look and feel, and they demand a certain level of excellence in their execution. Baby boomer churches adopted the aesthetics of the variety show, while the new emerging churches have a grungier, hipper market in mind, but both generations reflect the idea that the church should make an impact on the imagination of those in attendance.

The second trend is the reemergence of prerevivalist, confessional traditions in evangelicalism. As believers become more aware of their own history, they discover the awe and transcendence of worship before it was co-opted by the nineteenth-century revivalists. There is an aesthetic behind austerity, too, they discover, and a way to worship God by directing the imagination upward toward him. I am more in sympathy with this trend because it reaches back to the Christian past to recover what is lost rather than setting up a cycle of reinvention. I want more from a community of faith than the assurance that it is "not your father's church."

My own views aside, it seems clear that in each case the driving factor has been a sense of loss. There was a time, we tell ourselves, when we were in touch with something that we have somehow lost. What is it? The question is answered in a variety of ways, but I believe the thing that has been lost is imaginative communion with God. We were made to worship God with the whole of our being, and part of that being is creative and imaginative. As long as the message from the church was that creativity and imagination could only be expressed outside the congregation, then a false dilemma was imposed on artistic souls. The Puritan concept of vocation, which had made it possible for a banker or lawyer to feel that his calling was from the Lord, needed to be extended to include the novelist, the filmmaker, the poet, the actor.

Believe it or not, the Christian artist has something to teach the rest of the church. As Dorothy Sayers wrote:

> It is the artist who, more than other men, is able to create something out of nothing. . . . This experience of the creative imagination in the common man or woman and in the artist is the only thing we have to go upon in entertaining and formulating the concept of creation. Outside our own experience of procreation and creation we can form no notion of how anything comes into being.[2]

In other words, if we want to understand creation, we must explore creativity. That is beginning to happen now. Evangelicals have been waging a cultural battle for several generations, and while it has been successful on the political front, it is an utter and catastrophic artistic failure. The Christian message was being broadcast legislatively but not creatively. Today evangelical leaders recognize the need to influence culture not just in the corridors of power, but in the chambers of the imagination. We

---

[2]Dorothy Sayers, *The Mind of the Maker* (New York: Harper Collins, 1979), 28–30.

don't need Christian laws as much as we need Christian books and films and music.

Out of the Ghetto

But that raises another problem, because we already have Christian books and films and music—and the fact that they're Christian seems to be a drawback. Unbelievers don't read Christian books or watch Christian films or listen to Christian music (at least, not knowingly). They are written and filmed and performed for a Christian audience.

So the question we need to address is how to take the Christian imagination out of the comfortable subculture and into real engagement with the world. How can the Christian imagination be embodied and embedded in fiction and film? How can we use our creativity as a tool for witness?

There are two questions we need to ask: first, is the Christian imagination creative or didactic? Second, what is the anatomy of the Christian imagination?

[II]

Christian stories have a tendency to degenerate into sermons. I use the term *degenerate* not in a pejorative sense—sermons are not, in and of themselves, degenerate—but because the form and goals of a sermon are very different from a story. Storytelling is not, first and foremost, about persuading people of truth. Rather, storytelling lets them experience truth, specifically the truth of real life and the way ideas and actions operate within it. We don't tell stories to change people's minds. We don't tell stories to educate them. We tell stories so that they can picture reality as it is or how it ought to be.

During the course of their discussion of the film classic *Double Indemnity* (1944) in *A Panorama of American Film Noir: 1941–1953*, Raymond Borde and Etienne Chaumeton quote critic H. F. Rey's assertion that, in spite of its depiction of immoral deeds like lust and murder, the film in fact stands in the Christian tradition: "The devil is shown in the astonishingly erotic shape of Barbara Stanwyck, but this is merely to obey Christian tradition, which doesn't hesitate to show evil when it has to. . . ."

> In this film, it's a question of demonstrating that crime does not, and never will, pay. This is an intelligent propaganda piece which, far from

denying certain social defects, willingly describes them, the better to stigmatize them.[3]

Borde and Chaumeton aren't buying it, though: "It's true that Christian moralists depict evil whenever they deem it useful: yet rarely without 'morose delectation' (to borrow their language) and always in order to present a repellent image of it." Film noir, on the other hand, "tends to grant an attractive side to evil." At the very least, it calls into question the convenient distinctions between good and evil upon which the moralists rely. One thing Borde and Chaumeton have in common with Rey, though, is their association of Christians with moralizing.

Moralists of the World Unite

Not all moralists are Christians, though. Moralists of every stripe— Christian, atheist, Marxist, capitalist, and so on—depict the immoral in such a way that the audience gets the message loud and clear: "See what happens when you do this?" *This* might be adultery and murder, or it might be insensitivity toward animal rights. The point is that the immoral, no matter how seductive it might seem, leads to undesirable consequences. In other words, as Rey says, "crime does not, and never will, pay." The moralist's goal is essentially didactic, and depending on the moral system he advocates, thoroughly true and worthwhile.

It could be argued, though, that the desire to teach and the desire to do art are incompatible—or at least in tension. During the years I spent in writing workshops at the University of Houston, I remember how hard it was for student writers to make didactic fiction work. The moralist, to make his point as strongly as possible, is tempted to stream-line or "clarify" reality in such a way that it no longer rings true to the average reader. Instead, the audience feels patronized. One mentor of mine insisted that it just wasn't possible to write a political or religious story. After all, the reader's task is one of interpretation, and a moralist is forced to preinterpret the story for the reader—in essence robbing him of a cherished prerogative.

To succeed, art needs to leave interpretation to the interpreters.

This might seem to preclude the possibility of Christian art entirely, except for the fact that not all Christians are moralists. What I mean by this is simple: there is a rationale for the depiction of evil (or sin, if you

---

[3]Raymond Borde and Etienne Chaumeton, *A Panorama of American Film Noir: 1941–1953* (San Francisco: City Lights, 2002), 146.

will) in art apart from the didactic impulse to warn the reader to avoid it. This rationale, far from conflicting with the goals of art, is essential to them. What is it? It is the representation of reality. As we have seen, Christian doctrine teaches that man is created in God's image but fallen—indeed, that the world itself is corrupt as a result of this fall. There are no good guys, no white hats or horses. Everyone is tainted by evil and no one can be accurately represented without its inclusion (which is why the innocence of some Christian attempts at fiction ring so false). It is in this context of corruption that the gospel is offered—without the fall, there is no call for redemption. Evil is, in this sense, a necessary aspect of human existence and a necessary component in any representation of reality. Evil is a necessary part of the Christian story.

Art under the Sun

A model for this view of reality is found in the book of Ecclesiastes, where life "under the sun" is depicted without any Pollyanna pretensions—a fact that has made the book difficult for moralists to digest, resulting in some bizarre and entertaining efforts at harmonization. The Preacher depicts a world bleaker than that of the existentialist: "You're right, there's no meaning. It's all vanity. And you think you can create your *own* meaning? Sure thing, pal." It is this brutally honest view of life in a fallen world, stripped of all moralizing—all comfort, even—that the Preacher drives home. No strategy for success, no method for coping. Nothing under the sun can relieve the intense futility of it all—and yet, in the midst of the futility there is joy. There is a "good life" to be lived. There is a God whose purposes transcend the all-pervasive gloom. If a Christian artist could understand and attempt to capture this view of reality, if he could create a vision of things in which it is increasingly impossible to mistake anything good as something other than grace, then he could claim to be holding up a mirror to reality.

If the impulse to moralize fails anywhere, it is in its potential for neutralizing our receptivity to grace. There must be something deeply imbedded in our consciousness that tells us that, no matter what the moralists say, things are never as simple as mastering a few skills and avoiding bad decisions. Our knowledge of ourselves gives the lie to Pelagian self-help. Repentance is deeper than realization and resolution. Moralizing visions are not necessarily moral visions, and the moralist's representation of evil, like his representation of good, falls short of the reality we live with every day. It does not ring true. And if this false note deceives the audience into believing that its own shortcomings are consequently not immoral—or that there must be ultimately no morality—then the moralist's efforts might contribute after all to the downfall of the project he holds so dear.

Perhaps the greatest fault of the moralist is to suggest that, in such a world, an adequate moral framework can be derived by observing the outcome of moral choices. In reality, such an approach is as likely to affirm the utility of evil as to condemn it. So the Christian artist is well served to depict life as it really is, and to seek his moral framework from a transcendent source.

The Morality of Art

I am not denying the moral component in art (or in life), but simply making a distinction between morality and moralizing. Of course art is moral. We create conflict and force our characters to make moral choices with painful consequences. We punish them whether they do right or wrong to see what interesting results might follow. Our characters live in a world that works, not surprisingly, the way we think our own world operates—and in that sense we communicate a morality, a theology, whether we intend to or not. But we do not moralize. We do not tidy up the choices or introduce chance or providence to straighten the crooked lines. We do not supply the reader with a predigested interpretation of the story.

A good example of this is found in John Fowles's book *The Magus*. The preface to the revised edition makes it clear that Fowles is a committed humanist who would like to see religion and the myth of God abolished for all time. And yet his book, which was originally to be titled *The Godgame*, does not pursue this agenda without ambiguity. Some religious characters are treated with respect, and some loose ends are left that a conscientious humanist moralizer would not have abided.

You could argue that, in seeking to depict reality, Fowles has incorporated a vision that is not wholly consistent with his philosophy. Rather than seeing this as a mistake, though, I suggest that the Christian artist should see it as a model. Too often, we are afraid to represent anything that does not fit (or does not appear to us to fit) into "our" reality. Because our faith encompasses every aspect of life in theory, we are reluctant to show any instance where it does not seem to in fact—as if our selectiveness might shield God from unwelcome scrutiny. This, of course, is a failure of faith. If artists are moral philosophers, then great artists are the ones who are not afraid to let the implications of the drama stretch beyond what is dreamt of in their moral philosophy.

In his book *On Moral Fiction*, John Gardner stands in the tradition of Tolstoy, who was a champion of moral or "religious" art. Gardner gives this definition of moral art at the beginning of the book:

> The traditional view is that true art is moral: it seeks to improve life, not debase it. It seeks to hold off, at least for a while, the twilight of the gods and us. I do not deny that art, like criticism, may legitimately celebrate the trifling. It may joke, or mock, or while away the time. But trivial art has no meaning or value except in the shadow of more serious art, the kind of art that beats back the monsters and, if you will, makes the world safe for triviality. That art which tends toward destruction, the art of nihilists, cynics, and *merdistes*, is not properly art at all. Art is essentially serious and beneficial, a game played against chaos and death, against entropy. It is a tragic game, for those who have the wit to take it seriously, because our side must lose; a comic game—or so a troll might say—because only a clown with sawdust brains would take our side and eagerly join it.[4]

This heroic, even pagan, vision of the artist can be hobbled by the usual postmodern questions. Who are you to define art? Who gets to decide what improves or debases life? Isn't the "trivial" a marginalized discourse that needs to be brought back into the open? Gardner could be construed as an elitist—in other words, as someone who makes distinctions between what is done well and what is done poorly. But the idea that the artist has a calling, that there is a brave hopelessness to his task, that it is all somehow very *serious*—these all resonate deeply.

These are the motives of heroism that should fuel a believer's art.

Dogmatic Decisions

The Christian artist, therefore, must adopt a position on the subject of dogmatism. The sanctified bodice-rippers on the religious bookshelf are often thoroughly dogmatic. They try to drag readers kicking and screaming to the truth. Every so often the action pauses for another tear-jerking conversion scene. Now I am not against conversion, but the standard conversion scene from Christian fiction does not quite ring true even to believers. Ironically enough, the more overtly dogmatic the storyteller chooses to be, the less engaged and more isolated his work

---

[4]John Gardner, *On Moral Fiction* (New York: Basic, 2000), 4–5.

becomes. Polemical authors write for their own community and no one else.

That's why more sophisticated authors sometimes attempt to draw rather than drag their readers to truth. In my view, this is a legitimate option. It involves a certain amount of persuasion, but this is accomplished through the type of story the author chooses to tell and the way he chooses to tell it. In other words, the nature of the action leads the reader to certain conclusions, but these conclusions are not hammered home in the way the moralist would prefer. There is still some interpretation to be done, though it proceeds along defined paths.

The third stance the artist can assume is nondogmatic. In a sense, it is impossible to be nondogmatic. Whatever work we do is stamped by the one who created it, so our worldview assumptions are, to greater or lesser degree, embedded in our art. Even in art forms that do not lend themselves to narrative, such as music, it is possible to argue that some vestige of ideas remains (at the very least, dogmatism in music is as easy to sniff out as anywhere else). So the point of a nondogmatic stance is not neutrality. Rather, it is a conscious decision of the artist not to provide the reader with a roadmap for interpreting his work. The goal is to imagine creation, to present a compelling glimpse of a realized world, without interpreting it.

Because this is a question each artist needs to work out for himself, I will not suggest a final answer. I will note, however, that if we have confidence that the world we live in really was created by God, then an honest portrayal of that world is a witness to God, even if it comes without the markers and signposts that make that conclusion obvious. The question could be asked, if all the Christian author does is present the world as it really is, then how does that differ from any other artist's approach? It differs in this way: the Christian artist seeks to render reality *without suppressing the truth about it.*

When we assume that non-Christian art is a neutral and uncolored representation of the world as it really is, we only confirm that we have not grasped the essential message of the faith: that God has indelibly marked all that exists as his.

[III]

Is there such a thing as a specifically Christian imagination? I want to briefly argue that there is, and that it consists in four key components.

Obviously, it is impossible to pin down something as vast and consuming as the believing imagination under four headings, so this outline should be viewed as a starting point. The goal is to help Christians think about the way their imaginations uniquely witness to the gospel of Christ.

1) Christian Imagination Is an Image Bearer's Echo of the Creator

As often as I have made this point already, it bears repeating. Our explanation for why we are creative is that we are made in the image of God. All human creativity flows from this source. That means that as people who acknowledge the Creator, we should be unashamed of our imaginative urges—in fact, we ought to be in the forefront of expression. It also means that we should be as bold in art as we would be in theology. The Savior reigns over one just as much as the other.

Is aesthetic expression an act of worship? There are certainly times when the artist feels it must be. Sayers is right to say that artistic expression is our nearest analogue (apart from giving birth) to the act of creation. The exalted, absorbing state that artists call inspiration is the closest we can come to experiencing the reality of sovereignty in creation and freedom in the created without compromise or conflict. No, the human artist does not experience creation as God does, but through analogy he comes to appreciate what it must mean to say that God created the heavens and earth, and that he remains active down to this very moment in their every turn and tilt.

Because we are created in God's image, we ought to be creative. We ought to treasure the imagination and the urge to tell stories as one of the best gifts given to us by a loving Creator.

2) Christian Imagination Embodies the Biblical Worldview

Christian imagination can go where Christian rhetoric cannot. The biblical worldview gives the Christian artist an immeasurable advantage in that it provides what Chad Walsh calls the "roomiest dwelling":

> If Christian eyes can see more and see it more exactly, it should follow that the truth a Christian writer can portray will somehow get through, because it will ring true even in men who consciously reject the faith that offers the new eyes.[5]

---

[5]Chad Walsh, "The Advantages of the Christian Faith for a Writer," in *The Christian Imagination* (Colorado Springs: Shaw Books, 2002), 173.

What this suggests is that the Christian artist can transmit the truth about the world apart from dogmatism, simply by giving readers the experience of seeing the world through the eyes of faith. From a Christian standpoint, the artist can travel anywhere without fear of stretching beyond the boundaries of his ideology. No aspect of existence is beyond the scope of his inquiry; there need be no blinders on his imagination.

Archimedes once boasted that if he were given a lever and a place to stand, he could move the world. The Christian worldview is a place to stand—all the rest is, as the hymn says, sinking sand—and the Christian imagination is your lever. So take up the challenge and move the world.

3) Christian Imagination Is Incarnational

God became flesh and dwelled among us. He did this perfectly, without sin. Some early adherents, influenced by Hellenism, denied the possibility of the incarnation. Christ could not have been truly a man, for flesh itself is evil. For God to be embodied, to be incarnate, would be for God to become what is evil—inconceivable. What these Gnostics needed to do, however, was invert the argument. If God had indeed become man, then their notion that the flesh is inherently evil must be wrong.

The flesh is sinful, but not inherently. It is corrupted, like all of creation, by the fall. While we struggle against the sinful tendency of the flesh, the lusts of the body, we recognize that these propensities originate in the will and the mind. We are not perfect souls contaminated by stinking bodies. Rather, we are corrupted souls who have dragged down the bodies that contain us and the world we inhabit.

What does this have to do with art and imagination? It means that there is value and beauty in the physical world. Beauty, truth, and goodness do not need to be abstracted; we do not need to separate the ideal from the real, the universal from the particular, the abstract from the concrete. Stories are not messages hidden in character and plot—the character and plot are themselves the story. In short, it is good to be embodied and to celebrate the physical world God has created.

To be spiritual is not to be otherworldly. The Spirit is working in this world. To be eternal is not to be outside of time. God is working within and through time to bring about his purposes. Incarnation signals many things, but for the artist it is a clarion call for integration. Story is important. Plot is important. Character is important. These things are good and necessary in themselves; they are not merely the vehicles of meaning. A work of art does not need to be didactic in order to be true.

4) Christian Imagination Aspires toward Excellence

Charles Spurgeon confessed something in his *Lectures to My Students* that would shock many people today. He said that when a young man with a speech impediment came to him claiming to be called to preach, Spurgeon told him that his inability to speak clearly was a sign that he was not! If God had meant you to preach, the logic goes, he would have given you a voice for it. That sounds rather hard-hearted today. This is an age of empowerment. One of our fundamental assumptions is that you can do whatever you set your mind to. Want to be an astronaut? Want to be the first female president? Nothing is beyond your reach. And here is Spurgeon, supposedly a man of God, saying that a speech impediment is a divine signal that you cannot do what your heart aspires to achieve.

Spurgeon's concept of God's sovereignty had something to do with it, I imagine. It would have seemed like common sense to him that God, who had the power to do whatever he liked with us, would equip us for the task he called us to perform. There are exceptions to every rule, but by and large, we are called to go where our strengths lie.

A corollary to this is that we are called to do whatever it is we settle up with all of our hearts, to the best of our ability, to the highest standard of excellence. There is something in the creative urge of man that recognizes this. We have a passion not only to create but to do it well. We judge the success of a work of art, just as we would any other work, by what it achieves, by how high its excellencies reach.

Judge not lest ye be judged. Particularly within the strictures of the subculture, Christians are guilty of applying this concept too broadly. We are discouraged from making critical judgments about a work of art because it was created by a Christian. It is one thing to hold unbelievers' work up to a standard, but our own people should be treated better. Now, as far as handling every artist with compassion, I agree with the sentiment (though I fall short in its execution, as the reader of this book has already observed). But to fulfill the God-given mandate of excellence we must expect great things from the Christian imagination and not be satisfied with mediocrity.

As much as possible, the Christian artist must strive not only for moral but also for artistic excellence. He must be an able craftsman as much as a learned theologian—perhaps more so. If others will not take him to task where he falls short, then he must hold his own feet to the flame and insist on realizing a greater vision.

When God surveyed all that he had made, he pronounced it good. We are often in no position to judge our own work so objectively, but it should be our desire, the aspiration of our heart, to create things beautifully after the example set before us, to emulate Christ in this as we strive to do in all things.

If the biblical worldview provides a foundation for our thought, and wisdom erects a fortification of discernment around our mind, then Christian witness is the force by which the kingdom of God is extended. Our evangelism and apologetics are informed by worldview awareness and the spiritual and psychological complexities of the unbelief we battle. The same is true for the Christian imagination. It draws its strength from the deep truths embedded under the surface of reality. It builds up strength and is nurtured in the matrix of right belief and right practice until it bubbles up in force, inspiring intellectual and emotional and spiritual and artistic expression.

That witness, by God's grace, leads others to fear the Lord, and so the cycle continues. New believers grasp the underlying message of the faith; they grow in grace and wisdom until they, too, feel the unstoppable urge to share this profound knowledge with the people around them. And that brings more people to Christ. Seeds are planted; plants are watered and they grow. The air carries the seeds of their faith abroad. This is the organic, perpetual life of the church, the life of the body you are called to inhabit.

The Christian artist is not the first among believers. He should aspire to be the last. His work, like the work of evangelist and apologist, should be forged in humility and with the simple desire to present truth under glass for the enlightenment and perhaps the salvation of his reader. To God alone be the glory.

Epilogue
The Final Word

A little learning is a dangerous thing; drink deep, or taste not the Pierian spring: there shallow draughts intoxicate the brain, and drinking largely sobers us again.

ALEXANDER POPE, *AN ESSAY ON CRITICISM*

Approaching the Christian life through a three-stage cycle, with worldview, wisdom, and witness depending upon and encouraging each other, illustrates the beautiful wholeness of a much more complex reality. The problem with such didactic tools as my three-part structure, though, is that such organizing tools are often taken as exhaustive, as if there is nothing outside their boundaries. To reduce the whole of Scripture's teaching and the long tradition of Christian thought to three bullet points would be a disastrous fraud, which is why I have intentionally held back a final word until now.

What I have outlined in this book is true, to the best of my knowledge, but by no means complete, which is why, instead of reiterating my system here, I want to use this epilogue to introduce one of the many things I have omitted. But first, an illustration to demonstrate the difference between knowing and knowledge.

Miss Dashwood and the Colonel

The difference between knowing a fact and having real knowledge is perfectly illustrated in a scene from Ang Lee's film version of Jane Austen's *Sense and Sensibility*. It is based on a conversation between Elinor Dashwood and Colonel Brandon, a family friend with a one-sided romantic attachment to Miss Dashwood's sister Marianne, that originally takes place at the end of chapter 11 in the book. In condensing the speech, Emma Thompson (who wrote the screenplay and acts the part of Miss Dashwood) creates a poignant moment that has always stood out to me as one of the quiet highlights of the film. Here's how it reads in the screenplay:

> *Colonel Brandon [speaking of Marianne]:* She is wholly unspoilt.
>
> Elinor: Rather too unspoilt, in my view. The sooner she becomes acquainted with the ways of the world, the better.
>
> *Colonel Brandon looks at her sharply and then speaks very deliberately, as though controlling some powerful emotion.*
>
> *Colonel Brandon:* I knew a lady like your sister—the same impulsive sweetness of temper—who was forced into, as you put it, a better acquaintance with the ways of the world. The result was only ruination and despair.
> *He stops, and briskly remounts his horse.*
>
> *Colonel Brandon:* Do not desire it, Miss Dashwood.[1]

Elinor Dashwood is understandably frustrated with her sister's unguarded expressions of favor to another suitor, Willoughby, and Brandon, who suffers in comparison, might be expected to sympathize with her feelings. If only Marianne would grow up a little and show more reserve! Elinor is right, in a way. She knows how people should behave in society and sees clearly the awkward situation Marianne is creating for herself. But her knowledge is more conceptual than experiential, and like so many people operating on head knowledge, Elinor lapses into a sense of superiority. (She is, after all, "sense" to her sister's "sensibility.") Perhaps what her sister needs is a comeuppance, a better "acquaintance with the ways of the world."

But Colonel Brandon has tragic, personal knowledge of what such an acquaintance entails. The world is a harsh teacher, and he would just as soon see Marianne continue in ignorance. That's not what happens, of course, but Brandon delivers his sentiment with such moral force that there is no question he is in the right. It is one thing to contemplate such things in theory and quite another to experience them.

Elinor knows what learning the ways of the world entails, but Brandon

---

[1] *Sense and Sensibility* (1995), directed by Ang Lee; screenplay by Emma Thompson.

knows better. Or we might say, leaning once again upon 1 Corinthians 13:12, that Elinor knows in part, but Brandon knows fully. This, I would suggest, is the difference between knowing and knowledge. We can know things truly in concept, without knowing them fully through (among other things) experience, and that incomplete knowledge can lead us, as it does Elinor Dashwood, into desiring what we should not. A little learning is a dangerous thing.

The Hole in My Thinking

This is why, here at the end, I am compelled to shake things up a bit. There is a hole in my thinking, a glaring omission. In fact, there are more than a few. But the one I have in mind here must stand for the whole. If we are to put this book down with a deeper knowledge of worldview, wisdom, and witness, one thing must be added to the list: worship.

Worship is not, like the other categories, one of several stages in an interdependent cycle. Rather, think of it as an umbrella covering them all, an idea standing outside the construct, informing it, stretching it, and pushing it toward fulfillment. Worship is an ecstatic reverence for God expressed through thought and action and utterance. Worship is something we think and feel, something we do, at once an act of communication and communion. It is also a state of being. In worship we aspire toward our final state of glory, manifesting what is already finished of a work not yet complete.

At the outset, I insisted that a book like this cannot be read like other books, that it must be read alongside the Bible or it would make no sense at all. In the same vein, the cultivation of worldview, wisdom, and witness is like Miss Dashwood's dangerous knowledge until it is tempered with sincere worship. One path nurtures Pharisees, the other Christ-followers. Truly, this is theology that leads us to doxology. Or else it's no theology at all.

On Earth As It Is in Heaven

One of the most moving passages in Scripture is found in Revelation 4–5. Here, the apostle John describes a fantastic scene, the throne of God in heaven. The great throne is surrounded by twenty-four lesser thrones, where the crowned elders sit, and before the throne burn seven flames. It is a vision rich in symbolism—and, of course, the symbolism of this apocalyptic book is quite controversial among interpreters—but

when I read the description it has a literal, aesthetic force behind it. I
see the throne room as John describes it; I picture the unimaginable
creatures. And when they lift their voices in perpetual declaration, I read
with trembling:

> "Holy, holy, holy, is the Lord God Almighty,
>   who was and is and is to come!" (4:8)

When the creatures offer this praise, the elders rise from their thrones and
throw themselves on the ground, prostrate before God. They pitch their
crowns at his feet in homage as they, too, cry out in worship:

> "Worthy are you, our Lord and God,
>   to receive glory and honor and power,
> for you created all things,
>   and by your will they existed and were created." (4:11)

This ecstatic surrender is what all human worship strains toward. We
gather bleary-eyed on a Sunday morning and belt out a few out-of-tune
hymns, and there is no question but that our efforts are a poor shadow of
the heavenly reality. Modest as it is, our worship follows in the footsteps
of this high praise, and I have often found myself in church, marveling
at the thought that as the world spins, more believers rise and join the
perpetual (if imperfect) chorus, anticipating the day when every knee shall
bow.

And then the Lamb enters.

In Revelation 5, he enters at the last moment, just as all hope is lost. In
God's right hand is a scroll, and the angel at his side asks who is worthy to
break its seal and open it. No one is found who can open the scroll, a fact
that moves John to tears. But then one of the elders tells him to weep no
more. "Behold," he says, "the Lion of the tribe of Judah, the Root of David,
has conquered, so that he can open the scroll and its seven seals" (5:5).

When John turns, he sees not a roaring lion but a lamb, the creature
of sacrifice. The lamb takes the scroll, and as he does, the elders—fresh
from their worship of the Father—bow down to worship the Son. Their
words give a perfect encapsulation of the gospel of Jesus Christ, seen from
the perspective of eternity:

> "Worthy are you to take the scroll
>   and to open its seals,

for you were slain, and by your blood you ransomed people for God
    from every tribe and language and people and nation,
and you have made them a kingdom and priests to our God,
    and they shall reign on the earth." (5:9–10)

Reading these scenes, stylized and as laden with symbol and significance as a medieval mystery play, I am overwhelmed by the feeling that this is what matters, this state of confession, a never-ending tribute to the worth of God, as evidenced in creation and redemption, his making and remaking of us, driven by an unfathomable love.

When the elders worship the Lamb, they set off a chain reaction in heaven. The hosts of angels join the living creatures and the elders in an exalted refrain: "Worthy is the Lamb who was slain, to receive power and wealth and wisdom and might and honor and glory and blessing!" I can imagine John, his whole body vibrating with the thundering cry, trembling witness to an event his words struggle to contain.

But it isn't over. At the end of chapter 5, we see the fulfillment of a hope Jesus taught us to express whenever we pray. As the Lord's Prayer says, "on earth as it is in heaven." All heaven reverberates with praise, and all creation answers:

> And I heard every creature in heaven and on earth and under the earth and in the sea, and all that is in them, saying, "To him who sits on the throne and to the Lamb be blessing and honor and glory and might forever and ever!" And the four living creatures said, "Amen!" and the elders fell down and worshiped. (5:13–14)

This is the mystery, the vital element in our dogmatics, the univocal aim of our thinking, our living, our speaking. Whatever else flows from that worship, valuable as it may be, must never obscure the vital sense of awe in which we live, the tangible shadow of God's grace.

Nothing must ever come between our knees and the ground.

General Index

Scripture Index